THE SECRET WAR COUNCIL

THE GERMAN FIGHT AGAINST THE ENTENTE IN AMERICA IN 1914

by

Heribert von Feilitzsch

First Edition

Every effort has been made to locate and contact
all holders of copyright to material reproduced in this book.
For information about permission to reproduce selections from this book,
write to Henselstone Verlag LLC., P.O. Box 201, Amissville, VA 20106.

Library of Congress Control Number 2015917469

Keyword Data

von Feilitzsch, Heribert, 1965-

The Secret War Council: Germany's War in North America, 1914 / Heribert von
Feilitzsch.
p. cm
Includes biographical references and index.

ISBN 9780996955409

1.   United States – History – World War I – 1914 to 1917
2.   Germany – History – World War I – 1914 to 1917
3.   Mexico – History – Revolution, 1910-1920 – Diplomatic History
4.   United States – Foreign Relations – Mexico
5.   United States – Foreign Relations - Germany
6.   Mexico – Foreign Relations – United States
7.   Mexico – Foreign Relations - Germany
8.   Germany – Foreign Relations – Mexico
9.   Germany – Foreign Relations – United States
I.   von Feilitzsch, Heribert. Title.

www.felixsommerfeld.com

Printed in the United States of America

"Your Royal Highness surely is aware of how the situation in the United States has turned out. Instead of friendly sympathy we encountered utmost enmity and a wholly unexpected hostility. We are practically at war with the United States. Anything that the United States is able to do to disadvantage us she is doing: Deliveries of war materials of any kind to our enemies, granting large financial aid and credits, subjecting herself to English maritime regulations, which are mocking all principles of international law and are aiming at a complete isolation of Germany [...] I wished that [...] we would not let the clamor of the American press let us be thrown off the right course, which is the only one to lead us to success, namely the ruthless exercise of all our might – I am specifically thinking of submarines, flying airships and airplanes."

Head of the Secret War Council in New York,
Heinrich F. Albert to Prinz Albert Wilhelm
Heinrich von Preußen, May 1915

Praise for

The Secret War Council
The German Fight against
the Entente in America in 1914

"The Secret War Council is a carefully researched study of Imperial Germany's secret war against the still neutral United States from 1914 to 1917. Propaganda and sabotage, managed by Heinrich F. Albert, the financial agent of the German Emperor, finally forced President Wilson to enter World War I. An important contribution to our understanding of the casus belli 100 years ago."

Reinhard R. Doerries, *Professor of Modern History*, retired *Lehrstuhl für Auslandswissenschaft, Friedrich-Alexander Universität, Erlangen-Nürnberg*, author of *Imperial Challenge: Ambassador Count Bernstorff and German-American Relations, 1908 - 1917*

"Germany's underground American activities before the U.S. entered World War I never cease to be intriguing. Heribert von Feilitzsch puts us all in his debt by offering a thorough yet fascinating account rooted in German sources. Some of the material dealing with sabotage is exciting enough to serve as the basis for a movie plot."

Justus D. Doenecke, *Professor Emeritus of History*, retired, New College of Florida, author of *Nothing Less Than War: A New History of America's Entry into World War I*

"The author continues his in-depth studies using long-neglected and ignored German records, adding to our understanding of the Intelligence War in the US from 1914 - 1918."

Mark Benbow, Professor of History and Political Science, Marymount University, author of *Leading Them to the Promised Land: Woodrow Wilson, Covenant Theology, and the Mexican Revolution, 1913 - 1915*

For Fabian

TABLE OF CONTENTS

ACKNOWLEDGMENTS

FONDLY REMEMBER ADMIRING THE COLORFUL Austro-Hungarian army uniforms and the spiked helmets in my grandfather's closet. He was born in 1886 and I wish I had been old enough to ask him about his opinions of the Great War. His legacy instilled a strange curiosity in me. On the one hand, my grandfather still rode into cavalry battles on horseback, yet on the other, this world conflagration featured so many technical novelties, ranging from wireless communication and rapid-fire machine guns to submarines and tanks. Biological and chemical weapons of mass destruction entered the battlefields for the first time. Terrorism, insurgency, and separatism became commonly accepted tactics for war, now painfully ubiquitous for our generation. The fascination with a war that seems so far away, yet with so many parallels to our world today profoundly challenged me as a historian. Only the most careful attention to historical detail, unconstrained by ideology or preconceptions, allow for a solid and realistic analysis of the fascinating break between an older world and ours. Such thorough analysis is the goal of this book series, *The Secret War Council*®.

There are many people who supported me on this endeavor, certainly my beautiful and understanding family who had to suffer through periods of absolute preoccupation with *my spies*. Much gratitude belongs to the late professor Michael C. Meyer of my Alma Mater, the University of Arizona, who set me on the course of this research. Professor Reinhard Doerries, the preeminent scholar on the topic of German secret agents and Imperial Ambassador to Washington in World War I, Johann Heinrich Count von Bernstorff, gave me his time and kind feedback. Thank you! Charles H. Harris III and Louis R. Sadler, two scholars, whose work I admire beyond any other historical scholarship have helped me through my first book and remained good friends and great supporters of mine. Without their encouragement and example of how to write *good history* I might have given up long ago. Heartfelt thanks also to Professor Justus Doenecke whose work inspired me greatly and who agreed to review my early manuscript. His constructive feedback focused my arguments and improved my manuscript. I am honored and eternally grateful for his support. Professors Nicholas Stenecke and Mark Benbow also gave me valuable advice. Thank you!

There are no words that can describe the deep gratitude, admiration, and respect I have for my great friend, Professor Günter Köhler. He has the sharpest mind I know, the strongest willpower, and the most supportive and patient attitude for which any author can hope. His example is one of the driving forces in my intellectual life. To my late friend Dieter and countless other close friends who sat through seemingly endless dinner conversations and thesis testing, I remain deeply grateful. I thank my editors, Rosa King and Steve Devitt for making my words palatable to readers.

I am eternally indebted to the great and dedicated educators and intellectuals who sharpened my skills as a historian and businessman throughout college, graduate school, and beyond. Without the brilliant minds of George Brubaker, University of Arizona, John Rossi, Pennsylvania State University at Erie, Leonard Dinnerstein, University of Arizona, and Melvin Leffler, University of Virginia, my research would have stopped at the many dead ends through which I maneuvered in the years of writing this book. Equally important as my training in history was the MBA program I attended at Wake Forest University in Winston-Salem, North Carolina. Special thanks to Professors Bern Beatty and Jack Meredith who worked hard on sharpening my strategic thinking and thorough understanding of the inner workings of corporations. These skills allowed me to trace the various money trails so crucial in understanding the historical events described in this book.

There is a group of people who work tirelessly in the halls of our libraries and archives. Their knowledge of the nooks and crannies of tons of files in the National Archives, Library of Congress, Deutsches Bundesarchiv, and Archivos Municipales Chihuahua provide the keys to successful research. I can never repay the self-less kindness I have been shown over the years. I would like to especially mention Michael Hieronymus, Curator of Special Collections at the Benson Library of Latin American Studies in the University of Texas at Austin. His kindness, incredible knowledge, and experience with all kinds of crazy historians who peruse through the materials are unsurpassed. I also want to thank David Kessler of the Bancroft Library at the University of California at Berkeley. The Bancroft Library acquired the papers of Silvestre Terrazas in the 1960s. This collection and many more, such as the Holmdahl Papers and the German Diplomatic Papers, contribute to the valuable documentation of the Mexican Revolution. Thank you!

In the National Archives in Washington, D.C., I met several of the most dedicated, motivated, and knowledgeable archivists in the world. I am immeasurably grateful to Richard Peuser and his staff. They assisted me not only in finding documents I asked about but also with recommending archival materials of which I was not aware. These dedicated archivists have such admirable command over so many collections that they truly have the power to bring history into the light. Thank you! In the Bundesarchiv für Militärgeschichte in Freiburg, Achim Koch, Andrea Meier, and Jan Warssischek assisted me with great knowledge and dedication. I am eternally grateful for their courtesy towards an unknown researcher who barged in from overseas with little time and an insatiable appetite for obscure files.

Another acknowledgment goes to our advanced technology: the Internet has drastically transformed research capabilities of historians in recent years. Suddenly, digitalized FBI files, excerpts from books mentioning a certain name or fact, and catalogs of archives worldwide are at one's fingertips in the office. An especially valuable tool is the Google books program. Free of charge, I found the most incredible and interesting histories, PhD theses, diaries, and data collections such as the Prussian army lists digitized by Google. Thank you!

I have been able to locate the great grandchildren of Frederico Stallforth online. Believe it or not, Frederico Stallforth is available on You Tube, lighting a cigarette, courtesy of Mary Prevo of Hampton Sydney University to whom I owe special gratitude. She allowed a total stranger to spend weeks on end in her upstairs study and sort through her great grandfather's personal papers. We bounced ideas and impressions back and forth. I shared my drafts and opinions on Frederico Stallforth with her and her aunt, Lawrence Webster, who remembers Frederico all too well. Their insight, historical sensitivity, and above all, Mary's unwavering patience focused my research and sharpened my understanding of a very complex and colorful character.

There are many others whose patience, intellect, and support have accompanied my journey. First and foremost are the many readers who join me on my weekly blog with valuable comments and suggestions. You are the greatest motivators for my continued quest to write about the past. Please forgive me for not mentioning you by name. Thank you.

CAST OF CHARACTERS

Albert, Heinrich Friedrich German lawyer and commercial agent for the German government in New York during World War I. German Commercial Attaché 1915 to 1917. Head of the Secret War Council, the German clandestine organization in New York in charge of propaganda, economic war, sabotage, and finance during World War I. German Treasury Secretary and Secretary of reconstruction 1923.

Ballin, Albert Founder and chief executive of Hamburg Amerika Paketfahrt Gesellschaft (HAPAG). During the war Ballin was in charge of organizing the German raw material management together with other German industrialists. Many of HAPAG's sailors and employees were naval reservists and participated in German clandestine operations in the United States.

Bernstorff, Count Johann Heinrich

German ambassador to the United States from 1908 to 1917 and to Turkey from 1917 to 1918. After World War I, co-founder of the Democratic Party in Germany (Deutsche Demokratische Partei). Member of the Reichstag 1921 to 1928. Went into exile during Nazi regime.

Bielaski, Alexander Bruce

American lawyer and Chief of the Bureau of Investigation, 1912 to 1919.

Boy-Ed, Karl

German Naval Attaché in New York from 1913 to 1915. Then head of the *Nachrichtenabteilung* N in Berlin 1915 to 1918 (Naval Intelligence).

Bryan, William Jennings

American lawyer and Democratic politician. Ran as a candidate for the U.S. presidency three times. Served as Secretary of State under Wilson between 1913 and 1915. Resigned in 1915, campaigned on behalf of the American peace movement, and pursued law practice.

Buenz, Karl

German executive of HAPAG in the United States. Also former minister to Mexico and Consul. He organized the re-supply mission for the remnants of the German navy from the United States. Was convicted of falsifying shipping manifests and convicted to prison. He died in prison.

Carranza, Venustiano   Mexican politician from Coahuila. Led the Mexican opposition against Victoriano Huerta. Mexican President from 1915 to 1917.

Claussen, Matthew   German-American propagandist. Worked as an editor of the *New York Herald* before he joined HAPAG as publicity agent. In World War I Claussen headed the publicity section of the German press office in New York.

Dernburg, Bernhard   Imperial Secretary of Colonial Affairs 1907 to 1910. Head of German propaganda in the United States 1914 to 1915. German Finance Minister and Vice Chancellor in 1919. Member of the German parliament 1920 to 1930.

Ecker, Otto   HAPAG executive in New York. He is suspected to have been connected with the German War Department spy organization General Staff, Abteilung IIIb, Sektion Politik.

Ernst, Johannes   German businessman who operated in the United States under the alias John Simon. Became one of Albert's most important blockade runners. Ended up cheating Albert.

Francke, Kuno   German-American professor of history at Harvard University. Participated in the early German propaganda efforts. Also was Heinrich Albert's uncle.

Garrison, Lindley Miller

Lawyer and Democratic politician. Served as Secretary of War under Woodrow Wilson between 1913 and 1916. Felix Sommerfeld, a German agent, informed and manipulated him with selected intelligence on the Mexican Revolution.

Goltz, Horst von der

German agent with the real name Franz Wachendorf. Worked for Sommerfeld in Mexico before the war. Sent to sabotage the Welland Canal in 1914. Mission was aborted. Goltz ended in British detention and testified against German agents in the U.S. in 1917.

Haniel von Haimhausen, Edgar

German diplomat. At the outbreak of World War I Haniel was charge d'affairs at the German embassy in Washington until 1917. He became a delegate for the armistice negotiations in 1918 and became general secretary for Germany in the negotiations of the Treaty of Versailles in 1919. Represented the Weimar government in Munich between 1923 and 1931.

Hale, William Bayard

American journalist and author. Supported and became friends with Woodrow Wilson in 1912. Went on missions for the president to Mexico where he also met and became closely acquainted with Sommerfeld. Joined the German propaganda team in 1914 as an editor. Largely discredited for his support of Germany in the war, he moved to Europe for the remainder of his life.

Hatzfeld zu Trachenberg, Prince Hermann
Second counselor of the German Embassy in Washington. Was a member of the royal aristocracy of Prussia, and former member of the German parliament. His father had been German Foreign Secretary and German ambassador in London under Bismarck.

Heynen, Carl
Wealthy German-Mexican businessman with companies in Mexico City, Veracruz and Tampico who represented HAPAG and North German Lloyd in Mexico before the war. Came to the U.S. on orders of the German naval intelligence and worked for Heinrich Albert as his treasurer and logistics expert. Headed the management of the Bridgeport Projectile Company.

Hintze, Paul von
German career navy officer who rose to Rear Admiral before World War I. Headed Department N, the naval intelligence division. Changed careers to become a diplomat. Emperor Wilhelm II appointed him Minister to Mexico where von Hintze witnessed the Madero presidency and the coup d'état against the president. Commanded naval intelligence in North America including Felix Sommerfeld. Was succeeded by Karl Boy-Ed and became Germany's envoy to China 1914 to 1917. Became German foreign secretary in 1918 until the resignation of the Kaiser.

Hoadley, George W.

American businessman who served as the figurehead in Germany's acquisition and operation of the Bridgeport Projectile Company between 1915 and 1917.

Horn, Werner

German agent sent to blow up a bridge between the U.S. and Canada. Project was discovered.

Huerta, Victoriano

Mexican general and usurper of the presidency in 1913. Held responsible for the murder of Francisco Madero. Went into exile in 1914. Attempted a return to power in 1915 but was arrested in Texas.

Jebsen, Frederick

Flamboyant German businessman in California. Operated a fleet of freighters before the World War. Ran Karl Boy-Ed's efforts to supply the remnants of the German navy in the Pacific Ocean. Organized the ships *Annie Larsen* and *Maverick* that were to transport weapons to Indian resistance fighters. Fled to Germany and was killed on a submarine in 1915.

Koenig, Paul

German secret service agent (not to be confused with the submarine captain of the same name). Headed the HAPAG corporate security office in the Americas before World War I. Under military attachés Franz von Papen and Wolf von Igel, Koenig and his many agents in harbor cities on the East Coast collected intelligence, bribed various officials, hired and fired agents, and provided security for the offices of von Papen, Boy-Ed, and Albert from 1914 to 1918.

Mach, Edmund von

German history professor at Harvard and member of the German University League. Worked with Heinrich Albert on propaganda for Germany.

Merkel, Otto

President of the German University League and German agent in World War I.

Muensterberg, Hugo

German psychology professor at Harvard University. Member of the German University League and staunch supporter of Germany in the World War.

Neumond, Karl

German businessman who received a large order and finances from the Imperial War Department to ship supplies from the United States to Germany. In cooperation with Heinrich Albert, Neumond was very successful in this endeavor.

Papen, Franz von

German Military Attaché in New York from 1914 to 1915. After World War I German politician and member of the Prussian parliament. German Chancellor in 1932.

Ruerode, Carl

German-American export specialist for North German Lloyd. Joined Hans-Adam von Wedell in the German army's passport fraud scheme. Was arrested and tried as a German agent.

Schmidt, Hugo

German banker who headed the Deutsche Bank in the United States in World War I. As a secret agent for the German government he was a specialist in circumventing the British financial system when moving German government funds from Germany to the U.S. Interned in 1918 and released after one year.

Schweitzer, Hugo

German chemist, secret agent, and businessman. Managing Director of Bayer Corporation in the United States. Supported German clandestine operations in the U.S. Became Heinrich Albert's successor in 1917 but died that same year.

Sommerfeld, Felix A. German naval intelligence agent under the command first of Minister Paul von Hintze then German Naval Attaché in New York, Karl Boy-Ed. Chief of Staff for President Madero, chief of the Mexican secret service, 1912 to 1913. Chief weapons and munitions buyer for Pancho Villa 1914 to 1915. Pancho Villa's diplomatic envoy to the U.S. 1914 to 1915.

Stallforth, Frederico Mexican-German businessman from Hidalgo del Parral, Mexico. Became a German secret agent in 1913. Worked closely with Felix Sommerfeld, Franz Rintelen, Heinrich Albert, and Andrew Meloy. Had financial responsibilities in the German sabotage campaign in the U.S. between 1915 and 1917. Arrested several times during the World War. After 1919 he became prominent financier in the United States and Germany. Joined the OSS in 1942.

Tauscher, Hans German agent and representative of Krupp Arms and several other German arms manufacturers in the United States. Married to the famous soprano Madame Johanna Gadski. Worked for Franz von Papen during World War I.

Tirpitz, Alfred von   German Grand Admiral and Secretary of State of the Imperial Naval Office. Headed the buildup of the German navy before World War I. Despite being distinctly pro-submarine warfare in the German cabinet, his prioritization for ship building budgets neglected the submarine. He fell out of favor with the German emperor during 1915 and resigned in March 1916.

Viereck, George Sylvester   American poet, intellectual, and journalist. Published the German propaganda paper *The Fatherland* during World War I.

Villa, Francisco "Pancho"   Mexican general and revolutionary chieftain. Raised the largest army of the Mexican Revolution. Attacked the United States in 1916. Assassinated in 1923.

Wedell, Hans-Adam von   German-American businessman Franz von Papen hired to falsify American passports for German reservists trying to travel from the United States to Germany. He was discovered and fled. British authorities arrested him on the Atlantic and took him to England. The boat carrying Wedell sank in a German submarine attack, killing the agent.

Wilhelm II of Prussia   German Emperor 1888 to 1918. Presided over the outbreak of World War I. Resigned in 1918 and went into exile to Holland.

Wilson, Thomas Woodrow Democratic politician, educator, and intellectual. President of Princeton University. Governor of New Jersey, 1910 to 1913. U.S. President 1913 to 1921.

LIST OF ILLUSTRATIONS

PROLOGUE:
MINISTER WITHOUT PORTFOLIO

I T WAS ON A HOT New York afternoon of July 24th 1915 that Heinrich
F. Albert and George Sylvester Viereck rode the 6th Avenue
elevated train from their lower Manhattan offices to uptown.
Two U.S. secret service agents, Frank Burke and W. H. Houghton,
shadowed the pair. Viereck got off the train at the 23rd street
station. Houghton followed the propagandist. Burke stayed on and
watched Albert on the way home to his apartment at 105 East 51st.[1]

> [...] a young woman boarded the car and took the
> vacant seat beside Dr. Albert and began reading a
> book. To reach his home, Albert had to take another
> car at 59th str., but when the train reached that point
> he was reading and was not aware that the train
> had halted until it was about to proceed again. The
> stuffed brief case [sic] was between Dr. Albert and
> the side of the car. When it occurred to him that he
> must get off, he jumped up and told the guard to
> wait a minute. As he got to the platform, the young
> woman called that he had forgotten his brief case
> [sic]. Burke told the girl the case was his, grabbed it
> up and headed for the station platform by another
> exit from the car [...] Dr. Albert meanwhile was
> struggling to get back into the car, his passage
> impeded by a fat woman in the doorway. By this
> time Burke had reached the platform, looked back
> and saw that Dr. Albert was visibly agitated. Other

passengers on the platform provided Burke with some concealment, but the stairway leading to the street was beyond the excited German. Sparring for time, Burke partially concealed the briefcase under his coat, and leaning against the platform wall, acted as if he were having trouble lighting a cigar. Dr. Albert glanced hastily about the platform, then dashed downstairs to the street below. Burke followed him. Dr. Albert was in an increasingly disturbed frame of mind. He walked out into the street, the better to scan the line of pedestrians. As an open trolley car clanged past, Burke ran out and leaped on its running board. But Dr. Albert had seen him and began pursuit. Burke told the trolley conductor the man pursuing them was deranged, so the car did not stop for him.[2]

The *briefcase incident* uncovered the existence of an obscure secret organization called the War Council.[3] Agent Frank Burke and his colleague had, in fact, snatched the satchel of its chief, Heinrich F. Albert.

America was far from the Fatherland, even further after the British had cut the transatlantic cables between Germany and the U.S. in August 1914. Communication between the German embassy in Washington and the key government ministries in Berlin had effectively been reduced to routes that led through enemy territories. Important functions such as transmitting funds to support the remaining German fleet overseas, buying supplies needed for the war, or maintaining even rudimentary trade between the overseas trading partner and Germany, were imperiled. The Imperial German government held emergency meetings between government officials, industry captains, and the military in early August 1914. They hatched a plan to combine the interests of all parties; military, clandestine, and commercial, in an organization that would be headquartered in New York.

The Secret War Council, comprised of a group of diplomats, businessmen, secret agents, and propagandists, formed in late

August of 1914. It organized, financed, and implemented Germany's strategy towards the United States between 1914 and 1917 during the period before the United States actively joined the war on the side of the Entente powers. The head of the council, an executive by any modern definition, was Heinrich F. Albert. An anglophile government administrator with management experience, he had the support of influential members of the German government, the military, and industry leaders. Albert would prove to be an able executor of the tasks Berlin assigned to him – with the embarrassing exception of having his briefcase snatched.

The efforts of the Secret War Council included perfectly legal and peaceful endeavors such as fund-raising, sourcing of critical supplies for exportation, and propaganda. There was also a darker side to the Secret War Council's mission, one that American officials and the public realized only after the unfortunate incident on the *El*. Albert worked in the United States under the cover of purchasing agent of the German Empire without diplomatic protection. Immediately after the compromising contents of his briefcase donned the front pages of American dailies, Ambassador Count Johann Heinrich von Bernstorff took Albert under his diplomatic umbrella and made him "Commercial Attaché" in a preemptive move and, thus, saved him from certain prosecution. His two colleagues, Military Attaché Franz von Papen and Naval Attaché Karl Boy-Ed, both members of the Secret War Council, enjoyed diplomatic immunity from the onset. They directed a host of subversive missions for the Imperial German government under diplomatic protection.

Clandestine operations naturally revolve around military necessities. The German military wanted reserve personnel in the Americas, especially the officer corps, to return to Germany and join the military forces. The Imperial Navy had to supply the remnants of her fleet despite an effective British sea blockade that forced virtually the entire German merchant marine to seek refuge in neutral ports, including New York, Philadelphia, and Baltimore within weeks of the outbreak of the war. Although the dispatch of reservists to Germany and the supply effort would seem legitimate and non-threatening to the U.S. on the surface, both operations posed serious legal and ethical questions. The projects involved falsifying passports and export manifests, a violation of a host of American laws. Given the participation of Canada in the European war on an unprecedented scale, German clandestine missions also targeted America's northern neighbor with insurgent attacks. These attacks originated on U.S. soil, again violating the law and the spirit of American neutrality. British and French purchasing agents scoured the U.S. from the onset for vital military supplies. The Secret War Council not only had to counter the enemy's efforts to source supplies but also had to collect vital intelligence on the level and detail of American involvement in the Entente supply chain.

The size and effectiveness of Germany's secret service organization in the United States has largely been underestimated in the historiography. Authors of early works lacked full access to archival documents, partly as a result of effective British misinformation that crept into scholarship. Historians also missed the full extent of German activities in the U.S. A compilation of all the facts now available in archives had not been assembled as yet. For the first time in an English language publication, this book uses and correlates the extensive financial records of the Albert office. This author accidentally discovered these extensive papers in 1991 while trying to locate the actual contents of Heinrich Albert's briefcase. Given this new information, it is now possible to follow the money trail from the German government to its agents in the United States and all the way to Pancho Villa's Division of the North. Extensive debriefings of German agents by Justice Department officials in 1918, which are now public, confirm the facts contained in Albert's accounting records. Additional private and public collections further corroborate the German financial records and the statements of captured German agents.

It is not the purpose of this monograph to explore the origins of the First World War, nor weigh the questions of responsibility or guilt for the indescribable suffering that occurred in the wake of this war. Rather, *The Secret War Council* illuminates the activities of German agents in the U.S. in 1914, a critical battlefield of the Great War. This crucial time of German-American relations builds the foundation for a thorough understanding of the road that led the two nations into open confrontation in 1917. This little known group of agents, diplomats, and businessmen organized in the Secret War Council helped pave that road.

CHAPTER 1:
GERMANY'S MOBILIZATION
FOR THE GREAT WAR

WORLD HISTORY IS CREATED BY events that literally divide time: before and after. The Great War was such an event. Many historians have grappled with the question of how a conflict could have erupted that caused whole peoples to slaughter one another on such a horrifying scale. The belligerents claimed close to thirty million military and civilian casualties from 1914 to 1918. Who were these leaders that brought such a calamity upon the civilized world? Could the march into the abyss have been stopped? Why did nobody stop it? The war ended with more questions than answers: The *Polish Question*, the *Minorities Question*, the *Rhineland Question*, the *Lebensraum Question*, to name just a few. Shocking the world two decades after the Great War, a veteran soldier from Braunau am Inn, Austria, dispensed with these questions in his catastrophic and twisted way and precipitated the destruction of Europe for a second time in a single generation.

Since 1918 thousands of scholarly works have dealt with the unanswered questions of the Great War. Few have found good answers, and many refused to see the brutal and naked truth: The leaders and people of civilized nations in the cradle of European culture had built a *Maquina Loca*, a crazy train, boarded it, thrown the controls out the windows, and driven it into an abyss while fully conscious of the resulting mayhem.[4]

The special edition of the *New York Herald* broke a headlining story on June 28th 1914, a Sunday: An assassin had stepped in front of the royal carriage in Sarajevo, Bosnia and shot Archduke Ferdinand of Austria and his wife Sophie in cold blood. German

Ambassador Count Johann Heinrich von Bernstorff and his Spanish colleague, Don Juan Riano, who were meeting for lunch in the
Ritz Carlton in Washington D.C., received the news of the assassination and feared the worst.[5] However, as Count Bernstorff noted in
his war memoirs, the American public seemed less concerned and
"[…] as always, regarded European affairs with indifference."[6]

    While the murder shocked the world, the story competed
for headlines with the publication of Sherburne G. Hopkins' stolen
papers.[7] Hopkins acted as an influential mediator between the
American oil tycoon, Henry Clay Pierce, the Wilson Administration,
and the revolutionary leaders of Mexico, Pancho Villa and Venustiano
Carranza. First published in the *New York Herald*, Hopkins's correspondence with his clients and American government officials
revealed a daunting web of conspiracy and influence peddling in
the Mexican Revolution. However, more significantly, the fact that
the Mexican Revolution and American involvement in it received
as much mention as the Sarajevo murders, attested to the lack of
premonition of the impending global disaster.

    There was no hint of more serious consequences to the
Austrian scandal than perhaps some sort of apology, maybe even
some saber rattling or, at the very worst, a border skirmish far away
in the Balkans. A war of global proportions seemed much more
remote than additional trouble with Mexico. After all, on June 28th,
American troops still occupied the harbor city of Veracruz, Mexico.
The provisional president of Mexico and self-styled *First Chief of the
Constitutionalist Army*, Venustiano Carranza, had condemned the
U.S. violation of Mexican sovereignty, and threatened war. Pancho
Villa, commander of the largest army of Mexico, the División del
Norte, had opposed the First Chief and supported the United
States, thus becoming a hero in the American press.[8] As the Austrian
crown prince and his wife succumbed to their gunshot wounds in
Sarajevo, Pancho Villa and Venustiano Carranza moved toward a
superficial and ultimately flawed unity to overthrow the Mexican
usurper, Victoriano Huerta. A flurry of diplomatic efforts between
Mexican factions and the Wilson administration far eclipsed the
events in Bosnia on that fateful Sunday. It was a week before July
4th 1914, the great celebration of American independence.

Yet July 1914 became the most dreaded month for generations of world citizens. During that month, decisions on the highest levels of the Austrian, German, Serbian, Russian, English, and French governments outfitted the proverbial runaway train with explosives and sent it on its tracks to blow up the world. The question of who could have stopped this impending disaster is still vigorously debated within the historical scholarship. The arguments range from sole German war guilt to the school of thought that the English premier, Lloyd George, first voiced in 1920; namely, that "all nations tumbled into war."[9]

Whether the conflagration could have been averted or not, German Emperor Wilhelm II and his chancellor, Theobald von Bethmann-Hollweg, played decisive roles in taking the world to the brink, then lost control. With the blessing of the German emperor, the Austro-Hungarian Empire declared war on Serbia on July 28th 1914, exactly one month after the assassinations of Archduke Franz Ferdinand and his wife. After last minute talks between Kaiser Wilhelm and his cousin, Zar Nikolaus broke down, Russia issued orders for general mobilization. The move prompted Germany in turn to declare war on Russia on August 1st and France on August 3rd. Great Britain joined her ally France on August 4th. The Japanese empire followed suit on August 13th, which effectively expanded the *European* war into a *World* war. Rather than defeating France first and then attacking Russia, as General Schlieffen had envisioned, Germany faced a war on two fronts by August 3rd. Like Wilhelm's ancestor, the Prussian king Frederick the Great, the Empire now found herself in a self-inflicted, epic struggle for survival.

German mobilization involved not only the military, but all strata of society including the press, agriculture, industry, and commerce. Thus, Germany prepared for war quite differently than England, France, or later the United States. The Empire had planned for a two-front war for years. The Schlieffen Plan, which von Moltke the Younger had modified, called for a total war.[10] Within days, eleven thousand trains carried over three million men to the French and Russian fronts.[11] All strata of society participated in the preparation for war. Reservists from every town and village in Germany added three million men to the army. The press became heavily censored, and all industrial capacities, raw materials, mail service, and the railroads reported to the War Ministry. The military nationalized the production of food. Pre-designated ships of the merchant marine became armed raiders and auxiliary cruisers. While the operational control of the merchant marine rested with the Navy Department, the financial control was centered in the Department of the Interior.[12] Almost all the captains, most merchant marine officers, and many sailors were navy reservists.

On August 4th 1914, fifty-four German merchant ships tied up in U.S. harbors for the duration of the war to escape marauding British warships. The German High Seas Fleet, Emperor Wilhelm's crown jewel in the fight against the British Empire, remained moored in German harbors safe for a handful of sorties. England's Grand Fleet as well stayed safely anchored. Neither naval power wanted to risk its capital ships early in the conflict. While the German navy patrolled the German coastline and Baltic Sea, the British Admiralty instituted a *Fernblockade*, a blockade of Germany from the distance. Warships had mined passages and effectively patrolled the waters between the British Isles, Scandinavia and the German coastline, an embarrassing early "naval checkmate" for German sea power.[13]

The result of this blockade, which was illegal by international standards (since it did not effectively seal the harbors of the enemy but rather the entire northern European coastline including the neutral countries of Scandinavia). The British navy controlled sea lanes from the rest of the world to northern Europe and subjected all ships that carried freight to northern Europe to search and seizure. Unable to return to their call harbors, large parts of the German merchant marine remained in safe harbors around the world. Thus, thousands of German naval reservists stranded the harbors of New York, Philadelphia, Baltimore, and Newport News stood ready to serve the Fatherland, a deadly resource for German Naval Attaché Karl Boy-Ed.

Von Tirpitz's navy and Ballin's merchant marine were linked together as the symbols of German ambitions for being a naval super power. However, these links were more than symbolic. The two organizations, HAPAG's merchant marine and the German navy, cooperated all along, but when the war started, they virtually operated as one. Almost every officer of the merchant marine had served actively in the German navy or was listed a reserve officer. Most sailors on Ballin's ocean liners were reservists. HAPAG's second man in command was Director Arndt von Holtzendorff. His older brother, Henning von Holtzendorff, a commander of the High Seas Fleet between 1908 and 1913, had risen to the rank of Admiral. At the outbreak of the war, Emperor Wilhelm II called him up to become chief of staff of the navy. He was a fervent supporter of unrestricted submarine warfare in the war years. While Ballin and Tirpitz both had the ear of the Kaiser and counseled him on naval strategy, the von Holtzendorff brothers represented but one of many links between military and civilian authorities that reached deep into the German government.

German industry organized itself in the *Kriegsausschuß der deutschen Industrie* (War Committee of German Industry). "The committee advised the War Ministry on industrial policy, a role that gave this body vast influence not only over the general design and administration of policy, but also over the distribution of war contracts."[14] Industry heavyweights such as Albert Ballin, Gustav Krupp von Bohlen, August Thyssen, Georg von Siemens, Walther Rathenau, Carl Fürstenberg, Max Warburg, Philipp Speyer, Arthur von Gwinner, and many more coordinated and planned every activity of the German economy. "[...] the War Commission of German Industry [*Kriegsausschuss der deutschen Industrie*] has enabled the German Government to get all possible assistance from the railroads, shipping companies, banks, and manufacturing concerns."[15]

Unlike the decentralized economy of the United States, German industry was managed completely through trade associations which, in turn, were controlled by umbrella organizations. The German government and industry leaders immediately streamlined and centralized command and control of the economy for the war effort through these trade organizations. The German Department of War created its own umbrella, the *Kriegsrohstoffabteilung* (War Raw Materials Department), also known as KRA. In charge of organizing all the raw materials needed for Germany's war production was Walter Rathenau, a well know industrialist.

The Jewish businessman had approached the Imperial Department of War at the beginning of the war with a plan to "save Germany from strangulation."[16] He proposed to centralize management of the entire war production process under a single organization that registered, purchased and distributed raw materials. The registration and management of resources, a virtual raw materials agency, occurred not only in Germany proper, but also in occupied territories such as Belgium. The KRA registered, and then allocated raw materials to the companies that could use them most effectively for products the War Department needed. Rathenau convinced the German Minister of War, Erich von Falkenhayn, that this plan combined "the best aspects of the capitalist free-market system with the principles of collective management," which enabled a smooth and optimally calibrated war production process.[17]

The imperial government had already decreed that the war effort had absolute priority by August 4th 1914. The decree legalized forceful expropriation and suspension of the legal process.[18] Germany did not have a Commerce Department. As a result, the Interior Department oversaw the efforts of both the War Department's purchasing agency and the industry's war commission for procuring important strategic materials such as cotton, dye, and rubber, as well as arms, munitions, explosives, and related chemicals.

The *Zentrale Einkaufsgenossenschaft* (Central Purchasing Corporation) that also operated in the United States specifically sourced and shipped those materials, as well as foodstuffs, to Germany. German industry, via the large commercial banks such as Bleichroeder, Deutsche Bank, Diskonto Gesellschaft, and Dresdner Bank, provided the funding. Germany's main commercial shipping lines, the Hamburg-Amerikanische Paketfahrt Aktien Gesellschaft (HAPAG) and the North German Lloyd, as well as additional leased merchantmen, arranged for shipping. No other European country had organized as efficiently as Germany to support the war effort.

The British blockade of northern Europe attempted to place Germany in a stranglehold, just as Walter Rathenau had predicted. Historian Gerd Hardach explained in his book on World War I, "during the early months of the war Germany and her allies enjoyed overall superiority so far as war materials were concerned. Large industrial capacity, the full exploitation of technical innovations, and the ability to mobilize the country's economic resources for the prosecution of the war gave the German war machine a measure of superiority [...]"[19] Because Germany's war economy functioned efficiently from day one, the blockade, while pinching German pride and the civilian population, did not succeed in seriously hampering the war effort of the Central Powers for the first two years of the war.[20]

German industry had grown decisively in the twenty-five years leading up to the Great War. Historian Frederic Wile noted in his book Men around the Kaiser in 1913 that mining production had increased "six and one-half times" since 1871.[21] By the beginning of the war, German steel production surpassed that of Britain twofold. Wile wrote, "Germany's supremacy in steel, iron and coke is unapproached [in Europe] [...] She is now [1911] behind the United Kingdom only in the production of coal."[22] Most impressive was the development of German exports that delivered German-made industrial goods to peoples around the world. While the German population had grown substantially throughout the period of economic expansion, the output of German industry rested largely on the ability to export. International trade and the development of new markets for German products dictated foreign policy. This dictum covered the need to expand into colonies, as well as to develop bilateral trading agreements all across the world. While German colonies lagged far behind those of England and France in size, over twelve million people on a combined area of one million square miles lived under German colonial rule by 1914.[23] Germany saw the colonies as an important market for her products. The world market had taken on crucial importance for the German economy.

In 1917, the U.S. Department of Commerce published a fascinating analysis of German foreign trade methods used before 1914. Despite the bad blood between the two countries at that time, U.S. bureaucrats pointed to Germany as an example worth studying for any American merchant:

'World trade' and 'world economy' early fill the
mind of the German who intends to occupy himself
with commerce [...] He realizes that the world is
the market for German merchandise, and he makes
a study of the world [...] They become familiar with
foreign commercial conditions and customs procedure, with foreign languages, with the collection
of accounts in near-by [sic] foreign countries [...]
The German home market is far less valuable than
the American home market, and with the unceas-
ing progress of German manufacturing industry
has come the necessity of cultivating foreign markets [...] He [the German] knows that there are
German steamship lines having connections with
the foreign ports in which he is interested. He feels
confident that some German bank has established
connections there [...] Necessity, geographical
position, and diligent cultivation of foreign markets
have given the German trader a cosmopolitan point
of view.[24]

It is no accident that steel-magnate Gustav Krupp's parents both
came from Philadelphia, or that German Ambassador Count
Bernstorff spoke English before he learned German. Albert Ballin,
the director of HAPAG, had Danish parents and completed his
commercial apprenticeship in England.[25] Bernhard Dernburg, the
Secretary for Colonial Affairs, had completed a banking apprenticeship in New York and spoke English fluently. Even the emperor's
chief of the navy, Alfred von Tirpitz, was an admirer of everything
British and had sent his children to England to be educated.[26]

Even more impressive than the development of German
industry was the growth of the German merchant marine. Two
corporations dominated that market, HAPAG and North German
Lloyd. From 1886 up to 1914 HAPAG grew from twenty-six ocean
vessels to one-hundred-and-eighty with a gross tonnage of 1.5 million,[27] about half of the total German merchant marine.[28] HAPAG
liners carried 403,000 passengers and eight million tons of freight

in 1911.[29] The North German Lloyd moved 514,000 passengers and 3.6 million tons of freight in the same year.[30] By 1913, it had a fleet of 133 vessels with 821,000 registered tons. In short, the German merchant marine together with forty-one smaller lines, was second only to that of Great Britain at the outbreak of the Great War.

Albert Ballin was the civilian alter ego of Alfred von Tirpitz in the German Empire. Both men had realized their visions of a strong naval fleet for Germany. The pride of the Second Empire was split between the proud battle cruisers of the High Seas Fleet and the commercial liners, the largest of which, the *Vaterland*, Ballin had put into service in 1913. She not only represented the might of German engineering and ship construction, she was the largest ocean liner in the world, larger than the *Lusitania*, *Mauretania*, or *Titanic*. The *Vaterland* not only eclipsed the British liners in terms of size and power, but also in terms of design and luxury. While larger and wider, she approximately matched *Lusitania* and *Mauretania*'s speed.[31] Count Bernstorff commented after traveling on the mighty ship in 1914, "Germans who live at home can hardly imagine with what love and what pride we foreign ambassadors and exiled Germans regarded the German shipping-lines."[32] To Count Bernstorff and many others, the *Vaterland* was an ambassador in itself.

The SS *Vaterland*, confiscated by the US and re-named *Leviathan* after WWI. This picture is ca. 1925[33]

The huge German industrial conglomerates and their leaders had only one interest at the onset of the war: A short and successful campaign. As a team, the large German banks, the great shipping lines, the munitions, chemical, and heavy industries became the critical support pillars of the German war effort. Germany had stocked up on strategic supplies for years, especially arms and munitions. The British blockade hurt Germany's economy on the civilian side, as a result. Before the war, German trade with South America and Africa had provided important raw materials such as fertilizers, cotton, wool, rubber, coffee, and sugar. In 1914 and beyond, these supplies, as well as staple foods such as rice, corn, and wheat became scarce because of the blockade. The German merchant marine was rusting in neutral harbors, mainly in the United States, or had joined the moored High Seas Fleet in Germany's North Sea harbors.

The German government foresaw the possibility of restricted transatlantic trade. In coordination with Germany's industrial and financial leaders, the empire had organized and prepared for a wartime economy. Centrally managed, Germany's leaders artificially curbed inflation, rationed food and strategic supplies, pooled money for worldwide sourcing activities, and organized industry to dedicate all its resources to the war effort. It is this marked difference between the German and the American political and economic landscape that laid the foundation for a balanced understanding of Germany's strategy and actions towards the United States in the war years.

CHAPTER 2:
THE WAR COUNCIL ASSEMBLES

T HE GERMAN TEAM TASKED WITH organizing the North American front in the Great War began to arrive in the harbor of New York on August 24th 1914.[34] Former Secretary of State for Colonial Affairs, Dr. Bernhard Dernburg, accompanied Johann Heinrich Count von Bernstorff, the Imperial German ambassador. Other key members of the Secret War Council, German naval and military attachés Karl Boy-Ed and Franz von Papen, had already rented offices in New York in the previous weeks. The German government selected Heinrich Albert to head the organization in the United States. He was sailing on another steamer a few days behind.

Ambassador Count Bernstorff, a man of fifty-two years, had an imposing personality. Tall, erect, with a well-trimmed mustache, the edges of which curved slightly upward in the Prussian fashion, he was highly intelligent, had a winning smile, and charmed most whom he encountered, especially women. Having served in the United States since 1908, he was intimately familiar with the politics and culture of the country, not least because of his American-born wife. Born in 1862 in London, Count Bernstorff was the son of one of the most courageous politicians in the Prussian Empire. While Foreign Minister for Prussia, his father, Count Albrecht von Bernstorff, had earned the ire of Prince Bismarck in the Prussian constitutional crisis of 1859-1866. Overestimating his political strength, von Bernstorff resigned in a spat over the constitution with the expectation of forcing his will upon the Prussian government. However, the Emperor accepted Bernstorff's miscalculated challenge and appointed Otto von Bismarck chancellor and foreign minister. Count Albrecht von Bernstorff would criticize Bismarck's

Machiavellian style of governing for the rest of his life. The elder Bernstorff served as ambassador at the Court of St. James in London in 1862. For the first eleven years of his life until his father's death in 1873 Bernstorff grew up in England.

After moving back to Germany Bernstorff went to the humanistic *gymnasium* in Dresden from which he graduated with a *baccalaureate* in 1881. While his dream had always been to pursue a diplomatic career, the family feud with Bismarck made an appointment to the diplomatic service impossible. Therefore, he joined the Prussian military and served for the next eight years in an artillery unit in Berlin.[35] Bernstorff finally succeeded in convincing the Bismarck family to settle the dispute with his long-dead father, and he was accepted into the diplomatic corps in 1892. Count Bernstorff married the American-born Jeanne Luckemeyer, the daughter of a wealthy German-Jewish family from New York in 1887.

His first diplomatic assignment was Constantinople where he served as military attaché. The count became counselor of the embassy in London after a brief assignment to St. Petersburg. Before he took the ambassadorship in the United States, he served as consul general in Cairo. Despite the problems his family had with the Bismarcks, the young ambassador basically agreed with Bismarck's policies, in particular with the decision to found the German Reich without Austria in 1871.

The young count and his American wife fit into the Washington scene. Socially very active, the popular ambassador received countless honorary degrees from American universities including Brown, Princeton, and the University of Pennsylvania. He enjoyed private invitations from President Taft, and stood out for his diplomatic tact and intelligence. When the war broke out, Count Bernstorff was taking his annual vacation at his summer home on Lake Starnberg at the foothills of the Alps south of Munich.[36] He had left the United States on July 7th in a first class cabin on the behemoth HAPAG flagship *SS Vaterland*.[37] Despite the claims by contemporary reporters and scholars that the ambassador was "recalled," Count Bernstorff simply had gone on his customary summer vacation before the crisis in Europe took on the semblance of a world war.[38]

Johann Heinrich Count von Bernstorff[39]

In fact, the European crisis was not even on his mind as he wrote to a friend before he left, "The English and French Ambassadors are both going to leave, so that I really don't see why I should stay here, especially as the Mexican question may drag on for years."[40] The crisis in Mexico, the revelations of the Hopkins papers, and domestic concerns seemed far more pressing than the fear of a global catastrophe as a result of the assassinations in Sarajevo. However, while in Germany, the situation in Europe became more precarious, and in August 1914, Count Bernstorff was forced to interrupt his vacation to meet with his superiors in Berlin. There, Foreign Secretary Gottlieb von Jagow briefed the ambassador on the developing situation and issued marching orders for his wartime assignment in Washington. Sadly, Count Bernstorff's specific instructions have not been preserved, although his preoccupations and actions in the following years make them rather clear.[41]

Bernhard Dernburg had given up his illustrious banking career to become Secretary of State for Colonial Affairs in 1907. The heavyset, full-bearded figure, with clear blue eyes, attentive, with a friendly disposition, portrayed raw power, intelligence, and decisiveness.[42] Wildly successful as an innovative and daring reorganizer, the German banker had risen to stardom in German political and financial circles, en par with "Albert Ballin, Walther Rathenau, Max Warburg, Carl Fürstenberg, and Maximilian Harden."[43] The German Emperor had chosen this powerful Jewish banker specifically for the colonial secretary assignment because "[…] his distinguishing characteristic [was] *Rücksichtslosigkeit*, cold-blooded, unrelenting disregard for anything but his objective."[44]

Dernburg was looking for a new job in the summer of 1914. His political enemies, the legions of kowtowing Prussian bureaucrats the secretary had steamrolled throughout his career, had finally succeeded in having him fired from his cabinet post in 1910. It took the Emperor four years to find a suitable mission for his old friend who had used the forced break for extensive travels to Asia and touring on the lecture circuit.[45]

The beginning of the Great War provided the opportunity. The former imperial secretary, the "Captain without a ship," was to arrange for a large loan to the tune of $150 million in the United States and organize the sale of German war bonds on the American market.[46] The proceeds were projected to finance the expected cost of purchases of American goods Germany needed in the war years.[47] Nominally, Dernburg represented the German Red Cross in the United States, a designation causing great consternation when the American public found out that their donations financed the war effort instead of helping battlefield casualties.[48] As a banker, Dernburg had been overseas on numerous occasions, and even spent his banking apprenticeship at Ladenburg, Thalmann and Co. in New York.[49] He had also cultivated important contacts on Wall Street in his years as a banker, Colonial Secretary, and financier. He spoke excellent English. The imperial German government considered Dernburg an expert regarding the United States with the *chutzpah* to get things done. Unfortunately, much to the chagrin of Ambassador Count Bernstorff, diplomacy turned out not to be one of Dernburg's strong points.

Bernhard Dernburg, approximately 1915[50]

The designated head of the Secret War Council and the person officially assigned to purchase essential supplies in America arrived from Copenhagen on August 26th. The neutral Scandinavian

America Line steamer *SS Oskar II* tied up at its New York pier two days after Count Bernstorff and Dernburg set foot on North American soil.[51] Born on the 12th of February 1874 in Magdeburg, Germany, Heinrich Friedrich Albert came from a well-to-do household. His father, Friedrich, owned a private bank. Albert studied law after graduating high school with a baccalaureate.[52] He passed his bar exam in 1901. His career took him through various jobs as a legal assistant in the Department of Interior. He rose through the ranks as an administrator specialized on economic questions, especially the role of cartels in the German economy. He married Ida Hausen in 1905 with whom he had three children. Although often called *Dr.* Albert, he probably never pursued any doctoral studies.[53]

Albert received the rank and title of *Geheimer Oberregierungsrat* (Privy Chancellor) in 1911.[54] Albert's responsibilities reflected his pre-occupation with details and bureaucratic process but he also had managerial qualities. His talent for details, combined with fluency in English, secured him a managerial role in setting up Germany's exhibitions in the St. Louis and Brussels world fairs in 1904 and 1910, respectively. His responsibilities for the German exhibits brought the young lawyer in contact with officials from many realms of the Prussian economic and political power structure. Most notably, Albert worked directly under Clemens von Delbrück, who became Secretary of the Interior and Vice-Chancellor in 1909.[55] Their working relationship was close enough that the Secretary actually expressed to Albert's wife in 1915 that he "missed him."[56] Albert Ballin, the director of HAPAG also noticed Heinrich Albert and took a liking to this uncomplicated, meticulous, hard-working, yet decisive and results-oriented manager. Ballin invited Albert on a relaxing cruise through the Mediterranean in 1911, fully paid for by HAPAG.

The courtship worked. Albert signed on with HAPAG on April 1st 1914. HAPAG director Arndt von Holtzendorff appointed the German lawyer to become the private assistant to Director Dr. Otto Ecker for an annual salary of six thousand German Marks (approximately $30,140 in today's value before the war with deteriorating value thereafter). Ecker was slated to join HAPAG directors Albert Polis and Dr. Karl Buenz in New York that year. The contract ran for two years with the option of being extended.[57] Albert had become a protégé of HAPAG director Albert Ballin.

No records have survived confirming the suspicion that between 1904 and 1914 Albert also worked undercover as a spy for Germany. However, it is very likely that certain members of the team including the German administrator who assembled the St. Louis exhibits in 1904 had been German agents entrusted with gathering and reporting intelligence. Albert seemed to transition seamlessly from a successful government career, in which he rose to privy counselor, to moving into the private sector with HAPAG, and then back to working for the German government in the United States. Despite the lack of archival evidence (which is not unusual with respect to intelligence officers), Albert's career indicates that his true occupation was indeed in the intelligence sector. The various *career* moves were nothing but cover jobs for various intelligence missions. Certainly, one of the main responsibilities of his war assignment in New York was to establish command and control over secret service activities in the United States. Despite the British propaganda ridiculing German agents' skills in the U.S. during the war, which several scholars picked up unchallenged, it is unlikely that the German government would have entrusted this important function in New York to an amateur without any previous experience.[58]

Emperor Wilhelm II, through Albert's former boss, Secretary of the Interior Clemens von Delbrück tasked Ballin with creating and managing the Central Purchasing Agency for the German Empire when the war broke out. Ballin decided to put Heinrich Albert in charge of the critically important New York office. The war was just taking shape when Albert arrived on August 26th 1914, with his boss Dr. Otto Ecker and Director Albert Polis in tow.[59] Albert's wife and children remained in Berlin. The newly created *Zentrale Einkaufsgenossenschaft* (Central Purchasing Agency) reported to Albert Ballin, but was officially a department of the Interior Ministry.[60] Because of the re-organization of the German economy for the war effort, HAPAG's resources, human and otherwise, were entirely at Albert's disposal. Ballin and his managers opened their network of German-American merchants to the German lawyer, as well as business and banking connections. By the time the United States entered the war on the side of the Entente powers in 1917, Albert's New York office would have disbursed over thirty-four million dollars ($714 Million in today's value), a staggering amount that even baffled senior U.S. investigators at that time.[61]

Albert noted in his diary the frequent meetings he had with his superiors Ecker and Polis, sometimes including the Military Attaché Franz von Papen.[62] Notable also are entries in his diary referring to *reports* he filed with the Department of Interior in cooperation with the two HAPAG bosses.[63] The two managers sat in on various meetings with Hans Tauscher, the Krupp representative in the United States and secret agent of the German General Staff. Tauscher, a captain of the reserve (same rank as the military attaché but without General Staff training), was a well-connected arms dealer in New York. He represented Krupp, Mauser, and other German arms manufacturers with customers ranging from Mexican revolutionaries to the American government. Besides having made millions before the war, Tauscher was married to Johanna Gadski, a world-renowned soprano and New York social star. These discussions most likely centered on the purchase of ammunition and other war supplies. Even meetings dealing with propaganda, a field having nothing to do with the business of HAPAG, prompted their attendance.[64]

Clearly, Ecker and Polis had responsibilities far exceeding those inherent in their *cover* as HAPAG executives. The reports mentioned in Albert's diary have not all been uncovered. Fragments preserved in the National Archives in Washington D.C. indicate that Albert transmitted sensitive intelligence on a regular basis to the German military intelligence, the political section, *Abteilung IIIB* of the German General Staff. Count Bernstorff, the German ambassador, provided further evidence of the true responsibilities of the HAPAG managers in New York. He purposely misstated in his war memoirs that Albert traveled with him and Dernburg to the United States.[65]

The question begs why he would mislead his readers (and historians) regarding his travel companions in 1914. The ambassador probably sought to conceal the identity of the people with whom

Albert arrived. In reality, they were his intelligence handlers who traveled under the cover of HAPAG management. Count Bernstorff additionally identified Albert's employer as the Interior Department, although, strictly speaking, he worked for HAPAG. Though Albert was exposed later in the war, his two superiors at HAPAG, Ecker and Polis, remained anonymous, indeed to this day. Over the next years, Albert's reports passed through the Hamburg-America building in New York before they landed on the desks of his true superiors, who resided in Berlin. Heinrich Albert worked for the Secretary of the Interior, Clemens von Delbrück, but under the supervision of Otto Ecker and Albert Polis, he also reported to *Abteilung IIIB* of the War Department, as well as Department N, the *Nachrichtenabteilung des Admiralstabes* (German Naval Intelligence).

Albert did not fit the stereotypical, overbearing, and brusque Prussian militarist, the likes of Franz von Papen, whom the American papers took greatest pleasure in mocking during the war. He also differed significantly from the suave, aristocratic, and arrogantly cultured version of the Prussian diplomat, the likes of Count Bernstorff and Prince Hatzfeld. The *New York Sun* reporter John Price Jones described the privy councilor in his 1917 book on the German Secret Service in America:

> He was a tall, slender man, wonderfully supple-looking in spite of the conventional frock coat and the dignified dress of a European business man [sic]. His clear, blue eyes, his smooth face, thoughtful and refined, his blonde hair, and his regular features suggested a man of thirty-eight, or even younger, though you would look for a middle-aged or older man as selected for a position requiring so many nice decisions. When you entered his room – and few persons gained admission – he would rise and bow low and most courteously. He spoke in a soft, melodious voice, was deliberate in the choice of his words and encouraged conversation rather than made it.[66]

While he sketched Albert so aptly the reporter missed one important feature that characterized many a spymaster: He was also non-descript. No one noticed Albert. He was of average build, his dress fit the surroundings, his looks were average, and nothing about this man caused anyone but another secret agent to take note of him. One other characteristic would have endeared him to his nemesis at the Bureau of Investigation, Chief A. Bruce Bielaski: Frugality. When he returned to Germany and accounted for his expenditures and activities in the United States, he credited the Central Purchasing Agency "the difference of $1,177.86 [...] with reservation of a later decision as to whether this surplus from the funds of the daily allowances belongs to me personally."[67] He had not used a sizable portion of his $20 daily expense allowance.

Heinrich Albert in his office in April, 1916.[68]

Albert outlined his responsibilities for the Central Purchasing Agency in New York in draft chapters of an envisioned book. These *chapters* are spread throughout his archival files. His priorities included the obvious, *Reichseinkauf* (Purchases for the Empire), but also *Geldbeschaffung* (fund-raising),[69] *Aufklärungsarbeit* (education of the American public), *Schädigung des Feindes* (hurting the enemy),[70] leasing and purchasing of ships for transportation of goods to Germany,[71] insurance,[72] and maximum exploitation of the American legal environment.[73] He directed and financed each of these tasks from an administrative perspective, while others planned and executed the work. Despite Albert's nominally inferior rank to Ambassador Count Bernstorff, Secretary Dr. Dernburg, Consul Hossenfelder, Attachés Naval Commander Boy-Ed and Army Captain von Papen, they all had to come to Albert regarding clandestine work, and disclose their projects.[74] It was at Albert's discretion if they would then receive funding.

Former Secretary of Colonial Affairs Bernhard Dernburg headed the fund-raising team. He also involved himself deeply in propaganda efforts, especially after failing to raise the envisioned loan in the United States. *Hurting the enemy* belonged to the two military attachés, von Papen and Boy-Ed. Many scholars and journalists who wrote about the German clandestine operations in the U.S. between 1914 and 1917 mistakenly accorded Ambassador Count Bernstorff the command and control over the spy networks.[75] These assessments were based on contemporary newspaper reports, not the archival sources available today.[76]

The ambassador, for the most part, did not even have a right to know about, much less to direct these operations. In his full accounting to the German Department of the Treasury in 1919, the retired Commercial Attaché Albert softened his direct control over Count Bernstorff, Dernburg, and the military attachés as "collaboration" and "cooperation."[77] However, Albert not only financed their projects but also helped direct strategy. He was the paymaster for all military espionage assets in the United States (mostly naval), had his own network of agents, and was in charge of reports to the War Department's "political" intelligence section *Abteilung IIIB* and *Department N* of the navy.[78] Insurance, purchasing, and legal questions naturally remained Albert's domain.

Purchasing and fund-raising were intimately related. While still in Germany, Albert noted in his diary on the 10th of August 1914, that there was a promise of funds: "Authorization for me on Kuhn, Loeb and Co., 100 millions [sic]."[79] Sensationalist reports in newspapers and early books after the expulsion of von Papen and Boy-Ed in December 1915 fantasized of "millions", even "hundreds of millions" of dollars at the disposal of the German "fiscal agent" Heinrich Albert.[80] Much to Albert's surprise and disappointment, the actual numbers, which are recorded in his papers at the National Archives in Washington D.C., underscore the reasons for the urgency with which German officials pushed fund-raising.

Albert's three accounts, G. Amsinck and Co., Ladenburg Thalmann and Co., and the German Embassy/bond account showed inflows totaling $3.5 million between September and December of 1914. Early creditors amounted to three banks: Kuhn, Loeb & Company, the investment bank owned mostly by German financier and Dernburg mentor Max Warburg, Seligman & Company, and the Speyer banking house. Warburg, contributed a measly single million dollars, a far cry from the $100 Million guarantee given early in August. Seligman matched Warburg's loan. $500,000 came from Speyer, the balance were the proceeds from war bond sales.[81]

Albert explained in the draft chapters preserved in his papers that the financial situation he walked into was desperate and depressing:

> Shortly before the war Germany was the creditor
> of the United States. The exchange rate for cable
> stood at ninety-five and three eights [1 Reichsmark
> = 0.95 U.S. Dollars] in the week ending July 24, 1914.
> The beginning unrest led to a marked depreciation
> of American securities and repayment of balances.
> About eighty million dollars [$1.68 billion in today's
> value] must have been sold. The balances were
> transmitted telegraphically directly or indirectly
> to Germany. The fact that the exchange rate rose
> to one hundred and four [1 Reichsmark = 1.04 U.S.
> Dollars] in the following week, closing on August 1,
> 1914, shows that clearly. The result of these trans
> actions was that the German national economy had
> no balances and therefore no credits in New York.[82]

HAPAG had transmitted its U.S. cash reserves to Germany just before the outbreak of the war. Whether HAPAG managers expected a devaluation of the U.S. dollar and tried to shepherd profits back to the *Fatherland,* or counted on the German government to fund the enforced mooring of its ships is not documented.[83]

The Imperial War Department did take on some of the financing for HAPAG but not for charity. These funds would be at the heart of German clandestine operations in the first months of the war. While Russia, England, and France were able to raise large loans in the United States, the finances of the German Empire remained obscure to many contemporaries and historians. Wild speculations initiated by English propaganda and adopted in scholarly treatments clouded the true numbers for decades as a result. Most important for the understanding of German finances in the U.S. is a thorough understanding of the official-private relationship between German corporations and the government. During the war, any German corporation that could aid the war effort would be drafted. The connections linking the German government and these corporations started with the status of their employees. Most of the sailors on HAPAG and North German Lloyd ships became war draftees at the outbreak of the war. Therefore, responsibility for the stranded crews in the United States fell on German Naval Attaché Karl Boy-Ed, another key member of the Secret War Council.

Naval Commander Karl Boy-Ed has been portrayed in history as the alter ego of Franz von Papen – arrogant, militaristic, ruthless, not very smart, and dishonest. Indeed, his work in the United States put the naval attaché into situations where, by definition of his duties as the chief of naval intelligence for the Western Hemisphere, he violated American laws and the diplomatic code of conduct. He followed orders without regard to personal consequences for himself or his agents. His memoirs about the time in Washington indignantly called *Verschwörer? (Conspirator?)* do not reveal an inkling of regret over his activities in the war or feeling for the victims of his schemes. Scores of his co-conspirators and supporters lost their reputations, livelihoods, and freedom. Boy-Ed simply moved on under the cloak of diplomatic immunity. However, to judge him solely through the eyes of the eventual victors would not do justice to this complex and sophisticated man.

Karl Boy-Ed was born on September 14th 1872 in Lübeck on the German Baltic seacoast as the oldest of three children.[84] Karl's father, Karl Johann Boy, was a merchant in town. Ida Ed, Karl's mother was the daughter of the German parliamentarian, publisher, and newspaper editor, Christoph Marquard Ed. Karl Johann Boy and his wife Ida Ed separated in 1878 and Ida subsequently moved to Berlin with her son. There, she worked as a journalist and began writing novels. Ida's estranged husband forced her and Karl to move back to Lübeck in 1880. She continued her career as a writer and published an amazing volume of seventy novels and essays. She supported the early career of Thomas Mann and corresponded regularly with his brother, Heinrich, also a renowned literary figure. A major influence in the art and music scene in Lübeck, Ida supported the early careers of conductors Wilhelm Furtwängler and Hermann Abendroth. Thomas Mann regularly stayed overnight in the Boy-Ed household.

Karl joined the German navy at the age of nineteen. Rising through the ranks to become lieutenant commander, Boy-Ed served on dozens of naval assignments. He witnessed the American occupation of the Philippines in 1898.[85] Shortly before the Boxer war, Kaiser Wilhelm's brother, Prince Heinrich von Preußen, sent the navy lieutenant on a secret mission to assess the "value of the Chinese navy."[86] Boy-Ed considered his report a major accomplishment as a writer. Given the hostilities that broke out with China a year later, Boy-Ed's research certainly was timely. Between 1906 and 1909 the navy lieutenant served on the staff of Grand Admiral von Tirpitz. During this period, Boy-Ed took over the *Nachrichtenabteilung N* (office of naval intelligence) from Paul von Hintze.[87] After three years in Berlin and a promotion, Boy-Ed served as first officer on the *SMS Deutschland* and captain of the naval tender, *Hela*. He sailed on the *SMS Preussen*, the flagship of the second squadron in 1911, by then promoted to lieutenant commander.

Boy-Ed's navy career brought him to the United States in the beginning of 1912 where he became naval attaché responsible for the United States and Mexico. He traveled to Jamaica, the Panama Canal Zone and Mexico before he took over his assigned post in Washington D.C. in 1913. Funny, smart, cosmopolitan, extremely well read, and intellectual, he enjoyed a great deal of popularity and respect among American naval officials before the war. Boy-Ed, intellectual and reserved stayed mostly to himself, but was well-respected in military circles in the United States. The single Boy-Ed began dating the daughter of an Episcopal Bishop from Pennsylvania, Virginia Mackay Smith in 1914. The couple married in Germany in 1921.

However, not all was well with the German navy officer. Boy-Ed suffered from phagomania, a constant desire to eat. The disorder required tremendous self-discipline in social circumstances. Another, more severe disorder was insomnia. Boy-Ed could not get a good night's sleep. On the one hand, the handicap increased his productivity by leaps and bounds but on the other it wore on his health. The stresses of his New York assignment – and possibly an unexpressed sense of regret for the consequences of his actions – took a heavy toll on him physically and mentally. He admitted in his autobiographic sketch that as a result of his wartime assignment his nerves suffered a permanent "crack."[88]

Naval Attaché Boy-Ed started clandestine operations immediately at the outbreak of the war. The same was true for Franz von Papen, his army counterpart and another key player in the Secret War Council. Von Papen returned from Mexico on August 7th 1914.[89] The young military attaché cut quite a different figure from Karl Boy-Ed. Tall, handsome, and thin, the dashing officer made a splash in New York's social scene. While Karl Boy-Ed has largely disappeared from the pages of world history, Franz von Papen remains a highly controversial figure to this day, despised by some as a ruthless war criminal, considered a man of limited intelligence by others, a statesman by few.

Ida Boy-Ed and son Karl, ca. 1873[90]

Karl Boy-Ed[91]

Franz von Papen in New York in 1915[92]

The son of Friedrich von Papen zu Koeningen and Anna Laura von Steffens grew up on a large estate in Werl in the province of Westphalia. Keeping with tradition among noble families, the first son inherited the estate, the second joined the military. The Papens sent their son as a boarder to several military academies at the age of twelve. After graduation from *Gymnasium*, the young aristocrat joined the Düsseldorf Cavalry School as a lieutenant in the elite 5th Uhlan regiment. An expert horseman, the cavalry sent him to the Hanover Cavalry Riding School in 1902 through which he represented the German army in international competitions. During this time period, von Papen acquired a good knowledge of the English language as he spent considerable time in Great Britain.

He married Martha von Boch-Gelbau in 1905 with whom he fathered five children. Professionally, the ambitious young cavalry officer advanced his career when the army admitted him to the General Staff School in Berlin in 1908. In March of 1913, the now thirty-four year-old Papen completed his training and briefly joined the Great General Staff of the Army as a captain. The army assigned the staff officer to the embassies of Mexico and Washington as military attaché in December of that year. He arrived in the United States in the spring of 1914. Subsequently, he spent several months in Mexico and witnessed the American occupation of Veracruz in April 1914. World War I broke out while von Papen was still in Mexico. He rushed back to Washington in August.

The core German team that the imperial government had assembled in August 1914 to execute war-time assignments in the U.S. chose New York as its permanent base. Even the ambassador maintained a suite in the Ritz-Carlton in New York and a summer residence in Cedarhurst, Long Island. New York was the center of American political and economic power by the fall of 1914. During the first months of the war, the city bristled with foreign agents of all colors and backgrounds vying for financial backing, political influence, and intelligence on the opposition. The first floor of the Hamburg-America building, 1123 Broadway, which housed Dernburg and Albert's offices, became the headquarters from where the members of the Secret War Council began directing their work.

CHAPTER 3:
SETTING UP SHOP IN NEW YORK

T HE MOST PRESSING TASK FOR the Secret War Council became the support and supply of the German navy in the western hemisphere. Cut-off from their home bases, a few cruisers, a naval squadron on the Pacific under the command of Admiral Maximilian von Spee, and several commercial ships outfitted as raiders required coal and supplies. German personnel stranded in neutral harbors up and down the Atlantic and Pacific coastline also needed to be paid wages. Since the British navy patrolled the American coastlines, supply freighters had to somehow rendevous with the navy ships on the high seas. Aside from the real chance of British battle cruisers attacking and sinking the German ships, neutrality laws only allowed warships to take on enough coal and supplies to make it to the homeport. U.S. authorities refused to let belligerents use American ports as supply stations for conducting war operations. As a result, British ships used Canada and Caribbean dependencies as supply bases, while German assets were cut off.

Within days of German ships arriving in U.S. harbors on August 4th 1914, naval attaché Boy-Ed received funds to support the interned ships and cut-off German naval assets in the Atlantic and Pacific oceans. The money arrived through German businesses with offices in the U.S. such as the Bayer Chemical Company and Wessels, Kuhlenkampf, and Co. Bayer, a chemical company not only known for the development of Aspirin, but also with a veritable world monopoly on dye stuffs, had large currency reserves in the United States. When the war began, the chemical concern trans-ferred these funds to the German embassy. The German govern-ment reimbursed the company in Germany, thereby successfully

masking the money trail. The coordinator for requisitioning, organizing, and distributing these funds was a relatively non-descript
administrator in the German *Reichsmarineamt* (Department of the
Navy), Department B.I.2., Lieutenant Commander Franz Rintelen.[93]
Rintelen became a notorious sabotage agent in the United States in
1915. After his discovery and arrest in England, he spent four years
in an Atlanta penitentiary.

The Bayer Chemical Company, best-known for the Aspirin
medication, transferred $300,000 to Boy-Ed's accounts via the
Warburg Bank on August 5th 1914.[94] The U.S. chief executive of Bayer
was Dr. Hugo Schweitzer, a German agent on retainer by the War
Department since the early 1900s. For a decade before the war the
respected CEO was Germany's highest placed industrial spy in the
United States. The War Department called him back to Germany
in August 1914 to receive his wartime instructions. Schweitzer
returned to the U.S. on September 9th 1914 to begin his assignment
for the Secret War Council.[95]

Another financial agent was Gustav B. Kuhlenkampf, a
German citizen, avid sailboat racer, and personal friend of the
Mexican-American banker Frederico Stallforth, who also later
worked for Albert. Kuhlenkampf ran a commodity brokerage in
New York headquartered in Bremen, Germany. Mainly specialized
on coffee and sugar, Kuhlenkampf commanded an impressive
network of connections in the main countries exporting those
commodities, such as southern Mexico, Guatemala, Colombia,
and various Caribbean countries.[96] Shipping giants, such as the
North German Lloyd and HAPAG, transported the commodities to
Germany. Kuhlenkampf knew many of the steamship captains and
reportedly was close friends with the captain of the North German
Lloyd liner, *SS Kronprinzessin Cecile*, interned in Maine since the 4th
of August.[97] Without question, Kuhlenkampf worked with, if not
for, German naval intelligence.

According to a New York District Attorney, Karl Boy-Ed
deposited $750,000 in New York Banks in early September 1914.[98]
The money came from Kuhlenkampf, who told prosecutors in 1916
that "just after the outbreak [of the war]," out of the blue, his company received $750,000 ($156.7 million in today's value) from the

Deutsche Bank.[99] "Well, some time [sic] after that [the money arriving], it may have been a week or ten days, or longer, Captain Boy-Ed came to me and asked if I received money from Berlin [...]. I said, yes, we had received some money [...] he [Boy-Ed] told me that it was for him."[100]

Kuhlenkampf disbursed large sums to German consulates in San Francisco and South America for Boy-Ed, some to HAPAG to requisition one of their ships, and the rest to various recipients on the East Coast.[101] An investigator with access to Boy-Ed's financials showed that the North German Lloyd received $213,000 ($4.5 million in today's value) and HAPAG $75,000 ($1.6 million in today's value) in 1915.[102]

Heinrich Albert's files additionally show that Boy-Ed received $1.2 million ($25.2 million in today's money) on the 23rd of October 1914, independent of the other funds under the control of Albert.[103] The money came to the Riggs National Bank on accounts of HAPAG and was kept under the codename "Guidofonds."[104] According to an anti-German propaganda book published after the U.S. entered the war, Boy-Ed received a total of $3.3 million ($69.3 million in today's value) between July 24th and October 29th 1914.[105] Despite the obvious bias of the book, the listed financials include the documented $1.2 million with the correct date of October 24th. The numbers in this book likely originated from captured German files U.S. authorities leaked to the press after the declaration of war in 1917.

1914			
July 24.	Received from	National Bank of Commerce . .	$250,000.00
" 26.	"	" A. Vogel	70,000.00
Aug. 1.	"	" National City Bank	100,000.00
" 1.	"	" Speyer and Co.	100,000.00
" 2.	"	" National City Bank	200,000.00
" 3.	"	" Speyer and Co.	500,000.00
" 5.	"	" Bayer Co., Inc.	300,000.00
" 16.	"	" Kuhn, Loeb and Co.	35,000.00

" 24.	Interest			1,941.11
Oct. 26.	Received from National City Bank			300,000.00
" 27.	"	" Kuhn, Loeb and Co.		150,000.00
" 29.	"	" Kuhn, Loeb and Co.		1,250,000.00
Dec. 1.	Interest			5,253.00
				$3,262,197.11
Oct. 24.	Paid to Hamburg-American Line			$1,200,000.00
Dec. 2.	" "	"	"	" 1,961,365.36

106

Boy-Ed's accounts show that he signed out $3,000 ($63,000 in today's value) every two weeks, usually in $100 bills to pay sailors.[107] Crew salaries, payments for supplies for German raiders such as the SMS Dresden, and other clandestine operations in support of naval ships on the high seas amounted to $325,000 ($6.8 million in today's value) from August to November. The German naval attaché also sent an additional $160,000 (3.4 million in today's value) to the North German Lloyd, presumably to pay for crew and expenses there.[108] Franz Rintelen, the notorious naval intelligence spy who worked in the United States in 1915, boasted during interviews in May 1940 that he had three thousand sailors under his command to undertake sabotage activities.[109] Although it is questionable that Rintelen actually had command of all stranded German sailors, he does allude to a most important point about German operations in the U.S.: None of the HAPAG and North German Lloyd sailors were civilians during World War I.[110] They constituted a virtual German army on American soil under the German navy's command. Other, much higher disbursements are also recorded. These clearly financed many of Boy-Ed's clandestine operations, which he directed from his New York offices, room 809 at 11 Broadway.[111]

The key to funding of the Secret War Council, and especially the clandestine operations of the German General Staff entrusted to Military Attaché von Papen, consisted of placing millions of dollars of German war bonds in the American financial markets. However, the war bonds project, which Dernburg was to pursue, turned out to be an unmitigated disaster. American high finance considered the risk of a quick German defeat too great. The financiers refused to invest in the treasuries. Dernburg, who had brought $10 million in German war bonds with him in August, placed less than one million by October 1914.[112] Count Bernstorff informed Albert and Dernburg in a top-secret letter on October 17th 1914, that the German Treasury was withdrawing the war bond issue. "[...] Thought of secretly placing [the bonds] with Americans abandoned for now."[113] Money was short, yet Albert had the thankless task of plucking a supply line from the U.S. to Germany out of thin air. HAPAG needed to maintain its assets and help supply German war ships. The German government had to quickly organize a clandestine service and propaganda organization in the U.S. All these goals seemed jeopardized, if not impossible, when the German team arrived on August 24th and 26th.

Heinrich Albert, the forty-year-old lawyer and administrator immediately went to work. "Arrived, Hoboken 10.15; at [Plaza] Hotel 10.45. Conference with Count v. Bernstorff (12.30)."[114] Albert jotted down the gist of the briefing he received from the German ambassador: "False information as to public opinion against Germany. Kaiser to blame for the war; [as well as] violation of neutrality. Difficult connections [relationship] with Europe."[115] At 1:00 p.m. Albert met with Bernhard Dernburg, who occupied a suite of offices at 1123 Broadway. The meeting lasted until 3:30 p.m. Albert jotted down Dernburg's key points: "Money market in New York in a panic; no loans on account of neutrality; Red Cross only for America!"[116]

Albert had a brief conference at 4:15 p.m. with the managing director of HAPAG North America, Karl Buenz, and his legal counsel, son of the famous American statesman and civil war general, Carl L. Schurz.[117] Buenz had been German consul general in New York from 1900 to 1909, then minister to Mexico 1909 to 1910. He left Mexico for Germany in 1910 to recover from an illness. He came to the United States in 1912, to head the HAPAG office in New York. Due to his wide-ranging career in the diplomatic service, Buenz had over an amazing network of influential friends, financiers, and politicians at his disposal.[118]

That afternoon, the seventy-one-year-old executive most likely did not have much positive to say to Heinrich Albert. HAPAG liners lay moored and rusting in harbors all along the East Coast with crews strolling about the piers in boredom while, in theory, they had been called up for military service. The cash situation of the hitherto mighty international shipping line was desperate when Albert arrived in New York. While war ministry funds took care of the crews financially, the maintenance and mooring expenses of the fleet of ocean liners and freighters remained with HAPAG and the North German Lloyd. The shipping conglomerates tried to mortgage their ships, but other than selling them outright, they could not get any interest in the offer. Some of the ships did sail again in the fall of 1914, this time under the flag of the United States. The business was in shambles, and the longer the war lasted, the more permanent the devastating result would be for HAPAG. Ultimately, the war devastated the once proud German merchant fleet. It was an unmitigated disaster for HAPAG, Albert Ballin's pride and joy. Ballin committed suicide as a consequence. Heinrich Albert noted in his diary, "H.A.L. [Hamburg America Line] here almost bankrupt [in] opposition to [what] Polis and Ecker [claim]."[119]

Albert's first day in New York was not nearly done. He rushed to the German consulate just around the corner of the Hamburg-America building at 4:30 p.m. There, he met Erich Hossenfelder, the acting German consul general who had just returned to the United States in the beginning of August. Albert noted the gist of his conversation with the consul and his staff, "trade conditions since and [likely a transcribing error, probably read "serious" or "deteriorated"] as a result of the war. Possibility of obtaining credits in New York through payments, which would exonerate firms from debts in Berlin."[120]

A final visit at the Hamburg-America building, most likely to view his new offices on the ground floor,[121] rounded out Albert's first day on the job.[122] He sunk into his bed at the Plaza Hotel. His final notation for the day, "All must report: Dernburg on the financial situation. Waetzold [of the consulate] on the commercial relations etc. And who is to act?"[123] Astutely, Albert realized within a few hours of arriving in New York that the people in charge of organizing the North American front for Germany lacked direction. Someone had to take control.

Erich Hossenfelder in his office at the Consulate in New York, ca. 1914[124]

And take control he would... Albert met with all the team members within a week, assessing their personalities, abilities, and usefulness. Regarding Count Bernstorff he wrote, "Easy going temperament [...] talks too much, he does not allow others to put in a word; but nevertheless a capital fellow, wholesome and not too particular, perhaps somewhat too vain."[125] While he felt that Count Bernstorff lacked the sense of urgency that he considered essential at this juncture of the war effort, another foreign service

official aroused a special ire in the German lawyer: Erich Hossenfelder, the acting German consul general. Hossenfelder was an
unsympathetic, jealous, overweight, brutish-looking official who
had little interest in risking his comfortable position for the war
effort. He viewed Albert, who did not have diplomatic credentials,
with a good measure of suspicion. Albert only consulted him a few
times in August and in September of 1914, and then continued his
work with Hossenfelder's office through the fifty-six year-old Commercial Attaché Daniel Waetzold.[126] He described his disdain for the
U.S.-based foreign service officials, and Hossenfelder in particular,
to Director Lewald of the Department of Interior in December 1915:

> I am more and more convinced that our foreign ser-
> vice requires a complete overhaul, at least as far as
> the United States is concerned. I arrive at this judg-
> ment completely independent of [sic] the occa-
> sional differences with the General Consulate in New
> York, which are exclusively the result of the utterly
> unfit person of the current consul [Hossenfelder],
> as well as of the privately charming relationship
> with our ambassador [Count Bernstorff], for who
> I have gained a sincere and honest adoration [for]
> [...] As an outsider vis-à-vis the diplomatic and con-
> sular service [I am] free of inhibitory conceptualiza-
> tions, that are typical for administrators in this type
> of career as a result of tradition and upbringing.[127]

Albert reflected that his relations with Hossenfelder had
deteriorated to outright hostility when he wrote to his wife, Ida,
in August 1915, "[...] he is not only professionally unusable, but
also personally not a gentleman [...]"[128] Albert tried to get Consul
Hossenfelder fired with the active support of Karl Boy-Ed through
his connections with Berlin (Count Bernstorff would not hear of it).
However, at the same time he attested to overcoming his initial,
negative impression of the ambassador. In later years, he worked
productively with Count Bernstorff. Nevertheless, Albert remained
distrustful of the ambassador and his bosses in the Foreign Service

and never disclosed more than that which was absolutely necessary to him. Count Bernstorff claimed in his wartime memoirs that he had little knowledge of the clandestine activities organized by Albert, Boy-Ed, and von Papen.[129] The press and later scholars seriously doubted his statements. While he probably did know more than he would freely admit, Albert did not trust him enough to make him privy to many of his secret undertakings. The ambassador certainly would not have had much interest in the liability of knowing, either.[130]

While Hossenfelder and the foreign service staff in the United States certainly topped Albert's list of *persons to watch out for*, Bernhard Dernburg only took four days to ruin his relationship with the newly arrived lawyer: The overbearing former Colonial Secretary took Albert's room at the Ritz-Carlton Hotel ($4 per night), booted the lawyer out, and made him stay at the cheaper Hotel Martinique on 32nd Street and Broadway. Albert commented in his diary: "Dernburg takes possession of my room and in his shirt sleeves cuts a figure like a clerk. Disregardful and bad manners."[131]

Albert also remarked from his observations over the next days, that Dernburg and Count Bernstorff had their first run-ins which, given the former Colonial Secretary's history, was not particularly surprising. "No one is decisive; Dernburg must pay regard to Bernstorff, I to Dernburg and Hatzfeld, etc."[132] Hatzfeld referred to Hermann Prince von Hatzfeld zu Trachenberg. He was the sixty-six year-old second counselor of the German Embassy in Washington, a member of the royal aristocracy of Prussia, and a former member of the German parliament. His father had been German Foreign Secretary and German ambassador in London under Bismarck. Between the rough manners of Dernburg, the self-importance of Count Bernstorff and Prince Hatzfeld, the jealous and bureaucratic obstructionism of Hossenfelder, only a few avenues remained for Albert to put together an effective team.

Over the first weeks of his assignment in the U.S., Albert accommodated the people of *power*: Dernburg, Count Bernstorff, and Prince Hatzfeld. Dernburg proved ineffective as a fundraiser and seemed more concerned with assembling and publishing an English version of the German White Book, arguing the German side of the causes of the war. Too *busy* to do it himself, he forced the job on Albert.[133] While propaganda certainly needed to be addressed to counteract a very effective British publicity campaign, Dernburg brusquely tried to re-prioritize Albert's agenda.

None of Dernburg's connections on Wall Street resulted in raising a loan. The bad news from the German front accumulated, culminating in the retreat and entrenchment of the German armies of von Kluck and von Buelow in the second week of September. The Western Front, key to the Schlieffen plan for a swift defeat of France in order to confront the Russian front in the East, appeared to foreshadow an impending military disaster for Germany.

Albert noted in his diary, "horrible mood among all the Germans over the news, especially news that von Kluck is said to have been taken prisoner with 15,000 men [false report]. The nerves of some individuals have given way entirely, for example, Ecker, even Pohlis [sic]. I myself am at times so excited inside that I am aware of violent palpitation of the heart and a feeling of nausea [...]"[134] Albert continued to confide to his diary: "It was widely expected that Germany would be defeated in a very short time."[135]

The illusion of being able to find an underwriter for a $150 million loan, the American public's apathy in acquiring German war bonds, and the depressing financial situation of HAPAG and the Central Purchasing Agency led to desperate moves by Dernburg. In order to receive cash, he authorized a deposit of twenty-five million German Marks ($5.9 million, today worth $125 million) in German treasuries with Warburg in Hamburg to, in turn, receive a $400,000 ($8.4 million in today's value) credit at Kuhn, Loeb and Co. With a 6% interest rate. Even worse than the conditions of the loan, Albert could only access half of the credit. The famed $100 million loan Albert mentioned in his diaries as a commitment from Max Warburg, and which is touted in scores of contemporary and scholarly reports, amounted in reality to $1,200,000 ($25 million in today's value) requiring nearly $5.9 million ($125 million in today's value) in security deposits.[136] While refraining from directly criticizing Dernburg for the ridiculous conditions of the loan, Albert's assessment of Warburg's bank was that, while not hostile to Germany, it clearly engaged in "usury."[137]

Dernburg did manage to increase the donations to the German Red Cross. Most of this cash was diverted to Albert's accounts. He used the U.S. proceeds and credited the *loaned* money to the Red Cross in Germany. Red Cross collections raised an estimated $2.3 million between September 1914 and November 1915, $576,000 between August and November 1914 alone.[138] However, the Red Cross funds, as well as the paltry loan Dernburg received, in no way made up for the failure to raise sufficient funds that could finance wartime purchases in the U.S. Discredited before the German Treasury Department, the Departments of Interior and War, and unable to return to Germany because of the blockade, Dernburg thus shifted his efforts from raising a loan to dedicating himself entirely to propaganda.[139] Albert had to pick up the pieces and work with them.

Albert started with the civilian priority: food supplies. Meetings in the end of August between Armour & Company, a huge meat-packing concern in Chicago, and the German embassy had not gone well. On August 31st, Vice President Arthur Meeker canceled shipping insurances because of the tightening British blockade and the resulting liability for transporting orders that the German government had placed in the U.S.[140] Armour was nervous about openly trading with Germany and risking the loss of France as a major customer. Two weeks before Albert's entreaties, Armour had publicly courted the French government. The company offered $100 million worth of preserved meat to be paid however France desired.[141]

Rather than continuing meetings with Meeker in New York, which Dernburg and Count Bernstorff attended, Albert decided on September 3rd 1914 to go to Chicago. He set out to create an organization that could source and ship meat, flour, and grain to Germany under the radar of the American public and the British government. His superiors at HAPAG, as well as the German ambassador, gave their blessings.[142] On the recommendation of William G. Sickels, HAPAG director and protégé of Albert Ballin, Albert made contact with Paul Tietgens. Tietgens, a German commodities broker from Chicago who worked for a Hamburg trading house, knew all the major merchants in the Midwest. Albert signed him as his representative on a five percent commission.[143] He explained in one of the chapters of his envisioned book, "As shippers, there appeared the firms given orders by Tietgens [...] Money was supplied by the [Albert] Office. The shipments were consigned to the firm of Henius and Co., Copenhagen [...]"[144] The British quickly caught on to the identity of Henius in Copenhagen. Tietgens therefore received $5,000 ($105,000 in today's value) from Albert in November to start his own *neutral* company, called Larsen Export Co. Tietgens became one of the most effective, honest, and loyal trading partners of Albert in the war years.

The other major trading partner was K & E Neumond, a German company with representation in New York. Karl Neumond and his brother Eugene managed to organize a credit of fourteen million Reichsmark ($3.3 million, about $70 million in today's value) through the Diskonto Gesellschaft in Berlin at the onset of the war. The Department of War had awarded the merchants a 40,000-ton order for cereal destined for the German army. His credit approved, Karl Neumond moved to New York, while Eugene handled the European side of the business.

An astute businessman, Karl Neumond managed to ship via the neutral Scandinavian America Line using the Guarantee Trust Company of New York as a guarantor. Just like the shipments Tietgens organized from Chicago, Albert booked all available space on the neutral shipping line through HAPAG in New York.[145] By 1916, Neumond had shipped over half of the original order, 23,603 tons of food worth $8.5 million ($178 million in today's value) to Germany on seventeen steamers.[146] During the two years of Neumond's efforts, only three out of twenty shipments amounting to $800,000 ($16.8 million in today's value) were impounded.[147] Considering the circumstances that required each shipment to be cloaked in fake consignees, ownership, neutral logistics, and untraceable finances, Neumond's record is nothing short of amazing. The trader maintained a close business relationship with Albert throughout the war. Neumond found his company blacklisted as a result, and himself in Fort Oglethorpe as a prisoner in 1918. Albert's accounts in 1916 show that Neumond deposited profits from the sale of his exports to Germany to the tune of $157,000 ($3.3 million in today's value).[148]

Throughout 1915 and 1916, Neumond also received payments for selling blockade-running steamships that Albert had purchased. Thanks to the German loan, Neumond, as well as other merchants working for Albert, succeeded in financing the German purchases in the U.S. to a large degree, while providing cash for Albert's various clandestine undertakings.[149] Albert raised $29.6 million ($622 million in today's value) from the sale of goods during the period from June of 1915 to the end of 1916, which he sent to Germany or which were sold in the U.S. when shipping to Central Europe became too difficult. These proceeds also included income from the sales of ships and placement of German war bonds in the American financial markets.[150]

Albert spent the rest of September 1914 working with the different team members on the various responsibilities. He added an accountant to his staff on the 9th. The food shipments, while hampered by lack of financial liquidity, started to make their way to Germany. By the end of the month, Albert also had resolved the insurance question with a new underwriter.

Dernburg put together the *Press Bureau* on the propaganda front, headquartered at 1123 Broadway. Its members included Karl Alexander Fuehr (embassy), Prince Hatzfeld (embassy), George Sylvester Viereck (*Fatherland*), Alfred Cronemeyer (HAPAG), Matthew B. Claussen (HAPAG), Geheimrat Dr. Anton Meyer-Gerhard (Red Cross), and Julius P. Meyer (HAPAG). Heinrich Albert sat in on many of the meetings for financial decisions, as did Karl Boy-Ed (for interest only), and Ambassador Count Bernstorff as the titular head of all German operations in the U.S. Albert also attended separate meetings with Franz von Papen, the military attaché, Hans Tauscher, the U.S. representative of Krupp, and Count Bernstorff, to discuss procurement of munitions, especially of artillery shells.[151]

A most interesting meeting took place on the evening of September 22nd 1914 on the roof garden of the Ritz-Carlton. Count Bernstorff and Heinrich Albert met with Arthur Count Rex, the returning German ambassador to Japan, and Colonel Alexander von Falkenhausen, the German military attaché in Tokyo, who attended with his wife.[152] Japan had declared war on Germany on August 23rd, prompting the German ambassador to return home.

The outbreak of hostilities with Japan also precipitated the posting of an experienced diplomat and naval intelligence officer in the person of Admiral Paul von Hintze to China. A secret trip that von Hintze, Germany's envoy to Mexico, made in the fall of 1914 has prompted historians to speculate on the purpose and the people he met with. According to several conspiracy theories, von Hintze, who in 1918 became Germany's Foreign Secretary, had set up the bloody sabotage campaigns of 1915 and 1916 that culminated in the explosion of stored munitions in the New York harbor, on Black Tom Island, in the summer of 1916.[153] The damages from the explosion which eventually proved to be a German operation were staggering. Apart from the obvious loss of materials, New Yorkers awoke to an earthquake (estimated to have been 5.5 on the Richter scale) caused by the explosion, Ellis Island evacuated, the Statue of Liberty punctured with shrapnel, and most windows in lower Manhattan broken.

While von Hintze's fingerprints appeared nowhere in connection with the sabotage campaign of 1915 and 1916, the admiral was a high-ranking naval officer with far-reaching intelligence responsibilities. He might indeed have met the main actors of later conspiracies during this secret trip, such as Kurt Jahnke, Friedrich Hinsch (two German agents suspected to have caused the Black Tom explosion), Franz Bopp, Albert Kaltschmidt, and others.

Von Hintze was traveling through New York and San Francisco on the way to his new post in the middle of September. Though Albert did not mention von Hintze as a member of this dinner in the end of September, he likely attended. Around the time of the dinner, von Hintze was in New York, had meetings with von Falkenhausen, and turned over his naval intelligence responsibilities for the American theatre to Karl Boy-Ed.[154] It would be more than logical that he timed the secret trip to meet his retiring colleague from Tokyo and receive briefings on naval intelligence activities in the Far East, von Hintze's wartime area of responsibility. Von Hintze traveled from New York to San Francisco where he allegedly met the sabotage agent Kurt Jahnke, who ended up heading the naval intelligence organization in Mexico three years later.[155] There is no mention of Karl Boy-Ed at the dinner. While he certainly had meetings with von Hintze, Boy-Ed may have refrained from social obligations that evening. His younger brother Walter, a captain in the German artillery, had been badly injured and died just prior to the day of the meeting.[156]

Between his various responsibilities, both administrative and social, the many meetings and trips, Albert quickly showed strain. He worked through most weekends including Labor Day. He went out with his HAPAG bosses, Anton Meyer-Gerhard, Otto Ecker, and Albert Polis, or Prince Hatzfeld and his wife almost every night. While the German officials in New York wanted to make Albert's stay as enjoyable as possible, he did not particularly seem to enjoy their company. For example, after Meyer-Gerhard and Polis took him on a cruise up the Hudson, Albert jotted in his diary, "colossal heat, calm, dirt, on board very problematic food [...]"[157] He clearly felt uncomfortable in the heat wave that gripped New York until the end of September. "A colossal heat set in. The nerves often won't [function] any longer under the pressure of this climate. The stomach weak."[158] His weak physical condition seemed to crush his energy. He noted more than once that he was exhausted: August 31st, "Evening so tired out that at 10 to bed;"[159] on September 10th, "[...] I was weary (tired out) early to bed;"[160] on September 20th to the 23rd there are no diary entries, "Entries omitted on account of exhaustion."[161]

Obviously used to a higher level of luxury than the German government provided its expatriates, Albert complained about hotels – after Dernburg booted him from the Ritz – food, cleanliness, and trains.[162] Often, impressions of people with whom he interacted showed a bitingly cynical side of his character. Regarding the president of the Newspaper Association of Foreign Languages, he wrote: "An uneducated man of Austrian descent, who speaks neither German nor English correctly."[163] William Sickels, with whom he worked closely, invited him to his apartment for dinner. Albert remarked, "a very nice apartment; simple, charming wife (mistakes in speaking), nice boy (glass eye) [...]"[164] Finally, homesick and questioning his career, Albert admitted in a September 25th entry,

> I thought of my dear ones at home, of my 'Neele' [pet name of his wife Ida] whose face is a mirror of her tender soul, of the children and of my duties toward them. If there is ever a chance of getting free from the slavery of the ????? [naval intelligence work?] then it will be after my return; I must not overwork any longer, my character and my efficiency stand beyond all doubt; why prove it anew over and over again?! [...] but that does not hold true for the young –man's- Activity under Mueller [Admiral von Mueller and Albert's superior in naval intelligence?], I shall speak openly with [Clemens von] Delbrück how he wishes to make use of me in the meantime! Best of all I should like to become State Councilor of the empire.[165]

To deflect his misgivings about his assignment and compensate for the inadequacies of his New York accommodations, Albert diverted his interests by seeking out intellectual stimulation. He found this intellectual reprieve especially in the company of German and German-American scholars.

Carl Schurz, HAPAG's legal counsel invited him on September 3rd to a meeting at the German University League where Albert gave "a speech on the breach of Belgium [sic] neutrality" to its members.[166] The speech followed a slew of reports in the American press detailing despicable war crimes being committed in that small country. English propaganda made the most out of the stories, many of which were highly exaggerated or untrue. With communication channels under British control and censorship, the German officials in the U.S. did not have ready access to information from the front to counter the British claims. Eventually, Dernburg and his team tried to correct the allegations of war crimes and massacres, but the damage to the German image among the American public was done.

Schurz was a trustee of the German University League, along with the German-Mexican banker Frederico Stallforth, textile manufacturer Hans Stoehr, the Bayer Chemical Company's CEO in the

U.S., Dr. Hugo Schweitzer, merchant banker Adolf Pavenstedt, and a host of people who would work for Albert over the next years.[167] The leading organizer of the League was Otto J. Merkel, a German-American. Members included, among others, art history professor Edmund von Mach, psychology professor Hugo Muensterberg, whom Albert had met at the St. Louis world exhibition in 1904, Harvard University history professor Kuno Francke, and professor of Germanic philology Hans Carl Günter von Jagemann.

The speech was a success. A week later, Albert accepted a weekend invitation from Professor Francke in Cambridge. The Harvard professor was Albert's uncle.[168] Francke picked him up at the train station Friday evening, September 11th 1914. Albert stayed at the house of history professor Albert Bushnell Hart, who was about to leave for an assignment at the University of Berlin. The German lawyer relaxed on Saturday and Sunday, "reading, writing, sleeping!"[169] He mentioned in his diary a visit with von Jagemann where he enjoyed the contact with "young people," all students at Harvard.[170]

The second, more important reason for his visit to Cambridge revealed itself later in the fall of 1914. Influential members of the German University League formed the core personnel in Albert's propaganda organization, as well as the people charged with *hurting the enemy*. The group of scholars and associated members, knowingly or inadvertently, formed a tight network of connections that provided human resources, inventions, and a cloak of social acceptability for Albert and his group of agents. For all intents and purposes, the German University League became one of the most important resources for Albert's clandestine work that involved the German-American community in the United States.

It seemed that surrounding himself with intellectuals and scholars took the edge off the burden Albert felt by interacting with people whom he considered unsophisticated (including Dernburg). Albert Ballin also managed to take some strain off the young lawyer and added a unique perk to boost his comfort. Albert received permission on September 19th 1914 to take a suite on the *Vaterland* in order to make up for the rude eviction from the Ritz. "We are going on board the *Vaterland*, and indeed a kind of Fatherland [it

is], everybody speaks German, kindly service and treatment, [...]
charming rooms: living room, sleeping rooms, bath, real comfort,
fresh air, I draw a deep breath."[171]

Albert slowly settled into his wartime job in New York by
the end of September 1914. Though he proceeded to assemble an
organization that proved most effective, Albert remained a loner.
He preferred not to share his daily routines with anyone, typical of
a secret service agent. Shuttling between his offices in the Hamburg-America building, his various hotel rooms, the *Vaterland*,
apartments, and the Press Bureau at 1123 Broadway, none of the
people working for him understood the extent of his activities and
involvements. Historian David Wayne Hirst maintained that, to a
large degree, Albert's power exceeded that of Ambassador Count
Bernstorff and Bernhard Dernburg. "The clever hand of Dr. Albert
is discernible on every level, and there were few projects in which
he did not play at least a participating role."[172] Socially, he remained
available but aloof. He preferred to associate with people of intellectual capacity. Collecting a group of hard-working, smart, and
dedicated people to form his inner circle would become his main
activity in the next months.

Note of an informer to A. Bruce Bielaski concerning Heinrich Albert.[173]

Heinrich Albert in his New York office ca. 1914.[174]

Heinrich Albert in his office in New York, ca. 1915.
Note the portraits of Prinz Bismarck and von Tirpitz on the wall behind his desk.[175]

CHAPTER 4:
COTTON, COPPER, AND CONTRABAND

T
HE AMERICAN MUNITIONS INDUSTRY OUTPUT and capacities immediately occupied the attention of the Secret War Council. Great
Britain's lack of significant domestic production largely made her
dependent on American supplies from the onset of the war.[176] Germany, as well, initially hoped to source critical raw materials from
the United States. A survey of available raw materials in the German
Empire, which the German industrialist, Walther Rathenau, conducted for the German government in the beginning of August 1914, had
shown less than six months of inventories.[177] The German economy
had vast production capacities, as opposed to the British problem,
where munitions capacity simply did not exist and had to be created, especially after her main trading partners had become enemies.
However, without critical raw materials, such as wood pulp (used for
powder manufacture), rubber, cotton, wool, and non-ferrous ores
such as copper, Germany's industrial output was in danger. It comes
as no surprise that the competition for critical supplies between the
warring nations made the United States a commercial battleground
in the European war.

Within days of the declaration of war, Great Britain initiated a series of operations historian Nicholas Lambert correctly
identified as "economic warfare."[178] England was the center of
international finance at the outbreak of the war and possessed a
preponderance of control over the global "oceanic transportation
system."[179] British authorities quickly stopped virtually all transfers
of funds between the Central powers and neutral trading partners, such as the United States, and made it illegal for any British

merchant ship to transport goods for any enemy country.[180] The German government had anticipated such a move at least in part, hence the establishment of the Albert office in late August in New York. While historians rarely mentioned the financial stranglehold of Germany in their analyses until recently, the English blockade was a blatant and largely successful attempt to stop the movements of goods to Germany. The blockade resembled more an economic stranglehold of World War I era logistics than the traditional understanding of the word *blockade,* as Nicholas Lambert rightfully pointed out. The brilliance of British economic warfare was that it encompassed finance, logistics, and trade.

The British government declared the entire North Sea a war zone on August 5th 1914.[181] Just five years prior to the war, an international naval conference in London sought to define the rules governing a sea blockade. The resulting Declaration of London of February 1909 added to the vast body of international law on the matter. Ray Stannard Baker, a biographer of Woodrow Wilson, astutely remarked in his volume on the neutrality years that "International law, so called [sic], was merely a feeble and contradictory assemblage of precedents backed by no real sanctions."[182]

In fact, the British government never ratified the agreement, which complicated the adherence to the principles laid out in the 1909 document. President Wilson tried to settle the matter on August 6th 1914 and called on all warring nations to adhere to the Declaration of London.[183] Germany agreed, however Britain did not and announced modifications to the definition of *effectiveness* and *contraband.* The British attitude presented a serious problem for U.S. foreign policy, since the rights of neutral countries in this international conflict thus remained vulnerable.

The Declaration of London defined contraband in two distinct classifications. Absolute contraband consisted of materials that could primarily be used for the conduct of war,

1) Arms of every kind, including arms for sporting purposes and their unassembled distinctive parts;
2) Projectiles, charges, and cartridges of all kinds,

and their unassembled distinctive parts;

3) Powder and explosives specially adapted for use in war;
4) Gun-carriages, caissons, limbers, military wagons, field forges, and their distinctive parts;
5) Clothing and equipment of a distinctly military character;
6) All kinds of harness of a distinctive military character;
7) Saddle, draft, and pack animals suitable for use in war;
8) Articles of camp equipment and their unassembled distinctive parts;
9) Armor plates;
10) War-ships [sic] and boats and their unassembled parts especially distinctive as suitable for use in a war vessel;
11) Instrument and apparatus made exclusively for the manufacture and repair of arms and of military material for use on land or sea.[184]

The second classification was called conditional contraband:

> Articles suitable for use in war as well as for inoffensive uses may be declared conditional contraband when they shall have the special hostile destination specified above [...] Notification thereof must be given.[185]

This second classification became one of the flash points in the war, since it allowed a belligerent to declare any material or product conditional contraband. Both Great Britain and Germany published ever-expanding lists of articles considered conditional contraband. These lists included almost anything imaginable by 1915. Especially the inclusion of copper, cotton, and wheat in the latter part of 1914 seriously hurt American trade with Europe.

Also difficult to define was the question of destination. Even if neutral steamers from the United States or Latin America on the way to neutral ports of the Netherlands or Denmark had properly manifested payloads, British search parties argued the principle of *continuous voyage*, meaning "when the destination of contraband merchandise is established it makes no difference that the voyage of the goods includes or does not include transshipments [shipping to a port and from there to another] and stops or calls of the vessel in course of the route."[186]

No matter what the true destination, shipments to Denmark, Netherlands, Sweden, and Norway ended in prize court because of the assumption that the final consignee could indeed be the German government. Neutral streamlines had to contend with the ever-expanding lists of conditional contraband, which under the principle of *continuous voyage* ruined any effort to stay in the shipping business. This infringement on the rights of neutrals remained an unresolved issue throughout the war. The issue became even more complicated when both British and German merchantmen used neutral flags to hide the ownership of their vessels.

All contraband, as well as the ships carrying the materials, was liable to be seized if encountered near an enemy port. A third classification of free goods initially included copper, cotton, wheat, and fertilizers. If intercepted in front of an enemy port, the blockading power could seize these shipments, as well, but had to fully reimburse the shipper. All neutral shipping had to submit to search and seizure as it approached continental Europe. British authorities then had to decide whether to seize freight even if it had not yet been declared contraband. Consignees had to retrieve reimbursements for their confiscated wares in prize court, an arduous task for most.[187] The cost of detention until British authorities cleared a ship to proceed forced many neutrals to sell their loads in Britain, or face even larger losses. Food shipments to continental Europe, especially, came to a grinding halt because the British government did not have to seize the payloads. Customs officials simply waited until the food was spoilt.

Surprisingly, the German response to the British sea blockade did not at all match the pre-war propaganda of naval prominence. Germany engaged the British navy in the battle of

Heligoland Blight on August 28th 1914. After fierce fighting, the German ships retreated, thus ending Germany's early efforts to break the blockade. The High Seas Fleet remained anchored for most of the war. When the war started, only one German squadron patrolled the high seas, the East Asia Squadron under Vice-Admiral Count Maximilian von Spee.[188] Despite significant battle successes, Admiral von Spee's squadron eventually succumbed to superior British sea power. Virtually the entire German naval fleet, save for some coastal patrols, was either anchored or destroyed by the end of the year.

German naval strategists turned to the submarine as a weapon of choice against the British blockade. While the High Sea Fleet was ordered to remain in port, submarine construction became a construction priority.[189] Initially surprisingly effective, the submarine could not easily operate in observation of so-called *cruiser rules*, the international law that regulated sea warfare. Merchant ships, including those under enemy flags could be searched, seized, or destroyed. The law stated, however, that the crews had the right to leave the ship in lifeboats and be taken to a safe port or be taken prisoner. Neither procedure worked for the vulnerable submarines that only had the advantage of a surprise attack when submerged and hidden. Sinking ships without warning created an international outcry. In response, the German government required submariners to observe *cruiser rules*, which, of course, took the element of surprise of the submarine and made it vulnerable to ramming. This vulnerability caused the admiralty to question whether the submarine indeed presented the solution for breaking the British blockade.

While searching and seizing ships in international waters in disregard of *cruiser rules* was illegal, the British blockade did not stand up to international law, either. Declaring the entire North Sea to be a war zone, the British government violated two main pillars of international law with respect to a sea blockade: In order to be legal a sea blockade, "[...] it must be effective; that is to say, maintained by a force sufficient to really prevent access to the coast of the enemy."[190] Britain did not do that, but rather enforced its strategy by laying mines in the travel lanes that not only led to German but to neutral ports, as well. Dropping mines into shipping lanes represented the second violation of international law, since it was not allowed to blockade neutral ports.

Navigation through the minefields required assistance from the British navy for any ship, be it neutral or allied, thus causing the blockade to become illegal. The declaration of the entire North Sea as a war zone also constituted a gray zone in international law. International law typically did not cede the right of free trade in international waters to any belligerent. British patrols of American harbors represented another gray zone under international law. The men-of-war stopped and searched steamers leaving the U.S. east coast for Europe, albeit mostly in international waters. While the English patrols in front of Boston, New York, Philadelphia, Baltimore, Newport News, Charleston, and Jacksonville may have been legal under strict interpretations of the law, they greatly agitated and angered the American business community and the general public.

The American government faced a dilemma. As the most powerful neutral nation in the world, President Wilson felt compelled to defend the rights of neutrals. The British sea blockade effectively cut the traditional trade of the United States with Central Europe at the onset of the war. The New York Stock exchange had to close in a panic (and remained closed until limited trading resumed in November 1914; unrestricted trading did not commence until April 1915) in the first months of the war. The U.S. reeled from the shock to her economy.[191] Unemployment exploded from 4.4 percent in 1913 to 8 percent in 1914 and over 10 percent in the spring of 1915.[192] The international financial system seemed on the verge of collapse.

International shipping slowed drastically since companies such as the North German Lloyd and HAPAG had moored their steamers. The American South was especially hard hit because the war started before the annual cotton harvest. Suddenly, cotton piled up in U.S. warehouses. American cotton represented a major raw material for the large textile industries of Germany, Austria, Poland, and other central European countries. Germany, which had purchased 2½ million bales per year dropped out as a customer.[193]

The price of cotton fell to six cents per pound, less than fifty percent of the 1913 average.[194] In turn, Germany's virtual monopoly on dyes, potash (a critically important fertilizer), and lenses caused painful shortages for U.S. manufacturers and farmers. Government officials feared the worst.

However, U.S. trade with the Central Powers could not even touch the explosion of exports to England and France. The situation not only normalized, but the American economy saw the beginning of a huge boom by the second half of 1915. Factories for munitions and war supplies sprung up like mushrooms. The number of unemployed workers shrunk to the point that the American economy faced shortages of labor. Profits from exports sent the stock market back into positive territory. The brief recession had passed and it became clear that neither the Allies, especially England, nor the United States, could risk an interruption in trade caused by an export ban on munitions. Trade in lucrative war materials with England and France had replaced lost German demand and shipping capacity.

Three weeks after the European War had engulfed Europe in violence, Woodrow Wilson went before Congress on August 19th 1914, and declared U.S. neutrality in the war:

> The effect of the war upon the United States will depend upon what American citizens say and do. Every man who really loves America will act and speak in the true spirit of neutrality, which is the spirit of impartiality and fairness and friendliness to all concerned. The spirit of the nation in this critical matter will be determined largely by what individuals and society and those gathered in public meetings do and say, upon what newspapers and magazines contain, upon what ministers utter in their pulpits, and men proclaim as their opinions upon the street.
>
> The people of the United States are drawn from many nations, and chiefly from the nations now at war. It is natural and inevitable that there

should be the utmost variety of sympathy and desire among them with regard to the issues and circumstances of the conflict. Some will wish one nation, others another, to succeed in the momentous struggle. It will be easy to excite passion and difficult to allay it. Those responsible for exciting it will assume a heavy responsibility, responsibility for no less a thing than that the people of the United States, whose love of their country and whose loyalty to its government should unite them as Americans all, bound in honor and affection to think first of her and her interests, may be divided in camps of hostile opinion, hot against each other, involved in the war itself in impulse and opinion if not in action. Such divisions amongst us would be fatal [...].[195]

While the debate on the sincerity of President Wilson's declaration still rages, the United States did maintain a neutral stand in the strictest interpretation of the law between 1914 and 1917.

However, with respect to maintaining a spirit of neutrality, as outlined in Wilson's declaration, German-American critics of the time and scholarly critics since have raised convincing arguments against the existence of true neutrality. The British sea blockade allowed for a continuous supply of arms and ammunition to reach the Entente belligerents throughout America's neutrality period. J. P. Morgan's $12 million loan to Russia ($252 million in today's value) in August of 1914 added American financial power to the supply. More loans to France and Great Britain followed in 1915. Secretary of State William Jennings Bryan decried the one-sided support of the belligerents in a note to President Wilson dated August 9th 1914:

Money is the worst of all contrabands because it commands everything else. The question of making loans contraband by international agreement has been discussed, but no action has been taken. I know of nothing that would do more to prevent war than an international agreement that neutral nations would not loan to belligerents. While such an agreement would be of great advantage, could we not by our example hasten the reaching of such an agreement? We are the one great nation which is not involved, and our refusal to loan to any belligerent would naturally tend to hasten a conclusion of the war. We are responsible for the use of our influence through example, and as we cannot tell what we can do until we try, the only way of testing our influence is to set the example and observe its effect. This is the fundamental reason in support of the suggestion submitted.[196]

Neutrality in spirit rose and fell with the natural tendency of American corporations to maximize profits and the government's task to support this goal. The German Schlieffen Plan failed in the first months of the war for all to see. The German general, Count Alfred von Schlieffen, had designed a war plan in 1905 in case of a two-frontal war that required a quick victory on the Western Front to allow forces to redirect to the Eastern Front. This plan, with some modifications, constituted Germany's war strategy for World War I. However, within weeks of the start of hostilities, the unexpected resistance of Belgium slowed the critical advance on the Western Front and brought the German advance to a standstill. The empire could not win a prolonged war on two fronts. Thus, independent of any question of right or wrong, no financier in his right mind bet on the Central Powers with extensive loans in the fall of 1914. As the American economy recovered from recession and as American exports to the Entente powers eclipsed any pre-war sales to the Central Powers and their neutral neighbors, the spirit of neutrality succumbed to the Realpolitik of an export-based economic powerhouse.

It is doubtful that German officials in the United States, and Heinrich Albert in particular, believed initially that trade between the U.S. and Germany would continue unabatedly.[197] The early recognition that the United States, in the face of an effective English control of the seas, could not, and would not, declare a ban on exports to belligerents on both sides of the conflict (as Secretary Bryan had suggested), pushed the German officials in the United States to violate their obligation to respect American laws.

The United States had become a battleground in the war, thus opening herself to the repercussions of serving as a critical supply line to the Allies. Albert, an experienced lawyer, had no compunctions about the legality of the blockade and the environment within which he had to conduct his mission. He wrote: "What England is executing in Kirkwall and in the British Channel is not at all a blockade. It is only some kind of illegal strait control. The control does not lock down German ports."[198]

Albert noted optimistically, as a matter of fact, that German warships *freely* patrolled the Baltic Sea and the northern German coast. Thus, the British *Fernblockade* (blockade from the distance) would allow German warships to capture neutrals and tow them into German ports. Albert considered the tactic of shipping to enemy ports and, before the ships arrived there, of having the German navy seize them en route.[199] However, the timing had to be impeccable. The shippers had to either be part of the conspiracy, which would make them liable for criminal prosecution, or would have their ships and consignments confiscated as prizes. The Albert papers document at least one such shipment, the Norwegian steamer, *Eir*. Albert had her captured in October 1915 on the way from the United States to Norway.[200] His agent, "the representative of a New York firm [...] is alleged to have disappeared from Copenhagen."[201] Albert wrote in his memoirs, "[...] all these plans did not progress beyond the planning stage. There were always doubts."[202]

Albert had the official assignment to source and ship raw materials such as rubber, cotton, copper, and wheat. However, the inadequate funding by the German government (in part the result of British control of international finance, but also for lack of budgeting priority) and its lackluster effort to break the sea blockade raise the possibility of an entirely different purpose of the Central Purchasing Agency in New York. Ambassador Count Bernstorff wrote in his reminiscences about the World War, "All these enterprises, the purchase, sale, and shipment of foodstuffs and raw material

[…] had their political as well as their purely business side."[203]

Heinrich Albert, a trained secret service operative, under the cover of a commercial mission had the embarrassment of the Entente, political manipulation of the United States government, and the establishment of wide-ranging intelligence-gathering networks as his real purpose. Viewing Albert's activities under this assumption paints a radically different picture of his commercial efforts. Rather than concluding his commercial activities were a failure, the truth is that the mission accomplished almost everything it was designed to achieve.[204]

Albert's first commercial effort consisted of shipping foodstuffs to Germany via the Scandinavian-American line, a subsidiary of HAPAG. After the British seized two of their ships, the Gans shipping line took on Albert's orders. Albert succeeded in putting together loads for twenty voyages between September and November 1914, only four of which ended in prize court.[205] K & E Neumond shipped goods valued at 8.4 Million German Marks between 1914 and 1916, about half the 40,000 tons of food and supplies the Imperial War Department had requested. Only three loads, roughly 800,000 German Marks worth, ended in prize court. Albert's office received almost $1.7 million ($36 million in today's value) in profit shares from these shipments.[206]

Neumond's contract with the War Department was independent of the New York purchasing agency and concluded in the latter part of 1915. Albert's accounts are unclear about which shipments Neumond financed with his own credits, and which Albert underwrote.[207] Most importantly, for every ship and every load that the Entente powers seized, the German agents in the U.S. received more material that they used for propaganda against the enemy. The theme of *starving* German children through the illegal blockade countermanded the press reports of German atrocities in Belgium. Akin to a complicated game of chess, the German operation sought to create tension between the Allies and the United States. The U.S. government was inundated with complaints from German-Americans, American merchants (especially from the South), and merchants from neutral countries as the blockade choked international trade.

American businessmen often led dummy firms in the game to outwit the British authorities. Most of these businessmen were unaware that they were indirectly trading with the German government. Albert wrote about this tactic: "The Office [i.e. the Central Purchasing Agency in New York] could never appear as an active party on the outside. It could make suggestions, arrange for credit and furnish guarantees. But the business itself had to be concluded by others. The only possibility was this: existing American firms would have to undertake shipments. They must be brought to do this either by the Office or by confidential agents of the Office [...]"[208] The insurance aspect of Albert's operation was another important one since it further embroiled U.S. interest in the war against England in his schemes. Any non-contraband shipment that was bought by Germany and shipped there using neutral shipping lines automatically became subject of seizure. Albert, who successfully cloaked his involvement in the purchasing scheme, was able to purchase insurance for the merchandise through dummy firms. Albert wrote almost gleefully that clogging up the international prize court and redeeming American insurance payments for illegally seized shipments in England was "quick payment."[209] An irony of history, British seizures thus provided badly needed cash for German clandestine operations in the U.S.

The most successful opportunity to drive a wedge between the U.S. public, the U.S. government, and England in 1914 offered itself in the American South. The outbreak of the war had created a disaster for American cotton growers. The loss of sales for American cotton to Germany, Austria, and the neutral countries of Europe amounted to 859,000 bales in 1914.[210] "The result was a lively crisis," Albert commented.[211]

Commerce statistics showed that for the nine months between August 1914 and May 1915, cotton exports dropped from $542 million to $297 million.[212] Desperate to sell the fall harvest, the cotton lobby and southern politicians pushed the Wilson administration to influence the British to allow exportation of cotton to the Central Powers. Since it was used to manufacture uniforms, blankets, and other military textiles, the British classified cotton and wool as conditional contraband. The German government protested vehemently against this classification. However, the contraband classification had little to do with textiles. It stemmed from the fact that cotton was the main ingredient in the production of smokeless powder, widely used in artillery shells and cartridges of the time.[213]

Despite the arguably military application of cotton, the Declaration of London specifically excluded cotton and wool in their raw form from classification as contraband.[214] Under pressure from the American State Department, the British government relented on October 26th. Cotton became a free article and could be shipped to Germany. However, since German ships were moored and English ships would not transport cotton to Germany, the lack of shipping capacity posed a second, debilitating logistical problem. The cotton growers responded by pushing for re-flagging German ships under the stars and stripes to run as "neutral" steamers.[215] Albert and his bosses at HAPAG fully supported the scheme, of course. President Wilson signed the "Ship Registry Bill" on August 18th, permitting German commercial steamers to re-flag.[216] The American merchant marine added a total of sixty-two ships and turned them into American tramp steamers in the fall of 1914. Most had belonged to shipping lines that had gone out of business as a result of high insurance premiums and the disruptions caused by the war. Only five of the sixty-two had been German ships.[217]

American merchant houses were ecstatic about the opportunities of an enlarged American merchant marine. New York investor, and fabled *king of trusts* Charles Ranlett Flint voiced the enthusiasm of his fellow financiers.[218] "[He] said [...] that the opportunity afforded by the war to American commerce was a most unusual one – something that never could have been dreamed of, and would not have occurred in centuries of peace [...] It is an opportunity [...] to win back what we lost in the civil war."[219] Britain, which had dominated the South American trade, had every reason to fear a greatly expanded American merchant fleet. As a result, his majesty's government opposed the re-flagging of German ships not only to keep pressure on German war supplies and food but also to check the competition of America's vast economic capacities. Despite the "pro-German" shipping bill, only an insignificant eight ships found mention in Albert's accounts for having transported cotton to Germany.[220] However, a comment in his memoirs betrayed the true purpose of the 'cotton' conflict: "The agitation [of forcing the British to relent on the contraband status of cotton] was supported by the [Albert] Office with the greatest vigor by influencing the larger cotton exporters."[221] Albert pitted growers in the American South against the defenders of the British blockade and scored another win in the effort to discredit the Allies in the United States.

The cotton trade also revealed another strategy the Albert team pursued in the fall of 1914. The German agent admitted in his discussion of the cotton business that the large bales offered a great opportunity to hide absolute contraband.[222] Albert certainly never smuggled enough to constitute a real benefit for the German war effort. However, smuggling contraband represented an important means to test the British resolve and the efficiency of the sea blockade. The British consuls in the American port cities had the task of checking the bales to be loaded. Preventing smuggling is a difficult if not impossible task, as the fruitless efforts of the American Bureau of Investigation along the Mexican American border between 1911 and 1914 showed.[223] The British consuls also violated American sovereignty in this effort which, while sanctioned in higher up government circles, produced disfavor among American customs officials.

Though Albert clearly welcomed this friction between the American and British officials, there is evidence that the German officials indeed used the cotton trade for smuggling operations. Discussed in much greater detail later in this book, the German Department of War had decided in September of 1914 to attempt to corner the U.S. munitions market. The main agent in charge of this effort was Hans Tauscher, the arms dealer who reported to Military Attaché Franz von Papen. Albert's books show expenditures of $159,049 in October and November of 1914 to Tauscher and additional disbursements to von Papen.[224] Reimbursement requests to Military Attaché Franz von Papen show that Tauscher stored these arms and ammunition cases in warehouses in New York.[225] A June 1915 memorandum concerning a negotiation with M. Sulzberger, one of Albert's trading partners in the U.S., mentioned the transportation of "Goods for Mr. von Papen." The same document mentioned the chartering of SS Neuches [sic] and the SS Zealandia.[226]

It would have been easy for German agents to use cotton bales and other non-contraband freight to hide arms and ammunition, supplies of which were especially short on the front in the fall of 1914. Tauscher and von Papen purchased several million dollars' worth of arms and ammunition in the course of 1914 and 1915. Very little of these war materials could be accounted for after the war and in the archival documents. How were they disposed of? While most of it went to Mexican revolutionaries and Indian resistance fighters, Albert admitted in his manuscript that absolute contraband was indeed shipped to Europe. The claim gains credence considering that several former business partners attempted to blackmail him between 1915 and 1917. Albert wrote: "For shipment by the Office there were taken into consideration principally goods, which are considered as [sic] conditional contraband. Attempts were made to ship true contraband."[227]

The Scandinavian-American Shipping Line dropped all shipping capacities in October 1914 that Albert had reserved.[228] British agents in the United States had discovered the link between HAPAG, the Scandinavian-American Shipping Line, and Albert's office.[229] Two of Scandinavian's ships had been taken into British ports awaiting prize court proceedings. Any further dealings with Germany would have black-listed the company. Albert now switched to another line, the Gans shipping line. Gans, a German American who had been entangled in the Ypiranga case in the spring of 1914, took the risk to ship goods for Albert via Scandinavia.[230] However, this arrangement only lasted two months until the British got wind of the new relationship. Consequently, they intercepted $15 million worth of goods.[231] Gans had not only lost the prize court claims but also many of his ships by the end of the war.[232]

Albert seemed to be without shipping options by the end of 1914. However, the financial situation had improved sufficiently that he now chartered and even purchased ships for his ventures. Chartering American and neutral ships seemed easy enough. However, Albert quickly found out that most shippers did not want to take the risk of losing their freighters to the British. Albert succeeded in chartering a total of thirty-five ships, most under American flags, many of them as partial charters (not the full load capacity). He used German strawmen to found legal American companies on the German treasury's dime. Paul Tietgens received $5,000 to form the Larsen Export Company. The Central Purchasing Agency itself formed the American Export Company and capitalized it with $200,000 to finance charters.

Albert began purchasing ships when charter companies refused to deal with him and his strawmen, or demanded inflated rates. He organized his little steamer fleet under front companies, as well. The decision to buy steamers resulted from a meeting at HAPAG on October 1st 1914. "Yesterday with Sickel, [Julius P.] Meyer, Cronemeyer, [William Bayard] Hale, Lindheim [lawyer], [Matthew B.] Claussen [Publicity Agent for HAPAG]; contraband plans, especially fitting out a ship direct to Germany."[233] The first ship Albert purchased was the SS Wilhelmina. He organized the W. L. Green Commission Company as a cover. Albert used the New York representative of the Diskonto Gesellschaft, German-Jewish businessman Johannes Ernst, alias John Simon, as a front to complete the $175,000 purchase in December 1914.[234] The British seized the Wilhelmina without cause in January 1915 after only one run. Fortunately for the Central Purchasing Company, the prize court awarded the German dummy firm $280,000 in damages.

In a similar move, the Fiske Trading Company functioned as a cover for the SS Zealandia, an Australian steamer, which Albert also purchased in December of 1914. He paid $300,000 for the ship, which completed several runs to Europe as a blockade-runner. Like the Wilhelmina, the British seized her but had to yield to a prize court ruling, which favored the German owners.

SS Zealandia off Port Davey, Tasmania in 1933

The Interocean and Coastwise Steamship Company covered the operation of SS *Atlantic* for which Albert paid $700,000.[235]

SS *Eir* was another purchase. She sailed until October 1915 as a blockade-runner and was organized under the *Eir Aktiengesellschaft* (German for Stock Holding Company) with a capital of $408,000.[236] The German government *seized* the steamer flying a Norwegian flag in October, a move Albert carefully choreographed, thus capturing the entire cargo of cotton for Germany.[237] Four more ships belonged to Albert between 1914 and 1916. Once the blockade-running effort had run its course, all the freighters found new owners. Albert's accounting shows that the entire operation lost slightly over $80,000 not counting the commissions paid to the sales agents.[238]

Given the profit shares K & E Neumond submitted to Albert, the overall venture most certainly was lucrative, in addition to the positive effects on German propaganda efforts in the U.S. Deutsche Bank Director Hugo Schmidt described on December 8th 1914, the sum total of Albert's blockade-running operation between 1914 and 1917:

> $3,272,279 of wool, $287,250 of Jute, 419,759 bales of cotton [500 lbs. per bale at $0.733 per pound equals approximately $1,542,614[239]], $443,000 of canned salmon, $497,500 of rubber, $566,100 of dried apples, $255,000 of lard, $650,000 of copper,

$86,000 of wax, 18,700 bales of tobacco [171 pounds or 77.73 kilos per bale, $0.121 per kilo equals approximately $175,967[240]], 218,174 bags of coffee [$9.17 per bag in 1915 equals approximately $2,000,656[241]].[242]

Albert's office exported close to $10 million ($210 million in today's value) worth of conditional contraband to Germany, a pittance of pre-war trade between Germany and the United States, yet a respectable success given the environment in which he operated.

Besides purchasing and shipping foodstuffs and raw materials, operating and leasing his own fleet of commercial steamers, a less obvious facet of Albert's commercial venture has never been fully examined: Intelligence gathering. Through the effort of testing the British blockade and driving a wedge between the U.S. and the Entente, Albert built a formidable network of confidential agents, dummy firms, shippers, and fake companies. His most active partners were Karl Neumond, John Simon, Paul Tietgens, M. Sulzberger, and Theodore R. Lemke. Albert also maintained a multitude of dummy firms that only appear once or twice in his bookkeeping. Three of his business partners could not withstand the temptation of embezzling the clandestine funds Albert made available to them.

John Simon, who turned out to be a fraud, fell out with Albert over the sale of the SS Wilhelmina in 1916. The accountants of the Alien Property Custodian analyzed Simon and Albert's books in October 1918 and determined that the German merchant not only defrauded Albert to the tune of $400,000 ($8.4 million in today's value) on the sale of the ship but, in addition, owed Albert $626,442 (Over $13 million in today's value), a staggering amount.[243] Theodore R. Lemke skimmed approximately $50,000 ($1 million in today's value) from purchasing funds Albert had given to him. Finally, Albert accused the firm. Sulzberger and Sons, of embezzling $175,000.[244] Retrieving the funds turned out to be impossible, since the activities of the Central Purchasing Agency were to remain secret. Despite the impeccable relationship he had with Tietgens and Neumond throughout the war, Albert's disappointment in his trading partners tarnished his already pessimistic outlook on his job: "[...] personally this [the fact that he had been defrauded] was yet another deep disappointment[...]"[245]

Heinrich Albert mentioned in his diaries the many meetings with his HAPAG handlers in the course of which he authored "reports."[246] Regrettably, these intelligence reports to Germany have yet to be discovered. Consequently, the nature and volume of intelligence Germany gathered from Albert's activities can only be surmised. However, one thing is clear: no other German agent in the United States had inserted German intelligence tentacles deeper into the U.S. economy, particularly the financial sector and commerce, than Albert. The knowledge he and his superiors acquired allowed them to form, adjust, and often fine-tune the German efforts in the United States. According to the testimony of Friedrich Borgemeister and Carl Heynen, both of whom occupied key management functions in Heinrich Albert's office, roughly half of the $34 million disbursed between 1914 and 1917 went to commercial ventures.[247] The rest financed activities of propaganda, espionage, sabotage, and attempts to corner specific industries in the United States. While the American government sympathized increasingly with the Entente and, in the end, joined the war against Germany, Albert's commercial cover and activities laid the groundwork for his true, more clandestine mission in New York: *Hurting the enemy.*

CHAPTER 5:
WHITE LIES — BLACK OPS

E VEN BEFORE THE GERMAN SABOTAGE campaign against the United States started in 1915, agents of Germany and the Entente powers waged a clandestine war against each other in the United States. Historians, German propagandists, and various critics of the Wilson administration then and now minimized the impact and illegality of German clandestine operations in the U.S. in 1914. President Wilson came to the decision to enter the war on the side of the Allies in 1917 with a distinct sense that the national security of the United States was at stake.

A viable and sizable German secret intelligence organization existed in the United States even before the war. German agents commenced operations against the interests of the Entente powers in the U.S. from the onset of hostilities, often at the expense of American civil peace. While German activities in 1914 remained more or less in the shadows of public information, the increasingly flagrant violations of U.S. law throughout the course of 1915 caused a press frenzy. Consequently, many innocent German-Americans and members of other minority groups stood accused of being agents or sympathizers.

The legal framework of the United States that governed dealing with foreign activities on its soil was wholly ill-equipped to deal with the clandestine war between the belligerents in the country. Until the Espionage Act of 1917, foreign agents did not even have to register as such with U.S. officials. Therefore, clandestine operations, in which British agents shadowed German agents, or foreign agents manipulated the financial system and industrial production were, by and large, legal. Agents of the Bureau of

Investigations and the various secret services of the American government could monitor but would rarely interfere in the activities of foreign agents.

To an observer living in the post-cold-war era the matter-of-fact, in-plain-sight agitation of German agents in the U.S. is astonishing. There was little fear that the U.S. government would pursue German agents unless they violated existing law, mainly the Sherman-Anti-Trust Act and the Neutrality Laws. Franz von Papen characterized his legal understanding of violating U.S. law in his memoirs: "At the same time I wish to emphasize that neither activity [to be discussed in this chapter] endangered American lives or security, although, in the strictly legal sense, it was improper to use neutral territory as the base of such operations."[248]

Von Papen and Boy-Ed were already fully engaged in both legal and illegal operations when Ambassador Count Bernstorff, Secretary Dernburg, and Heinrich Albert arrived at the end of August 1914. First on the list at the onset of the war was the supply of German raiders in the Atlantic and Pacific oceans. While over fifty German ships self-interned themselves in New York alone to escape British attacks, several navy cruisers remained at sea:[249] The SMS Dresden, SMS Karlsruhe, and the SMS Leipzig, initially covering the Caribbean and South American region before sailing into the Pacific theatre. The SMS Leipzig joined the SMS Nürnberg and raided the pacific coasts of the United States, Mexico, Central and South America.

Two converted liners, Prinz Eitel Friedrich, and Kronprinz Wilhelm, also roamed American waters as auxiliary cruisers. These battle cruisers outfitted several German merchant ships with weapons and sent them on their missions to sink unsuspecting enemy steamers. They were the gunboat Eber and the converted cruisers Santa Luccia, Cap Trafalgar, Eleanor, Woermer, and Pontus.[250] The unarmored cruiser Geier self-interned on October 15th in Hawaii with engine trouble after raiding in the Pacific for months.[251] The SMS Planet, a German surveying ship self-interned in Guam and was also supported with Boy-Ed's finances. Both ships are listed in Boy-Ed's accounts.[252]

Boy-Ed's supply operations involved more than just a few

runs. The extent of the operation was revealed in the eventual trial of HAPAG managers who were involved in the false manifesting of supply cargo: Through HAPAG, and under the authority and collaboration of its managing director Dr. Karl Buenz, Boy-Ed leased a fleet of merchant ships. Purposely misstating their destination and purpose to American authorities, these supply ships met with German raiders on the high seas and transferred coal and other supplies, including arms to the battleships.[253] Boy-Ed's accounting dated November 7th 1914 lists $43,290 ($910,000 in today's value) for "coals and supplies for *D. Patagonia, D. Spreewald, D. Praesident, D. Stadt Schleswig.*"[254] Officers of HAPAG signed shipping documents with fictitious destinations and cargoes.

To the American courts, these false manifests presented clear cases of lying under oath. A total of twenty-seven ships are documented as members of the naval attaché's fleet.[255] Hints in Boy-Ed's accounting of expenses, salaries, and wages suggest that these vessels not only made single runs but that the operation was a huge and repeated effort with astounding success rates:

[November] 14 Supercargo Thurman, 'Nordpol' salary and traveling expenses... 600.00

[November] 19 Presumptive supercargo of 'Fanny Moll' traveling and salary advance. See receipts 600.00

[November] 23 Capt. Suhren Gladstone, Advance 100.00

[December] 2 [Capt. Suhren Gladstone, Advance] 10000.00

[December] 29 Advance to Cpt. Suhren (Gladstone) for possible payment of Panama Canal tolls through Henjes 200.00

[256]

"Supercargo" describes the German agent on board of each ship who had the authority to direct the captains and had responsibility for the payload. Without a doubt, a host of additional ships sailed under Boy-Ed's direction and finance. An article in the *New York Times*, dated August 22nd 1914, illustrates the semi-public operation:

> Philadelphia, Aug. 21. – The North German Lloyd steamship *Brandenburg* today took out clearance papers for Bergen, Norway, but was still anchored below this city at a late hour tonight. It is said that she has taken aboard 10,000 tons of coal. This has been placed everywhere, even being piled in the staterooms and on deck. The Captain explains that this big supply is necessary because it will require two months to steam to Bergen. It is also stated that enough provisions have been taken on board to feed the crew for a year. Considerable comment was caused by the character of the cargo, which shipping men declare contains many articles never before exported from this port for Norway. It includes sauerkraut, wůrst [sic], canned herring, canned sardines, and fifteen half barrels of beer. Canned goods of every description and other provisions, with smoking tobacco, cigars, pipes, wines, and liquors compose the bulk of the cargo in addition to the coal.[257]

She sailed on the 22nd, cunningly evaded the three British cruisers lying in wait, and offloaded her supplies to a German raider just off the coast of Delaware.[258]

The German navy had far more assets in the Pacific, which had to be supplied. The German agent in charge of leasing and manning the German supply ships on the U.S. west coast for Boy-Ed was Frederick Jebsen. The *Mazatlan* and another supply ship, the *Alexandria* belonged to Jebsen's front company for the German government, the "Northern and Southern Navigation Company."[259]

Jebsen was a shipping magnate in San Francisco with a colorful history. Born on May 21st 1881 in Appenrade, Denmark as the son of Michael Jebsen, a wealthy ship owner, Jebsen joined the German navy in 1898. He left as a lieutenant (*Fähnrich zur See*) in

1902 and immigrated to America. His father's business transferred to Jebsen's three siblings after Jensen Sr. passed away in 1899. A high-risk gambler, Jebsen invested in commercial steamers in the recession of 1908 just when investors exited the industry in droves. The money for his ventures came from his German brothers who had financial interest in all his undertakings in the U.S. According to the official German navy obituary, "[...] after working for a few years as a [commercial] captain, he started his own business first in Seattle then in San Francisco, and after a few disappointments became very successful [...] At the beginning of the 1. World War he supplied the German squadron of Count Spee with coal [...]"[260]

Young, six-foot, six inches tall, slim, with curly hair, single, and socially active, the flamboyant German-American investor turned the Jebsen Line into a fabulous success.[261] San Francisco papers marveled at Jebson's business achievements and eagerly reported on lavish parties the shipping magnate hosted on his vessels.[262] The "Adonis of the local shipping world" was hands-on, sailing on his ships to round up business in the middle of the Mexican Revolution.[263] His ships called mostly on the Pacific coast harbors of Mexico and Central America. Jebson lived in a "palatial" home in the nicest neighborhood of San Francisco, sharing the residence with Baron von Berckheim, a diplomat attached to the German consulate general.[264] For pleasure he competed in the California horse show circuit and was a member of all the right country clubs.

During one of his trips to Mexico in October 1913, Jebsen was arrested. Mexican authorities in Guaymas accused him of supporting the rebel forces with military supplies, a charge that might been well-founded. Guaymas, as well as Mazatlan, were critical port cities in the Gulf of California from where supplies flowed from American Pacific ports to revolutionary forces fighting in the Mexican states of Sonora and Durango. The San Francisco papers featured Jebsen's story, clearly worried about his fate. *The San Francisco Call & Post* featured the "idol of San Francisco society" on October 6th 1913, with a large portrait of him holding a caricature. It displayed him suffering in a Mexican jail and pleading with a mean-looking Mexican revolutionary.[265] Efforts of German minister in Mexico, Admiral von Hintze and the German consul in San Francisco, who was a close friend of Jebsen's, freed him.[266] However, it took until the beginning of December for Jebsen to return to California.[267]

Throughout his career, the shipping tycoon maneuvered through recession, revolution, and attempts of competitors in the coffee trade to outwit him.[268] The business flourished in the face of adversity, mainly because of its idealistic, dedicated, risk-taking, and creative leader. Jebsen, a naval reserve officer at the outbreak of the war, came under the command of Karl Boy-Ed. Immediately, his fleet of a dozen steamers, tenders, and schooners joined the supply organization of the German navy. Jebson's supply operations not only plowed the Pacific coasts of the United States, Mexico, and Central America, but also fueled and supplied German battle cruisers as far away as Singapore and the Philippines.

FREDERICK JEBSEN,
WHO IS IN GUAYMAS
POLITICAL PRISON

Frederick Jebsen, 1913[269]

Jebsen's ships sailed under the American flag for the most part. However he also maintained several traders under the Mexican flag for his business there. The leased steamer, *Jason*, flew the Norwegian colors. Jebsen purchased the ship in the spring of 1914, and renamed her *Mazatlan*. One of his first business ventures using the large steamer was with the German government. While fighting in the ongoing revolutionary war threatened the German colonies of Guaymas and Mazatlan, German envoy to Mexico, Admiral von Hintze, leased the *Mazatlan* to take German refugees to San Francisco. She took not only German, but also ninety-two American refugees on board on April 25th 1914, an operation that endeared the German shipper to the San Francisco print media.

The German navy turned Jebsen's fleet into the supply armada for the Pacific squadron when the war started.[270] Through a mishap, or through the manipulation of English intelligence agents, the *Mazatlan* and her colorful owner briefly crowned the headlines. When the *SMS Leipzig*, a light cruiser of the German navy pulled into San Francisco on August 18th 1914 to take on coal, she was only permitted a small amount as a result of the U.S. neutrality laws.[271] Jebsen and the *Mazatlan* received orders to secretly rendezvous with the warship off the coast of Mexico and top off the battle cruiser's hold. While loading 9,000 tons of coal in San Francisco, the "[...] *Mazatlan* mysteriously caught fire while he [Jebsen] was cavorting with girlfriends, allowing firefighters and port authorities to discover the illegal cargo. Nevertheless, Jebsen got [the] *Mazatlan* out of US waters with two prostitutes aboard and rendezvoused with [the] *Leipzig* at the Mexican port of Guaymas. There British naval intelligence observed the coal transfer from shore, having been informed by the *Mazatlan's* disgruntled telegrapher, an Englishman who had notified his country's consulate upon arrival in Guaymas."[272]

The next day, the British charge d'affairs voiced a determined protest against the activities of the *Mazatlan* for openly supplying the *SMS Leipzig* and *SMS Nürnberg* just outside the Bay of San Francisco, and further south along the Mexican coast.[273] Returning to his berth at San Francisco harbor a few months later, on October 5th, Jebsen allegedly was arrested and detained for "violating the 'white slavery' act."[274] Not a single newspaper carried the story, if it was true. It might just have been the latest effort of British intelligence to discredit Jebsen. Whether British propaganda or the embellishment of a historian, this nasty rumor entered the historiography as fact.[275] Jebsen sailed again within two weeks, further dispelling the rumor of legal troubles.

Despite the risk and the British attempts to sabotage the effort, supplying the German fleet was quite lucrative for Jebsen. Another cog in the wheel of Germany's secret supply scheme was the New York businessman Gustav Kuhlenkampf. His duty was to disburse money for Boy-Ed until the arrival of Albert in New York. He secretly transferred an estimated $600,000 ($12.6 million in today's value) to Jebsen in San Francisco ear-marked for supporting the German navy in the Pacific.[276] Boy-Ed's accounts also show a payment of $151,500 marked "for Manila" around the end of October.[277] With Jebsen's help, the German naval squadron under Admiral von Spee re-supplied in the Philippines in November for her last battle in the Falkland Islands.

Kuhlenkampf also sent money to buy supply ships. Jebsen's companies acted as fronts to arrange these purchases.[278] The *Mazatlan* was one of those ships. Originally, Jebsen had bought her in the spring of 1914 for $135,000. The low price resulted from the repairs she had undergone after she suffered extensive damage from a fire in March 1913.[279] When the war started, he turned the freighter over to the German navy for $80,000 ($1.68 million in today's value), $35,000 below his cost.[280] She registered under Jensen's Lloyd Mexicano S.A. as SS *Mazatlan*. She made two voyages in 1914 for the German navy. The second supply run ended her career as a German supply ship. "The ship's [...] voyage, under the name *Mazatlan*, began October 14, 1914, and after much involuntary service in Mexican waters, terminated October 8, 1915. The first vicissitude encountered on the journey was a requisition of the vessel by followers of General Carranza, during which she carried his troops and supplies. She then fell into the hands of supporters of General Villa. She was so held until October, 1915 when the sum of $15,000 was paid to the captors for her release."[281] By then the German Pacific fleet had been sunk in the Falkland Islands. The

Mazatlan changed owners again, was renamed *Edna*, and sold for $125,000. Jebsen allegedly made $50,000 profit.[282]

The whole supply scheme came into the open in the spring and summer of 1915. American investigators quickly identified HAPAG personnel at the center of the conspiracy. Although Boy-Ed's central role in the scheme became obvious, diplomatic immunity prevented his indictment. Instead, prosecutors honed in on the seventy-two year old Dr. Buenz, the Managing Director of HAPAG in New York. The estimated value of supplies, all of which was contraband by definition, and in violation of American Neutrality Laws, amounted to more than $1.4 million ($29 million in today's value) for the twelve ships American investigators had identified.[283]

This was only a fraction of the total value of supplies. Heinrich Albert's accounts for Karl Boy-Ed additionally listed the expenditures for coal for the *SMS Dresden* in Veracruz, Mexico. Amazingly, the German manager of HAPAG in Mexico, Carl Heynen, who ran Boy-Ed's supply operation from Veracruz, was never implicated in the scheme. This is especially astonishing since Heynen would join the Albert team in 1915 and became one of the key German agents in the United States. Boy-Ed's managing role in the supply conspiracy presented clear violations of several U.S. statutes, mainly conspiracy to commit fraud. Heynen kept the operation going with Boy-Ed's generous financial support until the last German ship had been expelled from the Atlantic.

The HAPAG managers in the U.S. did not fare as well. The project turned into Managing Director Karl Buenz's personal nightmare. He was tried and sentenced to penitentiary for conspiracy involving the false manifests in the fall of 1915. The proud diplomat and business executive remained free and under house arrest until his case wound its way to the Supreme Court. Finally, in bad health, Buenz started his sentence in 1918 but died in the Atlanta penitentiary two months after he was committed.[284] Boy-Ed, while mentioned in virtually all press reports as the mastermind of the scheme, never faced trial because of his diplomatic immunity. The German naval attaché dedicated his memoirs to Dr. Buenz and included a chapter on the trial itself.[285] The reader can clearly sense the amount of regret the naval attaché felt for having brought such trouble upon his friend. Boy-Ed's involvement with this and other infringements of American law eventually caused his expulsion from the United States in December of 1915. German officials in the U.S. and Germany saw the Buenz trial as a clear violation of American neutrality. While American authorities prosecuted the German supply organization, British cruisers patrolled the East and West coasts of the United States and openly received supplies from U.S. ports.

The supply of the German sea raiders paralleled with another illegal operation by the German military in the United States. At issue were the tens of thousands of German and Austrian military reservists and volunteers in the United States and Latin America that had been called to report to their consulates. The Austrian military planned to charter American or other neutral steamers on August 1st 1914, to carry their soldiers home.[286] However, the idea died before it even had a chance to thrive, since the United States refused to outfit such ships as a violation of the neutrality laws. Furthermore, the British blockade would have made certain that the reservists ended up in prisoner of war camps rather than on the front. The situation in New York in the first week of August resembled mayhem. Thousands of reservists chanting, *Die Wacht am Rhein* (*Watch on the Rhine*) marched up and down the streets in front of the overwhelmed German Consulate General at 11 Broadway.[287] New York police were called up to assure the separation of Entente and Central Power recruits.

The German Consulate issued instructions to regional consulates on the 6th of August not to send any more reservists. Local shelters had to serve as temporary housing for those who could not afford a hotel. It took over a week for the enthusiastic soldiers to finally return home, as transportation to Germany simply did not exist. Franz von Papen, the military attaché and his people scanned the lists of reservists for officers and individuals with special skills. He decided to find a way to bring reservists he considered *of value* to Europe: In order to leave the United States and not be discovered by British patrols he needed false passports. Considering the repatriation of officers an army matter under his personal responsibility, the military attaché proceeded from his office in New York to implement an audacious passport fraud operation. The German military attaché rented an office on Bridge Street, New York.[288] The American citizen and German Lieutenant of the Reserve, Hans Adam von Wedell, took charge of the operation. According to journalist John Price Jones, the German-American had been a reporter and lawyer before he joined von Papen's organization. Von Papen, in his zealous excitement to show his value to the German cause, made the mistake of ordering all consulates of the United States and Mexico to send German military reservists to New York.

Franz von Papen, undated picture around 1914 with reservists in New York.[289]

Without developing a plan for deal with these droves of German soldiers, his office on the twelfth floor of 60 Wall Street, called the *War Floor* by other tenants in the building, was suddenly inundated with visitors.[290]

According to Carl Ruerode, who worked for von Wedell, "there were at that time in New York between 60,000 and 100,000 German reservists who were unable to get across because of the British cruisers stopping all passenger steamers and taking from on board [sic] every male passenger of German extraction [...]"[291] British and Justice Department agents, who took note of the human traffic in and out of Papen's office, quickly traced the reservists to von Wedell's operation. The ones that did not come to Papen's office tried to catch him in the German Club. Scores of journalists and historians have used the fact that von Papen was easier found there than in his office to imply laziness, arrogance, and aloofness. The simple fact was that the military attaché, as well as the naval attaché and consul general, all rented suites in the Club and lived there.[292]

In addition to having to come up with a way to send the soldiers to Germany, von Papen's financial records show he had to provide for them while waiting in New York.[293] Von Wedell's office, where von Papen sent the reservists, outfitted the Germans with forged passports and paid their fare to Europe on neutral passenger liners. Von Papen wrote checks in November to the passport office amounting to $2,230 ($46,800 in today's value).[294] The German forgers obtained the passports several ways. The largest resource for American passports came from German, Austro-Hungarian, and Turkish immigrants in the United States. According to the 1910 census there were 254,000 German males, as well as 1.3 million German-born males in the United States.[295] The total number of people born in the countries of the Central Powers, not counting second-generation immigrant children, amounted to 4.2 million.[296]

Despite having received American citizenship, virtually all German-born citizens had to register with the local German consulates. German officials considered it the duty of any German to fight for Germany or, at the very least, donate the passport to those who would. Von Wedell's office simply had to change the photograph on the document, and ... voilà another 'American' sailed unmolested to Germany. Carl Ruroede Sr., who replaced von Wedell in December 1914, naïvely explained to an undercover federal agent how it was done:

We wet the photograph [...] and then we affix it the
picture of the man who is to use it. The new photograph also is dampened, but when it is fastened to
the passport, there still remains a sort of vacuum in
spots between the new picture and the old, because
of ridges made by the seal. Well, turn the passport
upside down, place it on a soft ground made with
a silk handkerchief, and then, taking a paper cutter
with a dull point, just trace the letters on the seal.
The result is that the new photograph looks exactly
as if it had been stamped by Uncle Sam [...][297]

His openness cost Ruerode his freedom a few weeks later.
German consuls, as well as von Wedell's office, also purchased passports from citizens of other neutral countries and first generation
immigrants. The 1910 census counted close to 1.4 million Scandina-
vians and Dutch in the United States.[298] Many of these immigrants,
however, were friendly to the Allied cause. The ones who agreed to
sell their passports received cash from Franz von Papen. The Germans traveling on these valued travel documents, in many cases,
were secret service agents.[299] Finally, von Wedell applied for an
American passport, using the name of a German-American who
was willing to *donate* his name. Instead of the real picture, the Germans sent in the reservist's photograph. The new passport with the
official stamp of the State Department and William Bryan Jennings'
signature were almost impossible to uncover as forgeries.

It is not known how many reservists the military attaché
sent to Europe. Newspapers reported that "between 800 and
1,000 German officers" went to Europe with von Papen's help.[300]
While the number cannot be verified and could have been even
higher, the effort and the cost involved in the scheme substantiate the assumption that the majority of the reservists were indeed
officers. Von Papen himself claimed that he "[...] arranged for the
manufacture of false passports for some of the key German personnel clamouring to return and serve in their country's armed
forces."[301]

Hans von Wedell got cold feet in November 1914. The State Department refused to process several of his passport applications. Suspecting his discovery to be imminent, he panicked when the British arrested one of his clients, a Dr. Stark, with a forged passport. He went into hiding for most of December until he finally obtained a forged Mexican passport from the Mexican consul, Juan Urquidi, a close friend and relative of Frederico Stallforth.[302] Whether Stallforth, who worked with Bernhard Dernburg at the time, had anything to do with getting the Mexican consul's support is unknown but likely. Reluctantly, and only after von Wedell's wife protesting vehemently to the military attaché about her husband's predicament, von Papen supplied money for him to go to Europe.[303] He received $300 "journey money" and his wife $800 to carry information to Europe for the German officials.[304] The German agent left New York on January 2nd 1915 on the SS Bergensfjord of the Norwegian-American Steamship Line. While sailing out of New York harbor, agents of the U.S. Secret Service stopped the ship, specifically looking for von Wedell.[305]

Not knowing what the suspect looked like, they missed him in the lineup. However, four German reservists, one from New York and three from Chile were caught in the dragnet. None of the four spoke English. Their passports, while prominently displaying the official seal of the Department of State, clearly proved to be forgeries. With the four suspects under arrest, the agents allowed the ship to continue. Von Wedell had slipped through, but the trip proved to be his demise in any case. The royal navy ship HMS Viknor intercepted the Norwegian-American liner. The British officers who boarded the ship had been in contact with New York officials, identified, and took von Wedell off the liner for further questioning.

Apparently, neither his looks nor his Spanish supported the Mexican passport under which he traveled. The Viknor struck a mine and sank on January 15th 1915, on the way to port. Von Wedell drowned.[306] The hapless forger had explained his sudden departure in a letter to German ambassador Count Bernstorff dated December 26th 1914. The document, which the U.S. government obtained a few years later, clearly implicated the German embassy and military attaché von Papen, in particular.[307]

Von Papen's captured checkbook showed payments to von Wedell in the months of November and December documenting his salary and travel expenses to escape to Europe.[308]

Carl Ruroede Sr. took over from von Wedell after the latter went into hiding. Ruerode had met von Wedell in the offices of the freight forwarding company, Oelrichs and Company, where he handled legal and illegal shipments from Albert.[309] The eighteen-year veteran of the North German Lloyd, HAPAG's main German competitor in the city, did not last long either. He had left his employ to work for von Wedell in November and continued to run the forgery operation from a new office on Whitehall Street. Unbeknownst to him, the U.S. Secret Service, with the support of British secret service agents, shadowed the forgers and kept the new office under surveillance. Hot on the trail of von Wedell and armed with the evidence of the four arrested reservists, federal agents came straight from the *Bergensfjord* and took his office apart. Ruroede, his seventeen-year-old son, as well as one other employee in the passport office came under arrest.[310] The four German reservists received a slap on the wrist with fines of $200 each for possessing forged documents. However, Ruroede did not get off that easily. A federal judge convicted him in March 1915, and imposed a sentence of three years in penitentiary. The former shipping agent spent the rest of World War I in federal confinement in Atlanta, Georgia.[311]

The passport scandal became a public relations fiasco for Germany. The American public took great offense in the fact that German officials, in the person of Franz von Papen, directed illegal operations in the United States. Von Papen did not smuggle reservists out of the country alone. Stories of Germans receiving legal and illegal support for their journey home from German consulates all around the country became wide-spread. The difference in von Papen's case was that a high official of the German diplomatic corps was clearly implicated. The trial and conviction of the conspirators caused the press to pay close attention to the German officials freely operating in New York.

The issue of German-Americans lending their American passports to the German government also raised public suspicions about the loyalty of the *hyphen* citizens. First generation

German-Americans were caught between the appeal by German officials to join the German cause, even if that meant breaking the law, and loyalty to their adopted homeland. Most German-Americans remained more American than German to the disappointment of von Papen and his colleagues. However, the cloud of doubt hung over their heads throughout the war and resulted in serious cases of discrimination and mob justice. While Boy-Ed's illegal operation to supply warships received bad press as well, the question begs whether the negative publicity was worth the results of the operations. In the case of Boy-Ed the answer must be affirmative. On the other hand, in the case of von Papen's scheme through which a handful of German reserve officers joined the war effort overseas, the damage to public relations did not seem to outweigh the benefits.

CHAPTER 6:
KRIEGSNACHRICHTENDIENST

A S EARLY AS MARCH 1914, Franz von Papen, on orders of the General Staff of the Army, established an American-based service organization, called the *Kriegsnachrichtendienst*, the *War Intelligence Agency*.[312] Von Papen's superiors wanted to put Hans Tauscher, the Krupp agent in New York in charge of the office. However, Tauscher, a multi-millionaire in his own right and husband of the famous opera star Johanna Gadski was not interested in taking a $238 per month job. Consequently, von Papen suggested to his superiors finding someone else.[313]

His choice was Wolf Walter Franz von Igel.[314] The twenty-six year-old German from Posen, Germany had worked as a banker for the German investment bank, Conrad Donner, in the city.[315] Von Papen also suggested three vice consuls to his superiors to run the *Kriegsnachrichtendienst* in strategic U.S. cities. The consuls he most likely referred to were Franz Bopp of San Francisco, Carl A. Luederitz of Baltimore, and Hans Kurt von Reiswitz of Chicago. All three, as well as scores of people working with and for them, were indicted and convicted for their parts in Germany's clandestine operations in the U.S. between 1914 and 1916. The new organization definitely was in operation by the outbreak of the war. Von Papen asked his colleague, Boy-Ed, on July 30th to run the *Kriegsnachrichtendienst* while he was on his way back from Mexico.[316] Von Papen's intelligence agency in New York transmitted critical, military-related information to several intelligence agencies in Germany.

German agent Franz Wachendorf, alias Horst von der Goltz, also mentioned the existence of what he termed "Intelligence Department of the General Staff," likely the same organization in his memoirs.[317] The intelligence von Papen collected in North America went to the *Political Section of the German General Staff, Abteilung IIIB* (Department IIIB) in Berlin. Von der Goltz' memoirs confirm this hierarchy. The *Abteilung IIIB* in Berlin was collecting information on issues of policy, political developments, politicians, and activities of third countries. Papen wrote in his memoirs "[...] the whole responsibility for keeping Germany and her allies informed of politico-military developments in the North American continent devolved on me."[318]

German intelligence-gathering in North America was not confined to the German General Staff alone. The German navy operated a similar organization specialized on naval intelligence, which was called the *Nachrichtenabteilung des Admiralstabes* (Department N). The German naval intelligence office under Commander Walter Isendahl was mainly interested in any information related to other countries' naval operations, port installations, defensive positions, and supply chains. Department N also received copies of von Papen's reports to the his superiors containing political and military intelligence of interest to the admiralty.

In countries where the German government did not station military attachés, the local naval intelligence officer in charge provided reports to both Department N and Department IIIB. Before the war, naval intelligence had been charged, for the most part, with intelligence operations on the American continent. The General Staff order from March 1914 that triggered the establishment of the *Kriegsnachrichtendienst* clearly showed a change in intelligence strategy for the American continent. The order established an additional intelligence organization next to the traditional naval intelligence agency.

A few weeks after his return from Mexico on August 7th 1914, von Papen also hired the whole Department of Police of the HAPAG. The superintendent was Paul W. Koenig, who now became the military attaché's main agent.[319] Koenig noted in his diary, "Aug 22 [1914]. German government, with consent of Dr. Buenz [Managing Director of HAPAG], entrusted me with the handling of a certain investigation. Military attaché von Papen called at my office later and explained the nature of the work expected. (Beginning of Bureau services for Imperial German Government.)"[320] Koenig was a broad shouldered, street-smart ruffian, five feet seven inches tall, had a fair complexion, brown hair, and dark eyes. He weighed 160 pounds.[321]

"P. K.," as journalist John Price Jones called him, was "[...] a sort of boss, an unmerciful autocrat in the lower world, physically fearless, trusting no man and driving every man to work by the use of violent abusive[,] language, boastful of his skill, physical prowess and his craft."[322] A drooping black mustache emphasized the defiant demeanor of his face. He was born in Rheda, Westphalia in 1882. Koenig worked for the Pacific Mail Steamship Company in 1907 and sailed on the SS Manchuria, as well as the SS City of Para.[323] His employment with HAPAG started in the following year. He listed his occupation in 1909 as "purser" traveling on the HAPAG liner, SS Amerika.[324] The Alien Property Custodian's office found that he worked in "[...] the auditor's department, and a while later started the company's bureau of inspection. This position evidently carried him to Colombia, South America, where he was known to be seeking affidavits involving an officer on one of the boats running into Cartagena."[325] It is not clear when he married. Martha Thorstedt, his wife, likely came from a Norwegian immigrant family in Quebec.[326] Martha was eleven years his junior.

The Koenigs moved to New York in November of 1912 where he founded the Bureau of Investigation for HAPAG.[327] All steamship lines employed investigators to handle cases of smuggling, theft, stowaways, and the like. These detectives also had responsibilities for background-checking of crew members and watching over their behavior while on land. Koenig's organization blossomed. "[...] on May 13th, 1913 we moved to an office on the 4th floor of 45 Broadway, room 82, and around March, 1914 we secured an additional office No. 83 directly adjoining the other one [...]"[328] Koenig employed approximately twenty-five detectives, many of them former Pinkertons, with offices right next to where Heinrich Albert settled in August 1914.[329] The Bureau of Investigation estimated that he had an annual salary of $3,100 ($65,000 in today's value), a proud sum for the times.

According to his immigration forms, Koenig was an American

citizen, although the actual citizenship applications that would have been filed sometime between 1904 (first arrival) and 1930 have not been preserved if they ever existed. Koenig declared on the 1930 U.S. census to have been naturalized in 1915, which definitely was untrue.[330] The Mixed Claims Commission archives reveal that he applied for citizenship between 1928 and 1930.[331] It remains unclear whether Koenig was a German or an American citizen in the First World War. Considering the lack of an early citizenship application, the statements Koenig himself made on immigration forms, from being a German and an American citizen to even being born in the United States, it is likely that Paul Koenig was a German citizen throughout the First World War.[332]

Paul Koenig, ca. 1915[333]

Koenig brought many talents to the German officials to be an effective secret agent: He was a trained investigator and intelligence analyst.[334] He knew every nook and cranny, every dive, crook, and deal-maker in the New York harbor. He also ran an existing detective operation in the greater New York area that he easily transformed into an intelligence-gathering apparatus for von Papen. Koenig was discreet. He knew how to get information and from whom to get it. While there is no evidence to suggest any blemishes on his police record before the war, Koenig was no stranger to applying pressure to men if the situation required it. As *New York Sun* journalist John Price Jones put it, "He knew wharf rats, water-front crooks, and was thoroughly acquainted with their schemes [...] He understood thoroughly how to handle men of the rough type."[335]

The main problem of the "Westphalian" as his subordinates called him was that his rough treatment of people not only affected those he had to investigate but also his own employees.[336] They hated him, which ultimately proved to be his downfall. Koenig headed three divisions of the Investigative Bureau, the Pier Division, The Special Detail Division, and the *Geheimdienst* (Secret Service Division), subordinated to the *Kriegsnachrichtendienst*.[337] Police Captain Thomas J. Tunney, the head of the New York Bomb Squad, described Koenig's organization in detail in his war memoir, *Throttled*:

> The functions of his departments were clearly defined. The pier division guarded the piers and vessels of the Line, and furnished him information of sailings from the New York waterfront, which he in turn passed on to the naval attaché, Boy-Ed. Through this division he was able to keep in touch with the waterfront element for whatever service of violence might be necessary, and to keep a fairly complete record of shipping. The special detail division was assigned to the guarding of von Bernstorff's summer place at Cedarhurst, Long Island, Dr. Albert's office in the Hamburg-American

building, von Papen's office at 60 Wall Street, and the Austrian consulate in New York.[338]

The Secret Service Division conducted counter-espionage, intelligence gathering, and special assignments as the military and naval attachés saw fit. Koenig had devised an elaborate system of case numbers (*D-cases*), a hierarchy of knowledge (*need-to-know basis*), and used dozens of aliases to camouflage his own involvement in the missions. Von Papen described the aspects of Koenig's job in his memoirs, "[...] the task of obtaining all possible information concerning shipments of war material to Europe. In this he was most successful, and I was able to keep the General Staff constantly posted as to their quantity and nature."[339] Koenig also had charge of protecting the German officials from espionage by Entente agents. In this capacity he trained the military attaché on how to shake a shadow. "We used to go to one of the big department stores, get in one of the lifts, change at different floors, and go up and down until none of the original passengers were left with us. Then we went down again and left the building by another door."[340] Koenig was a master when it came to exposing opponent shadows. Thomas Tunney, the New York chief of the bomb squad wrote admiringly,

> Koenig, a man of keen animal senses, was unusually quick in discovering his shadower. It used to confuse certain agents considerably to have him disappear around a corner, and when the agent quickened his pace and swept around the same corner after him, to have Koenig pop out of a doorway with a laugh for his pursuer which meant that the day's work had gone for nothing. I have known men who were excellent detectives and poor shadows. Sometimes they were too large and conspicuous, sometimes they were over-zealous, sometimes they excited suspicion by being over-cautious; rare enough was the combination of artlessness [sic] and skill which made a man a good shadow, told him when to saunter away in the opposite direction, when to pass his

man, and how to efface himself. It is, I think, the instinct of the good fisherman who knows just how much line to run out, and just when to exert the pressure. For Koenig was a slippery fish.[341]

Koenig's inner circle consisted of his wife and Frederick J. Metzler, who had worked himself up to become Koenig's personal assistant. Metzler's father, a German immigrant worked as a shipping clerk for HAPAG.[342] When Frederick Jr. was only fifteen, he joined HAPAG in the auditing department headed by Paul Koenig.[343] Metzler was born in the United States and had just turned eighteen when the war started. Another German-American, Henry (Heinrich) J. Wilkens, had big responsibilities in the office. Bureau of Investigations detectives described him as "5'-11", 35 years of age [in 1915], light complexion, slim build, 155-65 lbs, light brown hair, somewhat sunken cheeks, wears glasses, smooth shaven, speaks with a German accent, and good dresser [...]"[344] Wilkens originally managed the guards in the harbor as head of the Pier Division. Having received a raise from $3 per week to $20 in September 1914, Wilkens joined the Division for Special Details, the guards assigned to the German attachés' offices, the German and Austrian consulates, and the HAPAG offices. Koenig assigned Wilkens to watch over Heinrich Albert's offices.[345] His cover was administrative assistant.[346] Only Koenig had the combination to the safe where "all of Koenig's private secret reports etc. are kept [...]" He trusted no one![347]

While Koenig seemed to be closest to von Papen, and likely kept a majority of the gathered intelligence on file, von Papen received information from many more sources. Karl Boy-Ed, who ran his own intelligence agents, supplied his colleague with pertinent data.[348] He forwarded a report from Felix A. Sommerfeld on the 11th of November, for example, to the military attaché with "compliments."[349] This report from Sommerfeld, who together with Hans Tauscher probably had the best intelligence on Entente purchases, seems to be one of the few remaining specimens of a weekly report the German filed with the naval attaché. A second report to Boy-Ed with further information on arms contracts for the

Entente reached von Papen's desk on November 29th.[350] Agents of the American Bureau of Investigation, who came into possession of these reports, later accused Sommerfeld of having been in contact with von Papen.

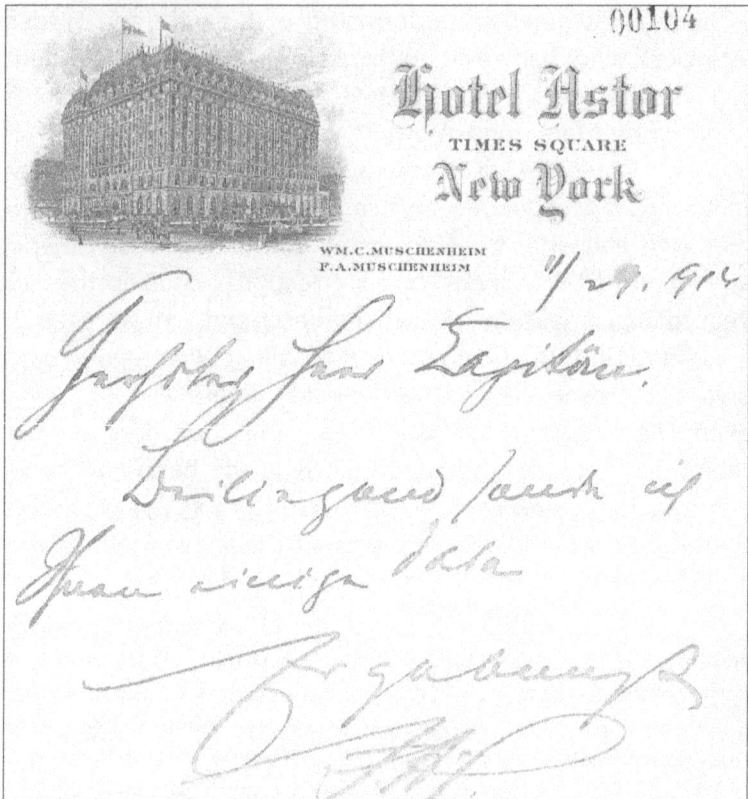

"Geehrter Herr Kapitän, beiliegend sende ich Ihnen einige Daten[.] Ergebenst, FAS."
(Dear captain, attached I am sending you some data [.] Your servant, FAS.)

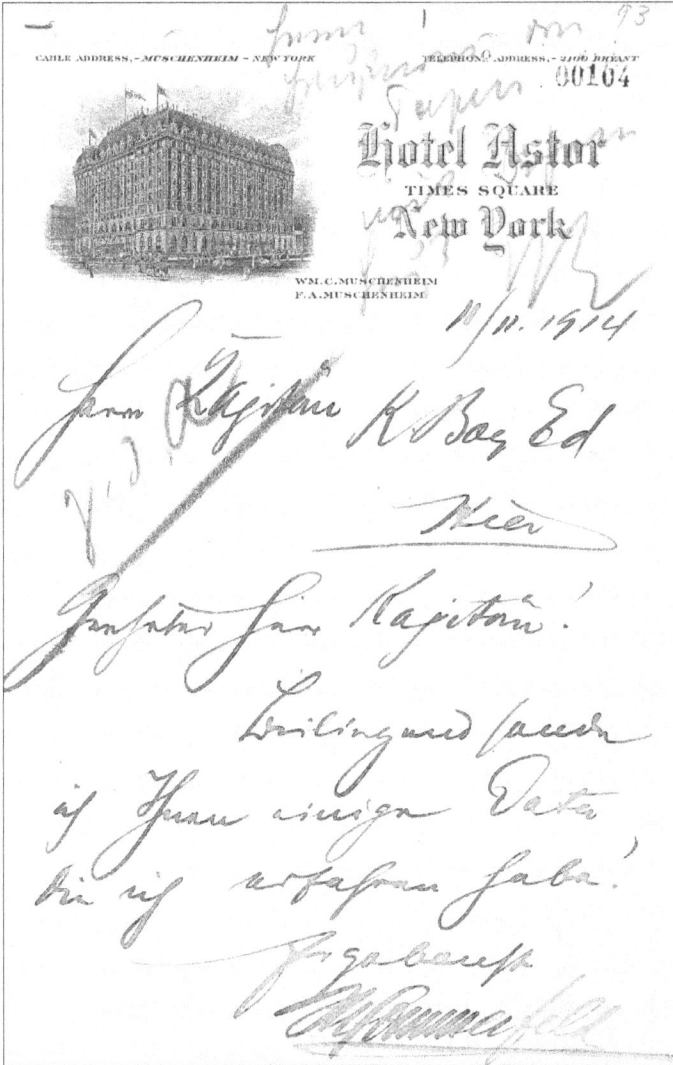

"Geehrter Herr Kapitän! Beiliegend sende ich Ihnen einige Daten, die ich erfahren habe! Ergebenst, F. A. Sommerfeld." (Dear captain! Attached I am sending you some data I found out about! Your servant, F.A. Sommerfeld)[351]

Sommerfeld emphatically denied the charge. He had addressed the second report as *"Geehrter Herr Kapitän."* The American translator made this into "My dear captain," which is technically correct, but the naval rank of *Kapitän* (Commander) referred to Boy-Ed, not to von Papen. If Sommerfeld had addressed von Papen, he would have written *Hauptmann*, which refers to the rank of army captain. Sommerfeld indeed never reported intelligence to von Papen, as far as the archival files reveal. He still gathered intelligence just for the naval intelligence, of course. He lied about this fact in his interrogation on 1918.[352]

Given the great human resources available through the moored German merchant marine and ocean liners, Paul Koenig had no problems hiring the eyes and ears he needed for his intelligence-gathering. The *Kriegsnachrichtendienst* employed similar groups of agents in the other harbor cities. German consul Carl Luederitz organized and transmitted intelligence on Allied shipping in Baltimore, where most of the North German Lloyd liners awaited an end to the war, to von Papen's office. The captain of the SS *Neckar*, Friedrich Hinsch, conducted the actual intelligence-gathering. He worked for Karl Boy-Ed starting the end of September 1914.[353] Most productive was Theodore Otto, a German-American doctor from Allentown, Pennsylvania who transmitted frequent updates on arms shipments for the Entente to von Papen.[354] Apparently, he was very well connected to the steel companies operating in Allentown that supplied munitions factories up north.[355]

Similar to Theodore Otto, Otto Heins, the General Manager of the Robert Bosch Magneto Company, furnished much pertinent information on allied contracts.[356] Heins had access to intelligence because his company supplied magnetos, igniters, lights, etc. to American companies. George von Skal, who worked for Franz von Papen, accused Heins of supplying the enemy. In a spat between Karl Boy-Ed, who likely had Heins on payroll as an informant, and von Skal, the matter was brought to Heinrich Albert to settle.[357] Albert, after initially threatening Heins with legal consequences for materially supporting companies producing materials for the Entente, sided with Boy-Ed, probably after the latter identified Heins as his agent.[358] Heins furnished regular intelligence reports to Albert from then on, and seemed to continue his business with U.S. companies as a quid-pro-quo.[359] Hans Tauscher also provided intelligence to von Papen. Next to Sommerfeld, Tauscher had the most connections to the industry.

Another source von Papen mentioned in his memoirs was

German-American bankers, who gathered the financial details on Entente contracts.[360] The most notorious case of German-American bank employees providing intelligence to von Papen was that of Frederick Schleindl. The twenty-six year-old German from Wildenstein, Bavaria had served in the 11th Bavarian Infantry Regiment until April 1912.[361] According to the Bureau of Investigations, the reservist took a two-year leave "to study in foreign countries," which brought him to New York.[362] At the onset of the war, he reported to the German Consul in New York, who assigned him to Paul Koenig. Frederick Metzler, Koenig's assistant described Schleindl like most of Koenig's agents, as young and non-descript, "[...] about 30 years; about 5 feet 8; about 170 pounds; light hair; smooth shaven, not sure [not self-assured]; full face [...]"[363] Schleindl clerked in the commercial credit department of the Rockefeller-owned National City Bank of New York, a key location for German secret agents to gather intelligence on the financial activities of the Allies. Koenig paid him $25 per week to provide copies of letters and telegrams with details of Allied munitions contracts to him.[364]

The arrangement came into the open in December 1915, when Koenig and a host of other German agents faced indictments for sabotage operations. Koenig's secretary, who tried to save his skin by becoming a star witness for the prosecution, had watched the bank clerk receive money and provide reports. Schleindl was tried and sentenced in 1916 to "[...] an indeterminate term in the penitentiary of not more than three years, which leaves him, of course, subject to parole at the discretion of the Parole Board."[365] The intelligence-gathering operations run by von Papen, Boy-Ed, and Koenig at the beginning of the war mainly served the purpose of understanding the impact of American supplies on the German front. However, the intelligence the Secret War Council gained also built the foundation for conducting less benign clandestine operations. Schleindl and others evolved from being informers in 1914 to becoming sabotage agents in 1915.[366]

Since the U.S. armament capacities at the beginning of the war were relatively small, the German officials in the U.S. became convinced early on that a cornering of the munitions and explosives markets was feasible. Count Bernstorff sent a report to the

State Department, seconded by von Papen, reporting to the German General Staff on September 10th and 12th 1914, respectively, and requested the go-ahead to "preempt purchase [by Entente of total annual production of artillery shells]."367 Von Papen claimed in his memoirs that he requested to "take over the total production of the munition [sic] factories of the United States."368 The cost of this venture amounted to "around $20 million" ($420,000,000 in today's value).369

The plan had been hatched in the Secret War Council. According to Bernhard Dernburg, it was Sommerfeld who "proposed at the time that Germany should try to conclude contracts for munitions with many of the [U.S.] arms manufacturers, and he believed he could keep these factories busy for eight months with $20 million [...] The infantry cartridge Mauser 7mm could all be sold off to South America and Spain, who are all using this make, and that with a profit [...]"370 Count Bernstorff, who clearly supported the request, notified both Bernhard Dernburg and Heinrich Albert on October 17th: "Please tell Mr. von Papen that I am trying to prevent the purchasing of munitions by the Allies in a different way, since we are not receiving a go-ahead with respect to this option from Berlin."371 The long-awaited but disappointing answer came on October 27th: "Munitions purchases are not viewed as practical."372

Von Papen considered the decision a huge blunder which, in hindsight it was, and for which the German government would pay dearly a year later.373 It was von Papen's opinion, and clearly that of Count Bernstorff, Dernburg, and Albert, as well as that of Tauscher and Sommerfeld, that an early contracting of American munitions factories would have effectively closed the U.S. market to Entente purchases. Albert wrote in his unpublished memoirs, "Undoubtedly the decision from Berlin [...] was a mistake from any point of view. At that time we could have achieved three things with a relatively small sacrifice: first, the supply of the Allies with ammunition would have been made more difficult; second, the American government would have been pushed into a neutrality that was not just theoretical; third, business connections with influential American companies would have been created, which [the companies] naturally would have been on the German side."374

Albert and his colleagues correctly ascertained that this strategy would have worked; however, only for a short period of time, namely the exact time it would take to add industrial capacity. Munitions factories had risen from the ashes of the American recession in the hundreds by 1915. Von Papen's idea might appear crazy and naïve in hindsight. However, considering the small munitions capacity of U.S. plants and the prevailing opinion among German officials, including members of the Secret War Council that the war would be over in a matter of months, lends credence to the realism of the idea. American manufacturers in the beginning of the conflict seemed hesitant to build up too much capacity, with which they feared to be straddled after a short war. Rather, they decided to increase the prices of their products. However, once construction of new factories began, the brief window of opportunity, namely to buy up most available munitions capacities in the U.S., came to a close. The New York team went back to the drawing board.

The intelligence-gathering activities of the two attachés in New York did not break American law *in the strictly legal sense*. However, Koenig and the regional consulates also vetted the scores of volunteers and reservists for use in clandestine operations. "[…] when strangers used to approach us with claims of having carried out this or that act on behalf of the Fatherland, Koenig was instructed to check up on them."[375] Once the *strangers* checked out as viable candidates for a clandestine mission, the German military attaché organized their finances and sent them on their way. The regional consulates supported the operations as best as they could. Consequently, von Papen and Boy-Ed's secret service staff, especially the agents attached to Koenig's organization, pursued the legal collection of intelligence only to a small degree. The Secret War Council now focused on attacking Great Britain from U.S. soil.

CHAPTER 7:
STOPPING THE GREAT ARMADA

T HE FIRST SERIOUS MISSION TO attack Great Britain from U.S. soil targeted Canada. The U.S.' northern neighbor had formally declared war on Germany on August 4th 1914. This fact is not surprising given that Canada was a British dependency. However, Japan joined the Entente on August 23rd and declared war against Germany, as well. German strategists suspected that the Japanese government would attempt to send Japanese troops to the west coast of Canada, and from there via railroad to east coast ports on to Europe. Canadian and Japanese enforcements for Great Britain had the potential to upset the balance of forces in Europe substantially.

Canada's mobilization for the war was nothing short of astonishing. The Canadian armed forces numbered 3,110 men with 684 horses on August 4th, the day of the declaration of war.[376] The Canadian ranks had swelled to 83,000 men by the third week of September, which shipped to Europe on October 3rd and 24th. The first contingent consisted of 31,200 men with arms, trucks, horses, and supplies. "It took three hours for the line of ships, more than twenty-one miles long, to steam through the harbor's narrow exit into the Gulf of St. Lawrence. Once in the open, the great armada reformed in fleet formation: three lines ahead, fifteen cables (3,000 yards) apart, each led by a cruiser, with the fourth cruiser bringing up the rear."[377]

By the end of the war, 65,000 Canadian soldiers had succumbed in the trenches of Europe. The question of what could be done to prevent men and supplies from coming to Europe from Canada arose for the German government. The British dependency had a relatively low population density, almost all of which was located in the southern portions of the country. The total population of Canada amounted to 7.2 million people in 1911, of which 490,000 were of German or Austro-Hungarian extraction.[378] The Canadian public feared the German element in the country at the outbreak of the war: "Many Germans were well settled in Canada before the First World War. However, about 18,000 Germans and 90,000 Austrians arrived in the country after 1901. The sense of threat, created when the War broke out overseas in August of 1914, was heightened by the perception that the German enemy was outnumbering Canadians who had been naturalized."[379]

This fear was well founded. German volunteers, as well as German war planners, including military attaché von Papen, eyed the infrastructure of Canada with more than just casual interest. Virtually all commerce took place via railroads or shipping through the Great Lakes. It comes as no surprise that von Papen sent Koenig to Canada to collect information on troop movements, on potential infrastructure targets, and the men and materials needed to mount an attack. He acted under orders from the German general staff. Investigators of the Mixed Claims Commission, set up after the World War to adjudicate claims of the United States against Germany for the war, concluded in the 1930s, "There had been communications with respect to sabotage in Canada [...] in 1914, where the Mobile General Staff instructed Papen to take action against Canadian railroads [...]"[380]

Given orders to prevent Canadian expeditionary forces from shipping out to Europe, Military Attaché von Papen and Naval Attaché Boy-Ed got to work. As soon as von Papen had hired Paul Koenig and his *detective agency*, he sent the secret service man to canvass the east coast of Canada. Historians who have dealt with Germany's efforts to stop Canada from bringing men and material to the European conflict have largely understated the magnitude of the Canadian effort or ignored it completely.[381] The German response, which many historians have cast aside as the work of a handful of amateurs, appears far less ridiculous in the light of the available facts.[382]

The intelligence mission consisted of estimating exactly

the extent of the Canadian mobilization, as well as identifying possible targets that would interrupt or sabotage the effort. For a period of five weeks, Koenig and his agents traveled in Canada on reconnaissance missions. Laureat Jean J. Leclerc, a garage owner in Quebec, rented cars to the German agents. He also repeatedly served as Koenig's driver on the spying forays.[383] In 1915, after Koenig's activities came to light, Leclerc testified against the German agent. According to the garage owner, Koenig and his associate Siegfried H. Mundheim canvassed the waterfront of Quebec "on several night trips."[384] "At first [...] I thought well of Koenig. I drove him around the Valcartier camp, about the wharves, along the water front, but one thing struck me – his trips were made mostly at night."[385] The majority of Canada's expeditionary forces converged on the Valcartier military camp starting in the beginning of September 1914.[386]

Mundheim had a unique background, which Koenig needed for his mission. According to the *Frederick Post* from December 28th 1915, Mundheim worked as a manager for the Cement Products of Canada, which had a factory on the island of Orleans.[387] This large island was strategically located at the entrance to Quebec harbor and formed one of the narrowest points in the channel. Koenig went there several times. According to Leclerc, the Germans investigated several other narrow points on the St. Lawrence river through which the troop ships had to move on their way out to sea.[388] While Koenig's orders to this effect never came to light, it seems likely that he wanted to block the St. Lawrence river at one of the narrow points to prevent the British troop ships from making it to the Atlantic ocean. He could have achieved that by blowing up a bridge across the river or sinking a barge in the shipping channel. It is hard to fathom another explanation for him and his agents canvassing the narrow points in the shipping lanes.

The Canadian chauffeur further described the extent of Koenig's missions in Canada. "Koenig [...] also paid numerous visits about the Ross Rifle Factory on the Plains of Abraham [on the waterfront of Quebec] [...] and about the Government arsenals on the Cove Fields [also in downtown Quebec], on Palace Hill and on the Cape [...] He asked many questions about the terminal and shipping facilities of Quebec Harbor, about the system of guards established since the war and was anxious to know what kind of a naval station Canada had at the entrance of Quebec harbor."[389]

Mundheim was not the only agent spying with Koenig on Canadian installations. Edmund Justice, a pier guard and Koenig *detective* in New York, joined P. K. and Frederick Metzler on one of the trips.[390] Koenig chose the two agents for the Canada mission because of their nationalities. Metzger was an American citizen. Justice had been born in County Cork, Ireland and had kept his Irish papers. Multiple support staff, safe houses, and financial connections provided the logistical backbone for Koenig's team in Quebec and Montreal. In the Northern and Midwestern states with heavy German immigrant density, every *Liederkranz* (singing club), *Stammtisch*, German Club, and veterans' club provided fertile soil for recruitment of volunteers. The U.S. government never named or prosecuted any of these peripheral people in the German plot. German agents paid lots of attention to the Irish-American community, which also rejoiced at the opportunity to hurt British interests.

The Canadian plot grew into much wider circles than the American authorities and subsequent historians ever realized. However, in all fairness, stories of German reservists organizing for an all-out assault on Canada was pure fantasy. A German, who called himself Max Lymar Count Louden, claimed in the fall of 1915, to have been commander of a strike force organized by "[...] a group of very wealthy German-Americans [who] created a fund of $16,000,000 with which to equip the expedition. As early as October, 1914, [...], they engaged him [Louden] because of his superior knowledge of military tactics to lead the invasion. Many secret meetings were held in New York. Plans for the quick mobilization and equipment of a full army corps of German reservists now living in the United States were completed and the invasion was to take place this spring."[391]

Although American newspapers as well as the English propaganda picked up this story with gusto, neither the German archives nor American investigative files contain any credible reports of von Papen sending weapons to singing clubs and Stammtisch crowds. It is certainly possible that von Papen and others having one-too-many beers in the German Club in New York contemplated the possibility of organizing a large force to invade Canada. However, there is no evidence these outlandish schemes ever moved beyond mere conversations.

The only loud voice to allege that such a plot existed was *Count Louden*. The swindler related this story in 1916 mainly to extract himself from a conviction as a fraud and a polygamist. According to an indictment in October of 1915, the *Count* had concurrently married as many as six women, all of whom he very professionally relieved of their wealth.[392] *The New York Times* reported in 1915, "According to the German records, 'Max Schiemangh' was born in 1869 in Staupitz, Saxony, (eighty miles south of Berlin) and studied at a military school. There he acquired the knowledge which enabled him to pose in any country he visited as an officer in the army of the country he had just left. He was dismissed from this school and then came to the United States."[393] Amazingly, his tales of German reservists marching in formation at German singing club gatherings all along the Canadian border persisted for years.

However, besides swindlers and narcissists taking advantage of the opportunity for publicity, real plots of German sabotage cells against Canada did come to light within weeks of the outbreak of the war. A small blurb in the *New York Times* on August 12th 1914, reported the arrest of four Germans on their way to Ottawa. William Lehmark, Oscar Hauser, Charles Wagner, and Oscar Seibel had entered Canada on a small paddleboat. They had with them two rifles, two pistols, one shotgun and a box with poison, gun cotton (nitrocellulose), and fuse.[394] The authorities discovered upon capturing them that only one spoke English, and none would reveal their mission. The capture of these four agents, who would spend the rest of the war as prisoners, was the first hard evidence of an active German cell of sabotage agents. The team had come from Philadelphia. The port of Philadelphia, like the ports of Newport News, Baltimore, and New York harbored several German merchant cruisers providing a potential army of recruits for the naval attaché Karl Boy-Ed.

A second German effort to infiltrate Canada on a sabotage mission launched on or around August 21st 1914. A German agent from Mexico turned up in von Papen's office.[395] Franz R. Wachendorf, alias Horst von der Goltz, placed himself at the German government's disposal.[396] Born on May 5th 1887 either in England or Germany,[397] he came to New York on the SS *Kroonberg* on May 21st 1912, if his story is credible.[398] He enlisted in the U.S. army in July 1912 as a private in the 19th Infantry Regiment in Leavenworth, Kansas.[399] He deserted from Company A stationed in Galveston, Texas, in April 1913, and went to Mexico.[400] Both dates and the fact of desertion match Wachendorf's own statements.[401]

The German naval intelligence agent Felix Sommerfeld, who while spying for the German government also headed the Mexican Secret Service at the time, recruited Wachendorf in May of 1913. Wachendorf was to serve in the Mexican secret service, while providing information to the German military. He joined the Constitutionalist movement under Venustiano Carranza which assembled in San Antonio at the time to mount the resistance against the Mexican president Victoriano Huerta.[402] Huerta had overthrown the democratically elected Mexican president Francisco Madero in a bloody coup d'état in February of 1913. Sommerfeld had been Madero's security chief when the coup took place. Now he had orders to join the resistance and organize a German intelligence network with the likely successors of the Mexican dictator.

Wachendorf recounted in his book that a German agent by the name La Vallee forced him to desert the army and work for the German government in Mexico. No record of a German agent named *La Vallee* has been found. A photograph in Wachendorf's book, however, identified his secret service handler: Felix A. Sommerfeld.[403] Nothing concrete is known about Wachendorf's work for Sommerfeld. According to his own recollections, he acted as a spy, was arrested and almost executed. Although entirely within the realm of possibility, none of these stories have yet been verified.[404]

Horst von der Goltz is in the back row, second from the left.
Next to him (back row, first left) is Felix A. Sommerfeld.[405]

Wachendorf's description of how he got from Mexico to New York at the onset of the European war rings true. According to the German agent, German Consul Otto Kueck of Chihuahua had sent him to New York. Kueck, a well-known German businessman in Chihuahua who had initiated Felix Sommerfeld into the world of spying had documented connections to the German secret service.[406] Just around the time of Goltz's story, Kueck found himself in big trouble in Mexico. After supporting President Huerta, the victorious Mexican general, Pancho Villa, expelled him from Chihuahua in August of 1914. Kueck stayed in El Paso for a few months, exactly when Wachendorf claimed to have met him and received orders to go to the U.S.[407] Kueck eventually moved to Los Angeles, where he died in 1915.[408] Whether Sommerfeld or, indeed, Kueck sent Wachendorf to New York, remains open.

Wachendorf did come to New York and contacted Frederico Stallforth who was working with Sommerfeld on supplying Pancho Villa's forces with arms and ammunition. "When he [von der Goltz] came to New York he looked us [Frederico and Alberto Stallforth] up [...]"[409] It is, therefore, certainly no accident that Sommerfeld worked with Stallforth and for the German government in New York when Wachendorf suddenly appeared. The German military attaché, Franz von Papen, assigned him to a sabotage team with a mission linked to the efforts of Paul Koenig.

According to von Papen and Heinrich Albert's accounting registers, sabotage agent Wachendorf received an initial payment of $100 on August 25th 1914, as well as subsequent payments of $200, $350, $600, and $150 between August 28th and October 1st.[410] These payments (close to $30,000 in today's value) were to finance an attack on a prime terrorist target in Canada: The Welland Canal.

The twenty-six mile-long waterway connects Lake Ontario with Lake Erie. The canal was the only sea-lane open to shipping from the western great lakes to the Atlantic Ocean, not only for Canada but also the United States. The Welland Canal served as a prime-shipping lane for grains and corn from the American Midwest and Canadian south during the Great War. It had been attacked by bombers twice before in its history; once in 1841 by a filibuster fighting British shipping, and the second time in 1900 by Irish separatists.

Von der Goltz later testified, "[...] von Papen asked me to confer with two Irishmen, who proposed the dynamiting of railway junctions, grain elevators, and the locks of the canals connecting the Great Lakes. It was hoped thus to terrify Canada, preventing the Dominion from aiding the mother country."[411] The two *Irishmen* were Thomas P. Tuite and John Devoy. Tuite, an American citizen and engineer by trade lived on 120th Street in Harlem. Devoy was the editor of a Gaelic-American newspaper, leading member of the Sinn Fein movement, and closely linked with von Papen.[412]

Also involved in the conception of the plot was Karl F. Buck. Buck was a German-born resident of New York who had received American citizenship in 1903.[413] He was a typesetter by profession and lived on the upper West Side.[414] Implicated, and possibly one of the original plotters also, was Ewald Hecker, a fourteen-year veteran of the 13th Dragoon Regiment of the cavalry with the rank of captain. He also spent two years at the German General Staff College and perceived his intelligence training sufficient to ask for an intelligence officer job with Franz von Papen after his return to

Germany in 1917.[415] His intelligence cover for his U.S. assignment matched that of Bernhard Dernburg, both *representatives* of the German Red Cross.[416] Vice-governor of German Samoa at the outbreak of the war, Hecker came to New York in August 1914 and worked closely with his former boss, Bernhard Dernburg, as well as Heinrich Albert.[417]

According to Wachendorf's testimony and memoirs, the two Irishmen introduced him to Charles Tuchendler, a twenty-seven year-old Austrian citizen who had moved from Berlin to New York in May 1914. The immigration record listed his occupation as merchant.[418] While Tuchendler clearly worked as an agent for either Koenig or one of his *detectives*, he made the assignment to Wachendorf appear to be purely by chance. According to Tuchendler, Wachendorf met him at a newspaper bulletin board in New York where both of them searched for the newest reports on the war.[419] According to Tuchendler's testimony at his trial in 1916, he had no other credentials for being hired than being from the *Fatherland*.

This image reflected what English propaganda wanted the American public to believe. When Tuchendler testified in 1916, Great Britain wanted to manipulate public opinion to support an American participation in the war against Germany. While the German efforts contained many errors in judgment, all the German agents observed some basic rules. One of them was the vetting of agents. Wachendorf admitted in his memoirs that the Austrian was an agent and "had already had some dealings with the two men who originally proposed the scheme."[420] Given the clout von Papen had gained with Koenig's organization, under no circumstances would he have hired a German adventurer from Mexico, given him a few bucks to assemble a team of amateurs with the sole prerequisite that they be German, and sent him with personally signed letters of recommendation on a terror mission to Canada. That chain of events, and the conclusion that German agents had been inept amateurs, had been a concoction of British war propaganda.

According to Wachendorf's story, he engaged Tuchendler to participate in the Canadian expedition for $2 per day.[421] After he had received his first payment of $100 on August 25th, Wachendorf went to Baltimore with his companion. The trip made little sense on the surface. However, just as Koenig was organizing cells of German agents on the moored HAPAG liners in New York, the same was happening in Baltimore where most of the North German Lloyd fleet had anchored. The trip to Baltimore also indicated that, despite his claims to the contrary, Wachendorf was never put in charge of the operation. Von Papen or Koenig sent him to meet with an existing cell of German saboteurs. The head of the Baltimore cell was German Consul Karl A. Luederitz. Wachendorf's exact role in the effort is not entirely clear; however, it seems that he told the truth to English authorities in 1915, when he said: "[…] He [von Papen] told me that I was to act as the go-between so that no one else would be connected with the affair."[422]

Certainly age or rank could not have been the reason for Wachendorf's selection. A twenty-three year- old would only have had a low rank (lieutenant) in the German army, if he ever served. Von Papen chose him for the mission for special skills. He was well-versed at handling explosives from his clandestine work in Mexico. Whether Wachendorf had some special knowledge of the American-Canadian border or spoke French is not documented.

Wachendorf and Tuchendler showed a letter of introduction from von Papen to Consul Luederitz when they arrived in Baltimore.[423] The consul passed the German agent on to one of the skippers of the moored Lloyd liners, presumably the SS Rhein, which had arrived on July 15th. The skipper detailed three sailors and an officer to participate in the operation with Wachendorf.[424] The German sabotage agent also received an American passport from Consul Luederitz with his mission codename, Bridgeman W. Taylor.[425] The German consul applied for the document on August 29th. The U.S. authorities issued it on August 31st in Baltimore, Maryland. Bridgeman W. Taylor's physical description is twenty-seven years of age, five feet, ten inches tall, prominent nose, fair complexion and oval face. The fictitious Taylor was born on July 16th, 1887 in San Francisco. The Maryland passport office forwarded the document to Baltimore attorney Frederick F. Schneider. Tuchendler, alias Charles J. Tucker, signed the sworn affidavit as a witness of the passport application. Tucker gave his address as 82 Wall Street, New York, not a residential area known to house recent German immigrants, but less than two blocks from Franz von Papen's office. Wachendorf and Tuchendler returned from Baltimore on August 31st. The sailors stayed behind for the time being. Three more conspirators joined Wachendorf in New York: Alfred E. Fritzen, Frederick J. Busse, and Constante Covani.

*The bogus passport of Wachendorf issued in Baltimore,
Maryland on August 29th 1914*[426]

Fritzen, a thirty-seven year-old German navy officer of
the reserve, had been a steward on the SS *Dwinsk* of the Russian-
American line.[427] He arrived on August 14th 1914 from Latvia on

an intelligence assignment.[428] Fritzen was assigned to Hans Tauscher, according to HAPAG files.[429] Busse was a manufacturer's representative with an office in Suite 406 of the World Building in midtown Manhattan, who in the past had also lived in England.[430] Whether or not Busse came from Koenig's organization in the first place is unclear; however, he did work for both Koenig and von Papen as a secret agent later in the war.[431] Von Papen's financial records show payments to Paul Koenig for "compensation for F. J. Busse" in July 1915.[432]

Constante Covani, twenty-six years old, "[…] was born in Lucca, Italy […] dark hair, dark complexion, good dresser, speaks good English, Italian, German, French and Spanish."[433] He had come to Boston from Genoa in 1906 to live with an uncle.[434] Covani had held multiple jobs; first as a clerk, then as a picture salesman, finally as a detective for Pinkerton's detective agency.[435] He listed his occupation as "foreign correspondent" on immigration papers in January 1914.[436] Paul Koenig frequently used Pinkertons' detectives, which might have brought him in contact with the Italian.

These five agents: Wachendorf, Tuchendler, Busse, Covani, and Fritzen constituted the core of the team to blow up the Welland Canal. There were other conspirators who figured into the scheme. The engineer, Thomas Tuite, assisted with specifying the amount of explosives needed, as well as the knowledge required to blow locks. Tuite's apartment in Harlem also served as a safe house. Wachendorf testified that a German with the name of Karl F. Buck provided the mailing address for his new passport. The information on the actual passport reveals that was not the case, although the German lawyer designated to receive the passport could have sent it to Buck's apartment in New York. However, apart from being a possible mail drop, Karl Buck had introduced Covani to Wachendorf.[437] While Wachendorf made himself out to be the leader of the group, it seems to have been Alfred Fritzen who had the most seniority and the highest military rank.

Within a week of his visit in Baltimore, the group of German sailors Wachendorf claimed to have selected came to New York. According to the self-aggrandizing Wachendorf, "[…] on my noticing that my movements were being watched, I sent them back to make the detectives think the enterprise abandoned."[438] Although there are no BI records or investigative reports to substantiate Wachendorf's explanation, British secret service agents watched von Papen's office, as well as the German Club where the military attaché and his colleagues hung around.[439] Theoretically, the British shadows could have picked out this particular twenty-three year-old among the hundreds of reservists who, in those early days of the war, called on von Papen to be worth investigating further. It just does not sound likely. Rather than Wachendorf being shadowed, it is more likely that to someone higher up in the conspiracy, like Fritzen, Hecker, Koenig, or von Papen made the decision that the German sailors were too conspicuous and ordered them sent back.

Nevertheless, the plot progressed in the following weeks. Wachendorf's account is that von Papen and Hans Tauscher attended multiple meetings with him and the plotters. Tauscher had a lot to lose and, thus, it is astonishing how carelessly he assisted in this scheme to attack Canada. Tauscher bought three hundred pounds of dynamite from DuPont on September 5th 1914, as the available documentation about von Papen's order shows.[440] Apparently, he told his contact there that he planned on extracting tree stumps on his property. The cost of the explosives amounted to $31 plus $0.13 for fuses.[441] Since Tauscher did not wish to have the dynamite delivered to his office under surveillance by the English secret service, he told the DuPont representative to consign the order to Bridgeman Taylor. Wachendorf, alias Taylor, picked up the box of "Straight 60%" dynamite on the 11th of September. DuPont delivered forty-five feet of hemp fuse two days later.[442]

The pickup location was a barge on the Hudson River. Bureau of Investigation agents reported, "Von der Goltz, Fritzen, Govani [sic], Tucker and Busse next engaged a motor boat, bought some old suitcases and went aboard a barge lying [on] the other side of the Statue of Liberty. The man in charge of the barge seemed to be expecting them, got the 200 pounds of dynamite, put the explosive into two suitcases and carried them to the launch to 148th Street. From there they took them down town in a taxicab. Half of the dynamite was stored under a bed in von der Goltz's room and the other half under a bed in Fritzen's room."[443] It is a long way from the Statue of Liberty to 148th Street. The barge was probably closer to the launch site on the Upper West Side or Harlem.

By the time the conspirators picked up the dynamite, Tauscher had also sent six guns to the plotters via a German safe house, Meyer's restaurant in Hoboken.[444] Wachendorf described the progression of the plot in his memoirs. The conspirators now stayed in "[…] a cheap section of Harlem. For von der Goltz, the spendthrift, the braggart, was seen no longer in the gay places of New York. He had spent all his money, and now, no longer of interest to the newspapers – or to the secret agents of the allies – had taken a two dollar and a half room in Harlem where he could repent his follies – and be as inconspicuous as he pleased."[445] He did not repent; he prepared the last details of his mission.

However, as with most of Wachendorf's embellished prose about his time in the United States, there always seem to be kernels of truth poking through the self-important mutterings that sprang from the agent. Not a single newspaperman had noticed the lanky German adventurer; neither did the police detectives of Tunney's New York bomb squad. If the plotters now moved to Harlem, they did not stay in a rented room; they stayed in the house of fellow plotter and engineer Thomas Tuite to make final preparations for their sabotage mission. According to Wachendorf, von Papen supplied them with detonators and wire, which he had stored in his room at the German Club.

Just as much of Wachendorf's story bristles with hair-raising details full of embellishments, so does this claim rub as unrealistic. It is utterly inconceivable that von Papen would invite three of the plotters to his apartment at the German Club, which he knew was being watched by British agents, to provide them with bomb-making materials.[446] Tauscher had easy access to those types of supplies, and it would have been more logical for him to supply all the needed accessories. Regardless, von Papen certainly sourced all the supplies from Tauscher. Whether von Papen really acted as carelessly as Wachendorf and the English propaganda suggested he did, it is certain that Hans Tauscher left his fingerprints all over the plot. He had a lot to lose as a respected businessman and as a key German agent in charge of much larger schemes than terrorizing Canada. His carelessness would ruin his hitherto comfortable life a year later when everything came out.

Paul Koenig, Frederick Metzler, and Edmund Justice left for Burlington, Vermont on the 15th of September.[447] Alfred Fritzen, Frederick Busse, Constante Covani, Wachendorf, and Tuchendler left for Buffalo, New York on the same day. Koenig's mission targeted the troop camp at Valcartier and the harbor of Quebec, where Canada's expeditionary troops made last preparations for shipping to Europe. Regarding the second team that included Wachendorf, the mission was to sabotage the Welland Canal, thereby creating a diversion while the primary team under Koenig sank a barge, or blew up a bridge to block the shipping channel. Both groups were armed and equipped, although the extent of preparations is only known about Wachendorf's team. Von Papen testified in 1932 that half of Wachendorf's dynamite remained in another German safe house, the apartment of "Martha Heldt, at No. 123 West 15th Street" in lower Manhattan.[448] Wachendorf wrote that he left "two suitcases" at the Heldt apartment. Originally, the two hundred pounds of explosives had been packed into two suitcases.

How much of the dynamite Wachendorf and his team actually took to the Canadian border is in question. It seems to have been a fraction of the two hundred pounds. It is curious that von Papen should mention the name of Martha Heldt and her address as a depository of the dynamite. Heldt, a reputedly gorgeous blonde, and her equally attractive roommate, Mena Edwards, allegedly entertained both Boy-Ed and von Papen lavishly causing a widely publicized "sexpionage" scandal.[449] Heinrich Albert also found himself entangled with Martha Heldt, although the newspapers did not specifically identify him as one of Heldt's customers. Apparently, she had joined Albert on a trip to St. Louis. The cryptic notation in Albert's diary for October 24th 1914 reads, "Sunday, Jefferson Hotel! Taken out by Hildegard [Wulfing] [...] in an auto! Supper old No. 827 with Mrs. Held[t] and Lacy (Forst); Peculiar feeling in St. L. [St. Louis] houses [...]"[450]

A few months later, Mena Edwards related intelligence gained at these supposedly wild parties at 123 West 15th street to agents of the Justice Department. Von Papen claimed in his memoirs, of course, that these stories were completely false. "I had never known a young woman of that name [Mena Edwards] in the whole of my life; nor had Boy-Ed and I ever taken her to 123 West 15th Street, occupied by a Mrs. Gordon or a Mrs. Heldt [...]"451 He might never have taken Edwards there (since she already lived there); yet, in 1932, the former military attaché made the mistake of testifying to the fact that he knew Martha Heldt and the address of her apartment, which confirmed the facts contained in von der Goltz' sworn statement. The looming question is: What happened with the dynamite that Wachendorf had not taken? Tauscher sourced the explosives for this particular mission. Rather than believing Wachendorf's story, it is much more likely that Martha Heldt's apartment served as the inconspicuous place where both sabotage teams stored and received their supplies. This theory also explains why investigators and British agents never found any dynamite at Martha Heldt's place or anywhere else. Koenig and his team had taken the remaining suitcases to Canada.

Fritzen, Wachendorf, Tuchendler, Busse, and Covani took the train to Buffalo, New York. They rented a room in a boarding house at 198 Delaware Avenue owned by Amos S. Guy. Guy later described "his transients as composing a jolly and noisy lot."452 Somehow, a watch went missing, prompting Wachendorf, alias Taylor, to cause a loud disturbance. The New York Times reported what happened next. Mrs. Guy, the landlady, "left her husband on guard while she went out and called in a policeman."453 The subsequent search almost turned into a disaster for the plotters, but, as the New York Times reported, "the dynamite was shifted just before a policeman searched their rooms."454 Whether the watch turned up or not has not been documented. Wachendorf, Fritzen, and the others stayed for four days in Buffalo and went on daily reconnaissance trips. According to Wachendorf's account, the German spy hired German-American aviator, monoplane builder, and part-time waiter Valentine Buettner, to help him investigate the locks along the canal. The two had met at Fels', a German restaurant in Niagara, where Buettner worked. Buettner, at one point, loudly told the chef in "idiomatic German" that a guest refused to accept his dinner.455

Wachendorf struck up a conversation and proceeded to take him into his confidence. Buettner procured a boat for Wachendorf and went with him to a "[...] light-house located where the small canal connects the Welland with Niagara Falls and surveyed the field with a view to determining how best to destroy the Welland Canal."[456] Buettner also agreed to store the dynamite at his shop. Apparently, restaurant proprietor Fanny Fels also stored the explosive suitcases at least for a short period: "I remember that they left some suitcases but I do not know what was in them. It frequently happens that guests leave they baggage here and I never question the contents of them."[457]

The German sabotage team stayed in the area around Niagara for ten days. Von Papen communicated with them through an Irish-American lawyer in Buffalo, John T. Ryan. Ryan had received a telegram from John Devoy, the *Gaelic-American* editor, on September 16th:

> Party who called is all right. I gave your address.
> Do all you can for him [Wachendorf]. Identify him
> at telegraph office. I will be responsible. Imperfect
> introduction due to my brother's death and hurry.
>
> John Devoy.[458]

Through Ryan, Wachendorf and his team received four hundred dollars in cash on the 15th and 17th of September.[459] However, the authorization for proceeding, the German agent claimed, never came forth. Wachendorf sent two telegrams to von Papen from Buffalo, "stating that he was awaiting instructions."[460] Von Papen, under the pseudonym *Steffens*, sent a telegram on September 24th without further explanation telling Wachendorf "can not do anything more for him."[461] According to the German agent, von Papen had abandoned him and his people without any reason. As a result, the entire mission fell apart. The truth was quite different. Tuchendler had already returned to New York by himself, while Wachendorf and Covani left the Canadian border for New York on September 27th. The one hundred pounds of dynamite stayed with pilot-waiter Valentine Buettner.

```
                  "Sept. 24, 1914

"John T. Ryan,
    "613 Mutual Life Bldg.     Buffalo, NY


"Please instruct Taylor [von der Goltz's
assumed name] can not do anything more
for him.
              "Steffens"
```

Steffens telegram to Franz von Papen[462]

The coordinated attack on Canada never occurred. Curiously, von Papen had cancelled the mission one week before the shipment of Canadian troops to England. The *great armada* sailed on October 3rd, not on September 24th as Wachendorf claimed. The German agent also claimed that he dismissed Busse and Fritzen while still in Buffalo, because of lack of funding. However, both men continued to work for the German secret service, which is widely documented in von Papen and Albert's accounts.[463] So, what may really have happened?

If the bombs had gone off at Welland in the last week of September, they would have generated the most impact and, quite possibly, jeopardized the assemblage of the troop ships. The glitch in the plan must have been a completely different one: The Canadian military knew that the Welland Canal was a prime target for terrorists. During the period leading up to the troop transports to England, "Canada formed a security service consisting of telegraph operators, customs and immigration officers, local and special police, military guards, private detectives and watchmen. This protective service was under the authority of Lt. Col. Percy Sherwood, Chief Commissioner of the Dominion Police. For the Canadian authorities the most important public utility that needed protection was the canal systems of Ontario and Quebec. The largest force used, one thousand, was deployed to protect the Welland Canal."[464] One convincing theory explaining the abandonment of the mission is that the Welland Canal team simply got cold feet.

According to Wachendorf's own testimony, it was he who

abandoned the project "Having meantime received privately information that the 1st Canadian Contingent had left Valcartier Camp, I knew that I should be recalled [...]"[465] Wachendorf wanted to abandon the project as soon as he understood the level of protection of the installation, and asked von Papen to do so. He wrote in his autobiography, "[...] von Papen should let us know when the Canadian troops were about to leave camp so that we might strike at the psychological moment [...] Then after a stay of several days in Niagara, during which we did nothing but exchange futile telegrams with Ryan and 'Mr. Steffens' [alias Franz von Papen] – we learned that the first contingent of Canadian troops had left the camp – and my men and I returned to New York [...]"[466] It is interesting that only two of his men returned to New York. The team split, indicating that Fritzen and Busse wanted to continue while Wachendorf and Covani backed out. Unable to coax Wachendorf into bombing the canal, von Papen instructed him to "Do what you think best."[467] Back in New York, von Papen reportedly questioned the German agent why he had not executed his instructions. Wachendorf blamed it on a misunderstanding and the lack of cooperation from the Buffalo lawyer, John T. Ryan.[468]

If the Welland Canal was that well protected, one can only imagine the security around the British fleet that was about to carry a whole army to Europe. Without the diversion that Wachendorf's team planned to execute, Koenig and his associates had no chance to get even close to the harbor of Quebec or the military camp of Valcartier in those last days of September. The same is true for any German raider that may have been dispatched to the Canadian coast. Steaming into the St. Lawrence or laying in wait at its mouth would have been sheer suicide. After Wachendorf and his men bailed, Koenig realized the futility of his mission and returned to New York around the same time.

Both sabotage teams were back in New York on October 3rd 1914 when, in the words of historian Brian Lee Massey, "[...] the entire Armada, containing the largest military force which had ever crossed the Atlantic at one time, set sail for England. In three long parallel lines of about a dozen ships each, with flags flying and signals twinkling, it made an imposing sight for the handful of people who saw it off. On October 6th the convoy was joined at sea by a ship carrying the Newfoundland Regiment. Before and during the crossing there had been much talk about the threat of German submarines but this threat never materialized."[469]

The Commander of Germany's submarine fleet, Admiral Hermann Bauer, did claim in his memoirs that U-20, a German long-distance submarine indeed had gone to Canada to intercept the Canadian troop transports. "U-20 [...] came back from its mission against the large Canadian transport near the Hebrides [...]"[470] The complete truth of what caused the sabotage mission to fail will never be known in its entirety. Wachendorf's later career as an author and key witness of the government against von Papen clouded the German military attaché's commentary. Von Papen explained to his lawyers in Berlin in 1916 that Wachendorf was an "[...] imposter. He was to get me information from Canada, as a result of which he went to Buffalo and hired two Germans named Busse and Fritzen. It soon became clear that he was only interested in making money, because intelligence he did not deliver. I therefore broke all connections with him in the end of September 1914. His claim that I personally equipped him with detonators and fuses is completely made up since I certainly did not have a depository of explosives-ammunition in my apartment in the German Club, nor did I in any way personally took care of such details."[471]

Von Papen was understandably angry when he briefed his lawyers. However, he might not have been that far off. The man, who claimed to be Franz Hobart Wachendorf, alias Horst von der Goltz, alias Bridgeman W. Taylor, remains an enigma to historians. No one could ever explain the origins of his curious names. Historian Johannes Reiling suspected that Bridgeman Taylor might have been the agent's real name and that he was English.[472] This theory seems far-fetched and is not documented. However, no archival records have turned up to define the true identity of the agent. .

What the records do show, however, is that almost all his biographical details are lies. There are no records that a Franz H. Wachendorf traveled to the U.S. in or around 1912. There is one record of Frank R. Wachendorf who served in the U.S. army in 1912 as a private in the nineteenth infantry regiment. Wachendorf mentioned that name and unit in his memoirs. No other record corroborating the identity of Frank Wachendorf have been found. He may have entered under a fourth name, real or assumed, which has not yet been identified by the authorities or historians. There is no Bridgeman W. Taylor who left any paper trail in England, Mexico or the United States.

Finally, the alias *Horst von der Goltz* prompted the very prominent German noble family of that name to vehemently protest having any connection to this agent. It is a twist of historical irony that von der Goltz is the only well-documented name for this agent. The English used this alias when they transferred him back to the United States in 1916.[473] Wachendorf also traveled under this name in 1922 when he promoted his book.[474] There is a remote possibility that Field Marshal Colmar von der Goltz, who had access to military records, extinguished the black sheep of the family from the face of his family history before he died in April of 1916. Were that true, descendants of the von der Goltz family will someday decide to lift the veil off this enigmatic agent.

After the failed bombing mission, Wachendorf received a final payment from von Papen on October 1st to finance his return to Germany.[475] Wachendorf claimed that the German military attaché asked to "present myself at my arrival at Berlin at the Section III. B. General Staff," the secret service division of the army.[476] The German agent procured a visa for Italy using the Bridgeman W. Taylor passport. He sailed to Genoa on the SS *Duca d'Aosta* on the 8th of October. He described in his book how he made his way from Genoa to Berlin. Rather than reporting to the General Staff, he wrote that he visited the Foreign Office in Berlin "to bring full details of conditions in Mexico and the United States to the War Office."[477]

None of this seems to be true. It is highly unlikely that if he had orders to report to Department III. B. of the General Staff, he would go to the Foreign Office, which did not even have a *War Office*, as he described in his memoirs. Wachendorf also asserted to have been received by Wilhelm II during this visit to Berlin. According to his memoirs, Wachendorf was given new orders for "crippling of the United States by a campaign of terrorism and conspiracy."[478]

Wachendorf, according to his own tale, gave himself up to British authorities on the passage back to the United States on November 7ᵗʰ 1914. Supposedly, he spent the next year in solitary confinement in Britain but, in reality, Naval Intelligence Director Sir William Reginald *Blinker* Hall's people turned him into a British agent.

Wachendorf's story, especially after his return to Germany, is full of factual inaccuracies and embellishments. While he could have received orders for a new mission, it is very likely that he never went to Germany. Rather, the British discovered Wachendorf on his way to Genoa. This possibility becomes especially real if Wachendorf's claims that he had been watched all along by British secret service agents, were true. British agents certainly had been present along the border close to what they knew was a prime target for German attacks, the Welland Canal. Having been watched there and on his way to New York, his voyage on the Italian liner likely was known to the British authorities in charge of stopping and checking ocean traffic. Were he caught, the British intelligence services could have sent Wachendorf to Germany as a British spy and, with much fanfare, arrested him on his way back to America. Wachendorf never admitted this, neither did the British intelligence services. The only clue lies in the British publication of documents captured from Franz von Papen in 1916. Von Papen's checkbook contained British notations for the American public to be able to understand the context of the payments. Referring to the check countersigned by Frederico Stallforth the British government noted:

> Cheque No. 22.
> Mr. Bridgeman Taylor: This person came over to England to offer himself for work under His Majesty's Government. His real name is Von der Goltz, and he is now in England.[479]

Like so many spy stories, Wachendorf's final mission remains shrouded in secrecy.

The fallout of the failed mission, however, proved to be devastating for all involved. Immediately, von Papen had to take care of Busse, Fritzen, Covani, and Tuchendler. Busse, Fritzen, and Tucker continued on as agents.[480] Covani, under his alias E. Gonzales, asked von Papen on October 19th to "[…] advise me of the possibilities of making use of my services abroad or here."[481] He gave as his contact address, "Karl W. Buck 843 West End Ave City."[482] Von Papen wrote Gonzales a check for $150 on November 24th, purpose unknown.

The eventual testimony of Wachendorf became a huge public relations disaster for Germany in general, and for von Papen in particular. Von Papen was evicted from the United States in January of 1916. The military attaché had to surrender his luggage to British officials on his way from the United States to Germany. Despite his status as diplomat, a British search party at Falmouth took his trunk, which the agents did not consider covered under diplomatic protection. The contents of von Papen's luggage were a boon for British intelligence. He carried secret and top secret files, including his checkbooks with stubs documenting payments to agents. These files corroborated Wachendorf's testimony to the British naval intelligence, namely that he had hired the agent and supplied him with money and other resources.

The concerted effort of September 1914 to simultaneously blow up the Welland Canal and block the shipping lanes in the St. Lawrence River, despite its failure, was one of the potentially far-reaching and ambitious clandestine missions in the World War. Never again would the stakes for inflicting damages on Canada be as high. The attacks on the Welland Canal and Paul Koenig's mission in Quebec have always been reported as separate plots. They were not. The details of this large-scale attack on the Canadian mobilization have never, and may never, fully come into the open. However, virtually all German secret service assets in September of 1914 seemed to be working on the same mission, which due to English and Canadian preparedness – and possibly the cowardice of Franz Wachendorf – failed before it ever took shape.

Subsequently, the British government presented the Agent Wachendorf to the American courts and an outraged American public, triggering the arrest and conviction of most of the plotters. Von Papen summarized the Wachendorf episode in his memoirs: "I admit that this was not a particularly intelligent piece of work on my part, and it must be put down to the confusion of those early days and my lack of experience in this particular field. Even success in the attempt would never have been worth the political risk involved. I soon learned my lesson, as Goltz turned into a petty blackmailer, who was always threatening some disclosure if I did not keep him sufficiently sweetened. I decided to look twice at all such plans in the future and to keep on the right side of the United States law."[483]

CHAPTER 8:
SABOTAGE OF THE CANADIAN RAILROAD

FRANZ VON PAPEN MAY HAVE looked twice at the plans after the Welland episode. However, no matter the intensity of his scrutiny the attacks on Canada continued unabatedly and unsuccessfully in 1915. Von Papen organized attacks until the American government ordered the German military attaché to pack his suitcases and return to Germany in the end of that year. As was the case with the passport forgeries and the attacks on Canada, neither von Papen nor his superiors in Berlin learned to weigh the political devastation they caused against the benefits their schemes could produce. The German General Staff ordered von Papen to attack railroad installations in Canada on January 3rd 1915.[484]

> B 386
> Transmitted 3rd Jan. 1915
> From Berlin
>
> To Washington
>
> With reference to my telegram, No. 257, Secret, The General Staff is anxious that vigorous measures should be taken to destroy the Canadian Pacific in several places for the purpose of causing a lengthy interruption of traffic. Captain BOEHM who is well known in America and who will shortly return to that country is furnished with expert informations [sic] on that subject. Acquaint the Military Attaché

with the above and furnish the sums required for the enterprise.

Zimmerman [sic]. [485]

Within weeks of the order the military attaché sent two sabotage agents, Werner Horn and Hans W. Boehm, to blow up railroad installations in the northeast.

Werner Horn's mission was to destroy a 110-foot bridge over the Saint Croix River between Vanceboro, Maine and St. Croix, New Brunswick. The strategically important bridge connected the Canadian Pacific Railway with the Eastern Maine Railway leading to the harbor of Bangor, Maine. Horn, an employee of a large coffee plantation in Guatemala, quit his job and travelled from Belize, British Honduras, to New York via Galveston, Texas in August 1914, in order to sail to Germany and report to his unit.[486] he went back to Guatemala after four unsuccessful weeks trying to find a ship that would take him. He did not get his old job back. Anxious to do something to aid his fatherland, he wrote to Ambassador Count Bernstorff "suggesting that a company of Germans in Mexico were preparing to seize Honduras [hopefully, he meant British Honduras – today's Belize] and asking for aid in the plan."[487]

Count Bernstorff's response, if he ever gave one, is not documented. Horn then came to Mexico City and reported to the German embassy there. The German authorities in Mexico sent him to New York via New Orleans at the end of December, where he arrived on December 26th 1914.[488] A tall, slender, good looking thirty-seven year-old with blue eyes, from the city of Stettin on the Polish border, Horn made a good first impression on people. He reported to the German consulate in New York, which in turn, put him in contact with the military attaché. Despite being a first lieutenant of the reserve in the German army, he did not receive a false passport, most likely because the fraudulent passport office had just been unveiled in the press. Rather than sending the reservist to Germany, von Papen decided to keep him around for clandestine missions.[489]

Amazingly, von Papen's saboteur, Wachendorf, and Horn had quite a few things in common. Wachendorf certainly exhibited delusions of grandeur in his descriptions of being a spy under direct orders from Kaiser Wilhelm II, and by adopting the identity of Field Marshal von der Goltz's offspring. To this author, Wachendorf was a pathological liar with a healthy dose of narcissism, but seemed otherwise competent. While no mental evaluation of Wachendorf has ever surfaced, U.S. authorities performed a psychological evaluation of Werner Horn while imprisoned. The results painted the picture of a disturbed personality. Horn aroused his American captors' interest in 1918 when he suddenly claimed to be the illegitimate son of German royalty (probably the Kaiser himself), and that he stood to inherit millions from his *real* family.

Werner Horn became more delusional by the day. An army doctor conducted a medical evaluation and found that while he was not dangerous, he suffered from metal afflictions. Prison guards and doctors in the Fulton County Jail where Horn served an eighteen-month sentence after his discovery thought that Horn faked mental illness in order to be released rather than being extradited to Canada where a new trial awaited him. However, the mental evaluation clearly identified that Horn's problems were rooted in the advanced symptoms of syphilis, a sexually transmitted disease he had contracted eighteen years earlier. "He talks sensible when being interviewed, but he has hallucinations. At one time he wanted to change his name to that of Prince [von der Goltz only adopted that of a famous general]. Another time he was inheriting ten million dollars and was going to divide it up among the internees[...]"[490]

Von Papen did not realize his charge's problems. After the military attaché received the order dated January 4th 1915 from the War Department to blow up railroad bridges in Canada, he remembered, of all people, the hallucinating reservist, who was likely living on the attaché's dime in a hotel on Staten Island, New York.

History: Infected with syphilis eighteen years
ago. Later took active anti-syphilitic treatment.
Thorough Wasserman examination this date negative.
About nine months ago developed gradually the delusion that he was an adopted son of his presumed
parents, really being the illegitimate offspring of
royalty. This delusion was later coupled with the
belief that he was possessed of practically unlimited
wealth. Aside from this there is nothing of importance in his history.
Examination: Physically normal in all respects
except slight Rhomberg reaction and slight exagger-
ation of knee jerks, nervous system. Delusion in
regard to parentage.
Conclusions: Patient is apparently in the early
stages of paresis, but there is not enough data
available to warrant confinement to an institution
for the insane. His ideas of responsibility are
normal and his being at large presents no menace to
the public on the basis of insanity."
          (Signed) "Theodore B. Appel, Lt. Col. Surgeon."

Werner Horn diagnosis by an Army Doctor in 1919[491]

Horn packed a suitcase on January 30th 1915, filled with sixty vials of nitroglycerin, maps and railroad schedules, as well as two armbands with the imperial German flag. He took trains from New York to Boston, and from there to Vanceboro, Maine.[492] The fact that the suitcase was filled with vials of nitroglycerin was incredibly reckless because it is such a volatile explosive. It can explode without ignition, for example, if a suitcase filled with it were to fall off the luggage rack in a train compartment.[493]

The source of the nitroglycerin is unknown, but likely came from the laboratories of Walter T. Scheele through Paul Koenig. The blasting caps were made by DuPont, and looked very much like the caps Tauscher had sourced a few months earlier and given to von Papen. Although Horn never disclosed the name of his secret service contact, it was undoubtedly Paul Koenig. He supplied the materials and a check for $700 to the sabotage agent.[494] Koenig, who kept meticulous records of his endeavors, listed Horn's mission under the coded file *D-case 277*.[495] Koenig's instructions to Horn were very specific as not to cause damage in the United States but to blow up the Vanceboro Bridge over the St. Croix River on the Canadian side of the border.

Upon arrival, Horn checked into a hotel directly below the bridge connecting Vanceboro with Canada. He reconnoitered the area on the morning of February 1st and promptly attracted the attention of local Sheriff George Ross, who stopped and interviewed him. Despite the suspicious behavior of Horn, the law officer let him go. That night, around 8:30 p.m., Horn, firmly believing that he was acting as a German combatant at war with the British Empire, slipped the armbands with the imperial flag on his coat sleeves, and left the hotel, nitroglycerin and all. Aubrey Take, the owner of the Vanceboro Exchange Hotel, where Horn roomed, described what happened next:

> I saw him in the hall on the first floor [on January 30th 1915], that on the following days I saw him several times walking up and down the hall and in the dining room, but that I never saw his baggage. That on Tuesday morning Feb. 2, 1915, I was awakened by the explosion on the Vanceboro Bridge, [...] and then looked at my watch and saw that it was 1.10 A.M., [...] I then put my head out of the door of my room which is opposite the bath room and saw Werner Horn standing in the door of the bath room with his cap and overcoat on apparently out of breath and very cold, rubbing his hands. I said 'Good morning,' and he said, 'Good morning' to me [...] I then dressed hurriedly, came out of my room and saw him again in the bathroom door; he said to me in effect, 'I freeze my hands,' and I told him to put snow on them and opened the bathroom window so that the snow could be obtained [...] I noticed the fresh tracks of a man leading from the direction of the bridge towards the hotel [...] I went as far as the pump house and there met Fred Mills, and asked him what had happened, he said, 'I think they have blown up the bridge.' [...] I found no damage

> to the bridge until I saw a part that is almost on the
> Canadian shore, in fact, the end post resting on the
> Canadian shore buttress was the one which was
> damaged. I noticed that some of the ties were splin-
> tered and that a number of them were gone entirely
> up to the rail [...] On showing him [Horn] his room, I
> noticed the flag on his arm and told him that he had
> better take it off; he grinned and put it in his pocket
> [...][496]

The weather did not support Horn's mission. "The wind was blowing an eighty-mile gale and the thermometer registered thirty degrees below zero."[497] Thus, the desperate attempts to thaw his hands in the hotel's bathroom. Instead of fleeing the site of the crime, Horn had become "physically incapacitated to some extent."[498] He resolved to stay for another, unscheduled night. Horn was arrested within hours. The Sheriff charged him with breaking several windows in Vanceboro but could not charge him with blowing up the bridge since the damage was on Canadian soil. Canadian authorities immediately tried to bribe the American lawman with one hundred dollars to take the prisoner to the other side of the border. Luckily for Horn, the officer refused. The attempt to bribe the American law enforcement became one of the main reasons why A. Bruce Bielaski protected the German agent later in the war and tried, albeit unsuccessfully, to block his extradition to Canada.[499]

The same severe winter weather that hampered and, ultimately, caused Horn's mission to falter also prevented first lieutenant Hans Boehm from succeeding. According to a report von Papen sent to the War Department, "a second mission that was started from Maine under the leadership of First Lieutenant of the Reserve Boehm collapsed as a result of severe frost."[500] Von Papen did not mention a very important detail: Naval Attaché paid Boehm $50,000 ($1 Million in today's value) for "special purposes" on January 7th 1915.[501] This fact proves beyond doubt that Karl Boy-Ed was very much involved in the planning, financing, and execution of sabotage missions. Boy-Ed recorded on March 26th the reimbursement of the entire amount from Boehm, who went on to Germany to take on his new assignment of supporting an Irish revolution.[502]

The General Staff tasked him to guide Sir Roger Casement's mission to land in Ireland in April 1916, which ended in disaster. British authorities arrested Casement immediately after a German submarine set him on land, and executed him a few months later. Boehm returned to the United States in October of 1915 on secret service missions involving sabotage until June 1916 when he returned to Europe. He remained elusive until the spring of 1917 when British agents managed to identify him on ship at Falmouth.[503] He spent the rest of the war in an internment camp. While Horn disappeared under the dusty bins of history, Boehm received a promotion to captain and an Iron Cross for his services.[504]

The Vanceboro Bridge (left) and Werner Horn next to Sheriff George Ross when he was arrested on February 2nd 1915.[505]

German attacks on Canada did not cease with the arrest of Werner Horn. Albert Kaltschmidt, a wealthy German-American business owner in Detroit, Michigan received $1,000 from von Papen on March 27th 1915, to destroy Canadian munitions factories and railroad bridges in Ontario.[506] The German consul in Detroit, Kurt von Reiswitz, had submitted Kaltschmidt's name to the military attaché. Kaltschmidt owned a machine shop in which bombs could be manufactured. He also had well-established connections within the German-American community, as well as the munitions manufacturers of the area on both sides of the border. It took until June and another payment of $24,500 ($515,000 in today's value) from von Papen to move on the sabotage operation.[507]

Sabotage agent and Kaltschmidt recruit, Karl Respa, along with a small group of conspirators, entered Canada in June, and dynamited a uniform manufacturing plant, the Peabody Overall Company, in Walkerville, Ontario. They also placed a bomb in the armory of Windsor, which turned out to be a dud. Respa and several co-conspirators were eventually arrested and tried. As was the case with von der Goltz and other sabotage agents, Respa begrudged being the fall guy for the whole operation, and switched sides to become the star witness against Kaltschmidt one year later. A jury convicted Kaltschmidt in 1917 for this and several other bombings in the Detroit area. Historian Grant Grams transcribed the trial of Karl Respa:

> During the trial Respa tried to demonstrate that he had been under Kaltschmidt's influence, 'that Kaltschmidt had scared him into being an obedient tool was the gist of much of Charles Respa's testimony. He said he placed the bomb at the Windsor armouries, but set it so it would not explode. When [...] asked why he left the bomb at all, he replied that Kaltschmidt would have been very angry. He wanted to avert Kaltschmidt['s] suspicion that he was to blame for the failure of the plot'. Due to the niggardly compensation paid by Kaltschmidt to those who actually carried out the espionage activities, many turned against him in court. Kaltschmidt was seen to be the mastermind of the plotters and was convicted guilty of three crimes. These were 1. organizing the bombing of the Peabody Overall plant in Walkerville, the attempt to blow up the Windsor armoury and a plot to destroy a Canadian

Pacific bridge in Nipigon, Ontario, 2. Conspiracy to bomb the Detroit Screw works and munitions plant, 3. conspiracy to damage the Saint Clair river tunnel, between Port Huron and Sarnia. Kaltschmidt was sentenced to four years in Levensworth [sic] and fined $20,000. Canadian authorities considered American justice light. Sherwood noted 'if the government should decide to bring this man [Kaltschmidt] back to Canada and try him for the indictment now pending against him, there is no doubt whatever if he were brought before the proper Judge (Sir Glenholme Falconbridge) he would receive a life sentence. This he is properly entitled to. [...] arrangements can be made to have Sir Glenholme on that circuit. I am satisfied nothing would give him more pleasure that pronouncing sentence on this scoundrel.'[508]

A third area, besides the east coast and the midwest, where von Papen wanted to attack the Canadian Pacific Railway was the Pacific Northwest. Papen's assistant, Wolf von Igel, sent $1,300 to the German consul in Seattle, marked "Angelegenheit" (German for "certain matter") on the day Werner Horn was arrested in Vanceboro.[509] The third set of German agents that infiltrated Canada a few months later once more did not blow up the intended targets.[510] The sabotage order against U.S. instead of Canadian installations had taken precedence by then. Paul Koenig himself attempted to destroy the Welland Canal in 1916, and failed again.

CHAPTER 9:
FREDERICO STALLFORTH — THE MONEYMAN

NOT IMPLICATED IN THE SCHEMES to destroy Canadian installation, but for the first time appearing as a paymaster for German agents, was Frederico Stallforth. Born in Mexico of German parents, Stallforth and his two brothers had lost most of their possessions as a result of the Mexican Revolution. Felix Sommerfeld introduced Stallforth first to the German naval intelligence in Mexico. After the overthrow of President Madero in 1913, Sommerfeld moved Stallforth to New York to help with the sourcing of arms and munitions for the Mexican opposition to the usurper presidency of Victoriano Huerta. When the war started, Sommerfeld himself transferred to New York and introduced Stallforth to Karl Boy-Ed and Heinrich Albert.

Within months Stallforth became an important asset for the Secret War Council because of his connection to both Wall Street and Mexican revolutionaries. As one of Albert's key financial promoters, Stallforth sold German war bonds very successfully (as compared to Dernburg) and raised money for the fledgling New York organization. Daring, slightly reckless, and with a charming naïveté, Stallforth took over more and more responsibility for organizing and paying German sabotage agents in the United States, especially after Albert's role became public with the briefcase affair. He played a key role in the financing of the explosion of Black Tom Island in 1916.

Stallforth testified in an interview with Counselor Frank L. Polk of the State Department in March of 1916, "[...] this Taylor [alias Horst von der Goltz alias Franz Wachendorf] was [...] introduced to me by my brother, who knew him in Mexico [...] My brother [German consular officer in Parral] advanced him [...] some money [...] when he came to New York he looked us [Frederico and Alberto Stallforth] up to have a check cashed for him. This was the check from von Papen [...] I therefore cashed the check and deducted the amount which Taylor owed to my brother."[511] Von der Goltz essentially confirmed the story to the British authorities on February 5th 1916; however, without mentioning a $35 deduction for old debts.[512] Stallforth also mentioned in his interview with Polk that he personally talked about the validity of the check to von Papen. "I went down to Mr. von Papen's office [...] I met von Papen and asked him about it and he said the check was all right [...]"[513]

Frederico Stallforth, unknown date. Photo courtesy of the Prevo Collection.

Frederico Stallforth (sitting) in his office in New York 1915.
Photo courtesy of the Prevo Collection.

Stallforth's statement contains several curious facts. The security around the office at 60 Wall Street was such that even the reservist and German agent Horst von der Goltz armed with letters of recommendation could not breach. Stallforth's office was not on Wall Street, but close by, which could explain the term "going down." The German agent and banker occupied an office with Andrew Meloy at 55 Liberty Street, ostensibly handling arms procurement for Pancho Villa. Clearly, unless he worked with or for von Papen, there is no reason, why von der Goltz needed Stallforth to cash the check, especially knowing that he owed money to the banker. Stallforth's recollections allow for the conclusion that he was working with von Papen on financial matters within four weeks of the beginning of the World War.

He had direct access to the military attaché. This also explains why he could cash a check for Franz Wachendorf, alias Horst von der Goltz. Von Papen stated to the lawyers of the Mixed Claims Commission in 1932, "[...] I sent to him [von der Goltz] [several remittances] through the medium of a New York banking house [...]"[514]

No. of Cheque.	Date.	Payee (and Object).	Sum.	Endorsements and Notes.
*22	1914. Sept. 1..	Mr. Bridgeman Taylor	..	Dollars. 200·00	G. W. Taylor; Bridgeman Taylor; F. Stallforth; German - American Bank; Second National Bank.

Stub from von Papen's checkbook, captured by Great Britain in 1916.[515]

The *banking house* as documented on the stub was Frederico Stallforth, who acted as a correspondence bank to the Deutsche Bank. It is quite likely that Stallforth acted as the paymaster for some of von Papen and Boy-Ed's agents. Stallforth admitted in his statement to the American authorities in 1917, that he met Karl Boy-Ed around the beginning of the war in the German Club.[516] A year later, Stallforth referred to Boy-Ed as his "superior officer."[517] He also claimed that he met Heinrich Albert "[…] at a meeting of the German University League, where he delivered a lecture upon the conditions in Germany […]"[518]

Albert gave the lecture about Belgian neutrality to the German University League on September 2nd or 3rd 1914, not in December of 1914, as Stallforth wanted American investigators to believe.[519] Stallforth had a vested interest in convincing the American authorities that he was not connected to the German sabotage ventures in the beginning of the war. However, all evidence available today points to the fact that by the time Stallforth cashed the check for Franz Wachendorf, he was firmly in the employ of the German government.

There are few financial records to substantiate the theory. However, von Papen, Boy-Ed, and Albert all cashed checks for significant amounts every week without stubbing the purpose, certainly allowing for the possibility that Stallforth received payments from them either for himself, or for those he was directed to pay. Finally, there is a curious entry in Stallforth's company financial records in 1921. One of the members of the sabotage team, Alfred Fritzen, owed Stallforth a whopping $5,150 [$108,000 in today's value].[520] When he borrowed the money is unclear; however, he was arrested in March 1917, and spent the rest of the war in a penitentiary.[521] This sum, rather than the few hundred dollars documented in von

Papen's checkbook may have been the real cost of the Canadian sabotage mission. This evidence clearly documents, at the very least, that Frederico Stallforth was intimately connected with von Papen's financial activities early in the war.

German efforts to hinder the movement of troops from Canada to Europe, and to affect in the slightest bit the national security of Canada failed completely, in the final analysis. Franz von Papen and Karl Boy-Ed neither had the experience nor the resources for organizing and commanding complicated plots, such as the twin attacks of the Welland Canal and the St. Lawrence River. The sheer size of the Canadian war effort, the British and Canadian preemptive moves to protect the troops and material ready to ship to Europe proved too much to combat for a handful of sabotage agents. The German military also failed to target the Canadian expeditionary forces from the sea with submarines. Just as many historians had, the German war planners underestimated the size and the impact of this formidable army entering the battlefields of Europe. Subsequent attempts to destroy rail lines and bridges failed but would not have had any impact on the European war in any case.

Without any real chance for success, these quixotic missions against Canada from U.S. soil turned captured German agents into tools for the English propaganda in 1916, and supported the British efforts to drag the United States into the European war. However, American and British authorities were also lulled into a false sense of superiority over an amateurish German secret service. German clandestine activities in the United States became much more sophisticated, well-funded, and effective, to a large degree because of the lessons learned in the attempted attacks against Canada as events of 1915 and 1916 showed.

CHAPTER 10:
"BLIND, DEAF, AND DUMB" [522]

ASIDE FROM ATTEMPTS TO THWART the British war effort through military means, the Secret War Council also had to counter the opposition's success in winning American hearts and minds for their cause. Public sentiment played a huge role in the decision-making process of the Taft and Wilson administrations. The German empire, which due to its form of government worried less over public sentiment in its decision-making process, virtually ignored the importance of propaganda in the United States. Naval Attaché Karl Boy-Ed correctly blamed public support of the eventual entry of the United States in the war. This was due, in large part, to the success of the English and pro-Entente propaganda.[523]

The German propaganda effort in the United States for the first three months of the war was under-funded, understaffed, and uncoordinated. Bernhard Dernburg, originally tasked to raise a large war loan for Germany and unable to travel back to Germany on account of the British blockade, took over the German propaganda organization in September 1914. It took several weeks for Dernburg to come up with a plan to reorganize, focus, and effectively orchestrate a German response to the superior British publicity campaign. He received help from an unexpected quarter: Naval intelligence agent Felix A. Sommerfeld.

Sommerfeld observed and was highly critical of the German public relations efforts in the beginning of the war. The agent who provided intelligence to Karl Boy-Ed, and with whom he had regular meetings, either contacted, or was contacted by, Bernhard Dernburg. During the 1918 interrogation of Sommerfeld by

American Justice Department agents, he recalled meeting Dern-burg in November 1914, although the meeting in reality occurred on September 16th on the occasion of Dernburg's speech on the roof terrace garden of the Astor Hotel.[524]

> I came into the Astor one night. There was a dinner party in one of the large dining rooms. There were lots of men in there in full dress, and I was standing at the desk, and somebody said to me, 'How do you do? And I don't know who it was, — some German from Mexico [i.e. Stallforth] [...] and turned around and he was standing with a man with a black beard and said,
>
> 'Your Excellency, I want you to meet Mr. Sommerfeld.'
>
> 'I heard a good deal about you.' [Dernburg said to Sommerfeld]
>
> I said, 'I am glad you have.'
>
> He said, 'I would like to talk with you.' He said, 'I am busy, but I will telephone you.'
>
> We finally agreed on two or three days later, eleven in the morning [...][525] I went to [1123] Broadway, and he said to me the following:
>
> 'Mr. Sommerfeld, I have heard that you know better than anybody here in this country the sentiment and the feeling of the Administration in Washington and the feeling of the country, because you come in contact with lots of prominent Americans in political life.'
>
> I said, 'Yes, sir; I know it pretty well.'
>
> He said, 'Will you give me a fair statement and opinion about everything?'
>
> I said, 'Yes, sir.' I said, 'First of all, Your Excellency, you must remember from now on that the time is past when deals are made under the table. You must put your cards on the table in Washington. You must write every letter to the

Government '—I was referring to the German government—'letters and telegrams, in such a way that tomorrow morning they can be published.'

He said, 'Do you mean to tell me you are going to publish diplomatic correspondence?' I said, 'There is no such thing as secret diplomatic correspondence,' and I told him how I had dealt all those years with Washington, how I would go to see Mr. [Lindley M.] Garrison [U.S. Secretary of War] and told him simply,

'Mr. Secretary I am placing the matter on the table. I have the cards on the table. I will tell you what I can do and mean to do;' and he would believe it.

I said, 'The other night I was standing in the hotel lobby and saw a newspaper man and said, 'Who is that man?' and he said, 'He is the German publicity agent,' – a man named Klauss [Claussen]; He used to be advertisement agent for the Hamburg-American Line, and I told him,

'Your Excellency, the best way to do that was not to have any German, but to have an American newspaper man, and give him all the telegrams about the war, and let him publish them,' and I said, 'They know what to publish. Don't tell him what to do and what not to do. They have the hand on the pulse of this nation every moment, and they know what to do [...]'[526]

Sommerfeld had an impressive resume for dealing with propaganda as a result of his work for revolutionary leader and later president of Mexico, Francisco I. Madero. Sommerfeld, officially an Associated Press reporter, acted as a liaison between the revolutionaries and the American press at the outbreak of the revolution in 1910. His task entailed controlling the press image of Mexican revolutionary leaders.[527]

He became a master at this job who understood that

propaganda was a crucial ingredient in any war effort. He focused on very distinct propaganda targets: The loyal military forces, the domestic public, military units of the foe, the international audience, and international governments. Messages were carefully designed and adjusted for each of those recipient groups. It mattered, who acted as a surrogate.

Most importantly, Sommerfeld understood timing. He and Sherburne Hopkins, Francisco Madero's lobbyist in Washington, had been impeccable in managing the many crises of the Madero administration. From the unseating of the Mexican dictator Diaz, the establishment of power in Mexico City, the many uprisings and attacks from old and new enemies from within, to the attacks from conservative political and business forces in the United States and England, the two men parried the opposition's strikes.

After Madero's murder in 1913, Sommerfeld and Hopkins also dealt with countless attacks on the Constitutionalist opposition they now supported. They tried to handle the frequent diplomatic blunders of Villa and Carranza. Given the personalities and discipline (or lack thereof) of their charges their efforts can only arouse admiration.

The biggest issues Sommerfeld and Hopkins managed were the international recognition of the Madero administration, the cooperation between the Justice Department and Mexican authorities to curb opposition all along the common border, the U.S. support of the Constitutionalist case against President Huerta, Huerta's ouster, and the legitimization of Pancho Villa.

Sommerfeld in particular succeeded in manipulating German foreign policy. His reports to Ambassador von Hintze had a decisive effect. Germany accepted and supported the Madero administration despite the conservatism of the German foreign office. Germany also broke with Huerta long before he was militarily defeated. Finally, Sommerfeld created a favorable impression of someone who at face value could not be further from the German idea of a statesman: Pancho Villa. With great skill, Sommerfeld and Hopkins influenced public opinion in the U.S. They managed press access and provided the *facts* for seemingly unbiased but in fact slanted reports furthering their cause. Only one devastating blunder discolored the otherwise clean record: The break-in at Sherburne Hopkins' office and the publication of embarrassing papers in the *New York World* and national dailies in June of 1914.[528]

Sommerfeld's success in handling international scandal, partisan attacks, political and diplomatic blunders by his own superiors followed a few, important principles:[529]

Rule number one: Limit access to information and control the message for each targeted channel. Sommerfeld practiced this meticulously much to the chagrin of journalists who sought access to Madero or Villa.

Rule number two: Preempt an attack, line up the important players beforehand and win the argument. This is the essence of his message to General Scott on January 6th. There are numerous examples in Sommerfeld's communications with Hopkins, Secretaries Bryan and Garrison, all preempting an attack from the opposing side.

Rule number three: Mold the message in such a way that the target audience understands it. Especially in the case of Pancho Villa this required a complete revamping of the personality for public consumption.

Rule number four: Control the message with surrogates who are beyond reproach. Sommerfeld used Army Chief of Staff Hugh Lenox Scott, Secretaries William J. Bryan and Lindley M. Garrison, special envoy William Bayard Hale, Minister Paul von Hintze, and dozens of carefully selected reporters and correspondents to articulate his message. Sommerfeld appeared in the forefront only in order to underline what had already been said.

From the onset of the Great War, the British and French governments succeeded in limiting the flow of information and managed each targeted channel in perfect execution of rule number one. English propaganda experts worked efficiently to turn the American public and the government against the German case. This was by no means a foregone conclusion. Thus, it is not surprising that Sommerfeld took more than a casual interest in the fledgling and amateurish attempts of German officials to countermand the highly successful British propaganda in the U.S. in 1914.

The important topics treated in the respective propaganda efforts at the onset of the war were relatively straightforward. A majority of the American public believed that the German Emperor had started the war. Demonstrations of hundreds of thousands of people on Times Square enthusiastically greeted the British decla-ration of war against Germany on August 4th.[530] The major dailies in New York made the sharp delineations of American public opinion on the day after the British declaration.

The *New York World*, owned by German-American Joseph Pulitzer, sharply criticized Germany's role in the war.[531] The *New York Tribune* voiced hope that England joining the war would keep international commerce afloat.[532] The *New York Evening Mail* adopted a wait-and-see attitude.[533] Hermann Ridder's *New Yorker Staats-Zeitung*, a German-American publication in German language, argued that England created the mess with all her bi-lateral treaties.[534] These manifestations of opinion occurred before the Central Powers and the Entente had cranked up their propaganda efforts. There were mass demonstrations for the British entry into the war. A lack of enthusiasm for the German cause extended to most editorial boards, even those controlled by German-Americans. The public reaction in the United States confirmed a general sense that Germany would fight an uphill battle in its propaganda efforts.

England successfully cut the German Atlantic cables at the Azores Islands on August 5th 1914. It was a brilliant move. Ambassador Count Bernstorff, still on vacation in Europe, left a gaping void in the leadership of the embassy. Not only was the German embassy cut off from instructions, but the sabotage also insured that virtually all information from Europe had to be routed via London.[535] British censors made sure to filter the facts when German armies violated Belgian neutrality in the beginning of August. Reports of unspeakable atrocities graced the headlines of American dailies. The extent of the German army's destruction of Belgium entered the news around August 16th. The invasion presented a clear breach of international law. Largely as the result of her actions, but also of British news manipulation, Germany appeared to the American public as a despotic bully pouncing on a weak neighbor. The largely pro-British editorial boards of American newspapers sided with the underdog and cheered the resistance of Belgian forces against the overwhelming German armies. The battle of Liège, a Belgian town near the German-Dutch border, became the symbol for the courage and desperate strength of Belgian defenders.[536]

English propaganda took advantage of the general impression that Germany was the European bully. British-controlled news reports from the front very successfully documented war crimes, crimes against the civilian populations, and the destruction of cities including religious and cultural monuments. The German side countered with *official* declarations that proved to be false and untruthful within weeks.

Instead of defending the indefensible atrocities in Belgium and the obvious trampling on international law, German propagandists could have exploited the whole issue surrounding the naval blockade and economic war against the Central Powers. The British stranglehold on international trade and finance captivated the American public. The sea blockade violated international law and, in particular, the right of American traders to roam the seven seas. The U.S. economy reeled from a financial panic and interruptions in trade, especially in the first months of the war. American editorials in the Midwest and South voiced their disgust at the British-caused troubles. The cotton market had virtually collapsed. The American textile industry came to a halt for lack of German dyestuffs. Product shortages affected average Americans. Apart from clothing, citizens could not even buy new glasses, binoculars, scopes, and cameras because virtually all lenses came from the fatherland. Prices rose to inflationary levels, while unemployment, especially in the south, the mid-Atlantic, and the midwest, further affected the American standard of life.

In fact, German officials violated all four rules in dealing with the effects of the British economic war. Rather than preempt waves of reports in American papers that detailed the Belgian atrocities, half-hearted denials issued by the German embassy in Washington did little to diffuse the reports emanating from or being censured in London. Worse, self-styled German-American leaders, mainly intellectuals and scholars working with or for American universities, took matters in their own hands, unable to look on as the German propaganda stumbled along.

German and pro-German scholars such as Germanist Kuno Francke, historian Edmund von Mach, psychologist Hugo Münsterberg, and political scientist John W. Burgess gave speeches, wrote articles and books with the purpose of *teaching* the American public about the superiority of German *Kultur*. Their message hardly reached an American public that was not interested in scholarly treatises on the thousand-year history that led to the war. Rather, these books produced a backlash from moderate and anglophile intellectuals, and fanned a public debate on the pages of American newspapers, which the German scholars lost miserably.

Cultural arrogance, combined with radical pan-German argumentation, turned off a public used to a political democracy and free market economy. Pan-Germanism lost even the few American newspaper editors that, in the beginning of the war, tried to see both sides. The same occurred with respect to editorials in German-American papers all across the country. Articles, some by the aforementioned scholars, attempted to justify German atrocities. While the target audience of these papers was the German-American community, papers such as the *New York Times* regularly quoted editorials from the *New Yorker Staats-Zeitung*. This occurred across the country.

While meaning well, these voices of the German-American community ignored the rules of choosing independent surrogates and adapting the message to the receiver. German-American scholars and intellectuals touted an image of arrogant cultural superiority. The German word for civilization, *Kultur*, evidenced in German music, literature, and science in a militaristic, Prussian interpretation of the state also meant "organized, scientific, efficient force – without the restraint of morals."[537] This principle of casting morality aside for the survival of a nation, although practiced by all warring factions, was indefensible for the American psyche. German-American scholars alienated scores of their own community and of the American public at large by touting autocratic rather than democratic leanings, and militarism. The German officials, so caught up in their intellectual exercises, ignored the practical topics that affected average Americans, such as food prices, employment, exports, and shipping.

The question of the so-called German-American, *hyphen-ated*, disloyalty had never before been an issue for a minority that was well integrated, productive, and respected. Now fears of the *other* imprinted themselves on the American public's mind. The question of whether German-Americans were German or American aroused the most primal of emotions. Within a few years, they manifested themselves in ways that would devastate the age-old and strong German-American culture in the United States. Historian Frederick C. Luebke defined German-American as all-American citizens of German extraction, most pronounced in the first, second, and third generations. He pointed out that, unlike its spokesmen, the majority of this large and diverse community indeed was American first and German second.[538] The sheer size of the German-American minority in the U.S. conjured up a sense of dread among Americans who doubted this minority's loyalties.

German-Americans constituted the largest minority in the United States, although this group was not at all as cohesive as English propaganda made it out to be. German communities included those united the Lutheran church, the German-American Roman Catholic community, the Amish and the Mennonites, both of whom had anti-war leanings. Poor laborers, farmers, and craftsmen had to worry more about their daily bread than joining a confrontation with the pro-British American movement. Many immigrants from the lower classes in Germany had changed their names and integrated fully into their communities as Americans. German merchants and traders, especially in the west and southwest, often were integrated in a way that there was no palpable difference from the rest of society.

These groups could not take sides for fear of losing their customer base. Thus, the raw numbers of Americans who identified their background as German, paint a superficial and wholly inaccurate picture. The 1910 census reflects that 8.2 million persons named Germany as their land of origin, of whom 2.5 million had been born in Germany.[539] In addition to the German communities, other minorities courted by German propaganda also had the potential of being perceived as disloyal to the United States: The Jewish community, in general, wanted Germany to win against Russia since

Jewish citizens there had few rights and were persecuted. The Irish and Indian communities sought independence from England and, as a result, were generally supportive of Germany.

The British propaganda effectively stoked the fears that these huge minorities would rise against their country of residence. The German mishandling of its own message greatly aided this effort. The American public swayed into doubting German-American loyalty over the course of the first year of the war. The German government understood clearly that the reality was different, but failed to assert the facts. Even before the war started, Ambassador Bernstorff had "[...]informed the Wilhelmstrasse that the majority of German-Americans were lost for the German cause as far as direct engagement was concerned."[540]

Consequently, German propaganda efforts not only targeted the American public in general but, in a huge and expensive effort, tried to secure at least ideological support among German-Americans. This effort confused the German message to the public at large and created a fertile ground for the other side to stoke the fires of chauvinism. Historians have difficulties to this day clearly delineating the super-patriotic, chauvinistic, even fanatical message meant for German-Americans from the moderate message. The moderate message that demanded *fair play*, portrayed the German empire as a pro-trade, peaceful, and largely democratic state, drowned in the sea of radical, pro-German pronouncements.

The German Chancellor Theobald von Bethmann-Hollweg gave a widely reported speech in the German parliament on August 4th, in which he blamed the war on Russia. This would be the last important news emanating from Germany for weeks to come. After the British navy cut the transatlantic cables on the next day, not only information from war correspondents was censored, but German officials in the United States, as well, were cut off. Lacking instructions or guidance from the Foreign Office, and, most importantly, intelligence support, which would have focused Germany's propaganda strategy in the U.S., the German embassy staff led by Charge D'Affairs Edgar Haniel von Haimhausen blundered the opportunity of shaping a convincing message. Though Haniel was a seasoned diplomat, he neither had the finesse, the experience, nor the immense respect that the German ambassador enjoyed in the United States.

Haniel gave one major interview in the first week of the war after Secretary of State Bryan had invited him for a consultation. During this interview, he floated for the first time Germany's assertion that French forces had moved into Belgium before Germany violated its neutrality.[541] Haniel gave short and evasive answers over the following days in brief press interviews, in which he appeared insecure, and did not at all make the impression of representing a major world power that "acted in self-defense."[542]

The confusion of the message had already started with the personnel choice of the German embassy in the first days of the war. Haniel von Haimhausen organized a small press office in New York under the direction of Heinrich Charles, Secretary of the German-American Chamber of Commerce. This Chamber of Commerce was a sham. The membership list consisted of four people, the most prominent of whom was Hugo Reisinger, a German-American art collector and philanthropist.[543] Reisinger likely only lent his name and had no influence on the propaganda efforts of the Chamber. He was traveling in Germany where he unexpectedly died in September when the war broke out.[544] Highly respected in the United States, Reisinger certainly could have added a moderate and perhaps effective voice to the German message targeting the American public. Instead, the German embassy allowed the first secretary of the Chamber to mold the message.

Charles had a long history as a provocative journalist desperate for attention. He publicly demanded to be deported back to Germany in 1910 since he felt persecuted – a plot to gain notoriety. Charles claimed that the German poet, Matthias Ringmann, not Vespucci, named America in 1507, per research seconded by historian Albert Bushnell Hart of Harvard University.[545] Despite his publicity stunts, he received only meager attention for his theory. Charles published the "Electro-Individualistic Manifesto," in 1913, a confusing pamphlet refuting Marx and Engels and claiming that the advent of electricity with all its applications would solve the social problems of mankind.[546]

The German embassy put Charles in charge of propaganda

efforts on August 5th. Predictably, the pronouncements of the provocative writer had a negative effect. His provocation of 1910, when he declared that he was "sick and tired of living in a barbarian land," earned him a sharp rebuke. It did not help, either, that Charles, who had lived in America for twenty years, never became a citizen.[547]

Charles claimed to speak for German-Americans, while in reality he was a mouthpiece of the German embassy. He filed a barrage of protests with the American government and copied the large New York dailies within the first two weeks of the war. He protested the cutting of the transatlantic cable. He made the case that the United States discriminated against Germany in the conflict when the United States decided to censor Germany's wireless stations at Sayville, Long Island and on Hickory Island near Tuckerton, New Jersey. The point was well taken since the Entente powers retained their transatlantic cables and had no need for wireless communication. However, the message fell on deaf ears. A respected, neutral surrogate would have saved the day. The German government disseminated a message from Chancellor von Bethmann-Hollweg to the American people on August 16th, vying for sympathy for a war brought upon Germany. However, the message got buried under the overwhelming pro-British reports in America's dailies.

Reiterating the point, Charles trotted out "Major Ulrich von Ritter of the General Staff of the German Army" to make "impartial presentations of German operations and military tactics."[548] The forty-three year-old Ritter (the nobility title had been accorded to him by the German-American Chamber of Commerce) had arrived on the 4th of August on the American liner SS *George Washington*, ostensibly to assist in the propaganda effort. Charles had explained to the New York press that the officer had arrived in the beginning of July to study rail systems in the U.S.[549]

The army major decried the British and French propaganda and explained the invasion of Belgium as a purely military necessity.[550] Charles published a pamphlet on August 21st, on the "Inside Story of Belgian Neutrality," authored by a "German military expert."[551] The efforts of the Chamber reeked of false propaganda. The variations of the message, from "Belgium, a military inconvenience," to "The

French invaded Belgium first," to "The British landed troops in Antwerp before Germany's invasion," all missed the point of what the American audience was interested in: What would German armies do in Belgium? How long would they stay? Would the civilian population be protected? Would indemnity be paid? None of regular Americans' concerns were touched upon. Instead, Charles and his embassy supporters underscored the image of Prussian militarism trampling on the rights of a free people.

Haniel supported a second, militantly German propaganda outlet: The weekly magazine, *The Fatherland.* Founded by German-American George Sylvester Viereck in the first days of the war, the embassy took over the financing of the fledgling weekly in the middle of September.[552] The headquarters of the three-man editorial staff were at 715 Broadway. Viereck, born in Munich, Germany on December 31st 1884, had made a name for himself in the United States as a poet, author, and playwright.[553] The important themes in his writings before the war outlined a devoted reverence to the German, Old World culture, and the need to instill German *Kultur* to America's civilization.

Viereck's father was the illegitimate child of a Prussian prince related to the Kaiser, a fact that the poet readily promoted.[554] He immersed himself in the study of Germanism in the 1910s and briefly taught poetry in Berlin. He used his various connections to further German-American cultural exchange. Also in 1910, Viereck published the journal, *Rundschau zweier Welten* (*Observations in Two Worlds*), with the former U.S. president, Theodore Roosevelt. Viereck raised the money to start the weekly magazine, *The Fatherland,* when the war started. Thirty years old, well-mannered, of small physical frame, the bespectacled German-American writer looked like a boy, his youthful and innocent appearance betraying none of his radical devotion to the German cause.

The first issue of the *Fatherland* appeared on newsstands on August 10th for five cents with a circulation of 25,000. Published in English, the magazine targeted the greater American public. The cover page announced the mission of the publication: "Fair Play for Germany and Austria-Hungary." The first page featured a poem from Viereck,

Wilhelm II., Prince of Peace
By George Sylvester Viereck

O Prince of Peace, O Lord of War
Unsheathe thy blade without a stain,
Thy holy wrath shall scatter far
The bloodhounds from thy country's fane!

Into thy hand the sword is forced,
By traitor friend and traitor foe,
On foot, on sea, and winged and horsed,
The Prince of Darkness strikes his blow.

Crush through the Cossack arms that reach
To plunge the world into the night!
Save Goethe's vision, Luther's speech,
Thou art the Keeper of the Light!

When darkness was on all the lands,
Who kept God's faith with courage grim?
Shall He uphold that country's hands,
Or tear its members, limb from limb?

God called the Teuton to be free,
Free from Great Britain's golden thrall,
From guillotine and anarchy,
From pogroms red whips that fall,

May the victorious armies rout
The savage tribes against thee hurled,
The Czar whose scepter is the knout,
And France, the harlot of the world!

But thy great task will not be done
Until thou vanquish utterly,
The Norman brother of the Hun,
England, the Serpent of the Sea.

The flame of war her tradesmen fanned
Shall yet consume her, fleet and field;
The star of Frederick guide thy hand,
The God of Bismarck be thy shield!

Against the fell Barbarian horde
Thy people stand, a living wall;
Now fight for God's peace with thy sword,
For it thou fail, a world shall fall![555]

This poem set the tone for German propaganda in the United States. Devoid of the sensibilities of the American people, fanatic in its prose, Viereck declared the German Empire the defender of western civilization, and touted a fight to the bitter end. The poem played on Kaiser Wilhelm II's declaration of August 7th: "We shall resist to the last breath of man and horse, and we shall fight out the struggle, even against a world of enemies."[556]

Articles on the next pages of the *Fatherland* followed the line of somehow proving a cultural superiority to the (by definition) uneducated and uncivilized American public. Professor of American History Hermann Schoenfeld argued that *Pan Slavism* caused the war. Editor Frederick Schrader argued in the article that followed that the "American people are [...] systematically drugged with the virus of Germanophobia, and taught to forget the traditional friendship of Germany, in the interest of Slavic supremacy [...]"[557] Harvard Professor and Heinrich Albert's uncle, Kuno Francke, had his article "Germany's Defensive Aggression" reprinted in the *Fatherland*. It had been published in *The New York Times* as a letter to the editor on August 6th 1914.[558] Professor Hugo Muensterberg, a key member of the German University League, contributed an essay asking the American press for "Fair Play."[559]

The message of the *Fatherland* echoed in letters-to-the-editor in all major New York publications. Professor Kuno Francke's letter from the 6th has already been mentioned. Professor Moritz J. Bonn of the University of Munich floated the *Russia is to blame for the war* theory in *The New York Times* on August 8th. Perhaps it is a curious coincidence that the political economist from Munich arrived on August 4th, on the same ship as Ulrich von Ritter.[560] Clearly, the German intelligence services were sending propagandists to the United States. One month after Bonn and Ritter's arrivals, two German agents, Isaac Straus and Arthur Meyerowitz, tasked to agitate the Jewish-American community in Germany's favor, also arrived in New York.[561] Heinrich Albert financially supported their endeavors.[562]

The second edition of the *Fatherland* appeared on August 17th, during a week busy with a flood of letters-to-the-editor to perceived pro-British papers, numerous editorials, articles, and commentaries. The *Fatherland* featured a follow-up article by Professor Muensterberg, in which he called upon the "silent majority" in America to support the German "underdog."[563] If Muensterberg actually believed what he wrote, he proved how hopelessly out of touch with the American public the German-American scholars were. *Fatherland* editor and drama critic Frederick Schrader argued in a commentary in the same issue that German-Americans, the largest minority group in the United States, overwhelmingly served in the U.S. armed forces. The article contained an implied threat against the American government not to dare to engage military forces against Germany.

The New York Times published the German "White Paper" on August 24th 1914.[564] The publication followed a day after the English "White Paper" appeared on the front page of the New York daily.[565] Professor Kuno Francke countered the British "White Paper" in the same issue of August 23rd with a full-page editorial: "Justice on German Side, Says Prof. Kuno Francke."[566] A *Times* editorial accompanied the publication of the German "White Paper," asserting its *lawyer-like* argumentation.[567] Charge D'Affairs Haniel von Haimhausen wrote the lead article in the August 17 issue of the *Fatherland*. Rather than point to the questionable legal issues of the British sea blockade or defend Germany's role in the outbreak of the war, or clarify the escalating battles in Belgium, the German diplomat cried foul over the British cutting of the transatlantic cable.

It may have seemed unnecessary to the reader that Haniel complained not to have received any instructions from Germany.

The badly conceived article made that clear. Haniel reinforced his ill-conceived message and forwarded a message from German chancellor von Bethmann-Hollweg to the *Associated Press*: "Germany is completely shut off from the rest of the world, and can neither send out news nor receive it. The Empire is therefore unable to defend itself against the falsehoods propagated by the press of the hostile countries. It can only defend itself by its deeds. The German people will be profoundly grateful for every effort to disseminate the real truth. (Signed) VON BETHMANN-HOLLWEG, Imperial German Chancellor."[568]

Of course, the deeds that followed were widely publicized and horrified the American public. Papers reported a massacre in the village of Dinant close to Liège where over six hundred civilians were slaughtered on the orders of the German commander, the same day of von Bethmann's boast that deeds would be Germany's defense. The German 1st army retreated two days later, on August 26th, after the Belgian army attacked from the rear. The retreating German forces under Major von Manteufel regrouped in the medieval town of Leuve (Louvain). The German forces razed the city, deliberately burning the library of Belgium's oldest university founded in 1425, and destroying 300,000 medieval books with an untold number of manuscripts. Additionally, several hundred civilians perished in the rampage. The rest of the population fled. Richard Harding Davis, an American reporter for the *New York Tribune* arrived in Louvain while the fires were still raging.[569] There was not much left to spin for the German sympathizers in the U.S.

An article in the August 31 edition of the *Fatherland* by Alexander Harvey accused the U.S. president of being an anglophile since his grandparents came from Britain, and that the true capital of the United States indeed was London.[570] These disparaging messages did nothing to convince Americans to sympathize with Germany. The opposite was the case: the embassy's public support of the *Fatherland* alienated the moderate and *fair-minded* Americans, as well as the U.S. government.

The core leaders of the Secret War Council, Albert, Dernburg, and Count Bernstorff, arrived in New York on August 24th and 26th. The day after his arrival, Heinrich Albert jotted down his first impression of the American press: "Achievement of Modern Civilization: Press! Make here a business act of news; the English language sheets [papers] out of bad, the German out of good; simply fabricated in order to make money (is also on the German side, six English Dreadnoughts destroyed?)."[571]

Albert was unfamiliar with the role of the American newspaper. Though a press existed in Germany, it was not independent. News came from the government and found its way into papers at some later date. Newspapers in Germany had none of the sensationalist bluster of the American boulevard press. German Naval Attaché Karl Boy-Ed illustrated the difference in his memoirs: "When we Germans were shot at without result, we reported: 'No military damage;' if the same happened to [the] English the German mortars either 'only tore to pieces an innocent small child' or 'a cow was killed'."[572] Street vendors in America blurted out the latest news holding up the evening edition of the *Sun* or special editions of the *World*. If the next day it turned out that the previous news had been wrong, another sensation would extinguish any lingering memory without correction. This basic understanding of how Americans absorbed their news did not exist for the German officials who would now be in charge of German propaganda in the United States. If it did, as Boy-Ed claimed for himself, for example, the lack of understanding in the responsible German government circles canceled any attempt to change the dynamic.

A few days after he had jotted down his first impressions, Albert made another astute observation going to the heart of the issues of the German propaganda: "Unfriendly attitude of press in part on account of [...] disconnectedness of the news; no German cable; feeling seems to be changing around; working up by press insufficient; no one is decisive (authoritative); Dernburg must pay regard to Bernstorff, I to Dernburg and Hatzfeld, etc. Articles are snatched up and printed instead of being spread systematically."[573] He correctly ascertained the lack of intelligence the Germans had on which to base their propaganda. Boy-Ed begged his superiors in Germany to send "much more news from Germany in any possible way [...] Special impressions are made if Americans and other neutrals report on Germany, her inner works and her war effort[...]"

More details have to be provided about the war effort, the common discipline, the caring for foreigners, the own soldiers, the insured, the enemies etc. [...]"[574]

Boy-Ed spoke to the use of proper surrogates and a targeted message, two of the rules that, in observance, would have greatly improved the German efforts to gain sympathy in the U.S. The opposite took place. Various German officials, volunteers, or self-appointed German propagandists mangled the message in individual and uncoordinated publications and speeches. The invasion of Belgium posed a huge problem for the German officials in the U.S. A continuous barrage of British reports of atrocities headlined the New York dailies, while reports from Germany did not arrive or, arrived censored, by the British days and weeks after the events. Worse, much of what the British reported was true. American correspondents traveling in Europe in many cases seconded the British assertions. Albert had doubts about how to counter with a pro-German message in the face of an "[...] attack of [sic] a small country that cannot protect itself, and monstrous destruction [sic] of the land, all arguments against this (Position of Belgium before the war, Agreement with France and England, Other encouragement from the French, Geographical position etc. [,] Attitude of the Belgian population etc.) have no weight [...] Bombarding from airships? And when justified, has it had any advantage, or is the latter in proportion to the unfavorable effect on public opinion?"[575]

Albert influenced the Secret War Council to recognize the need for a unified and clear message during meetings with Bernhard Dernburg, the HAPAG executives Polis, Ecker, and German Red Cross representative Meyer-Gerhard, as well as Count Bernstorff. Despite his personal doubts in the face of the horrendous reports of German war crimes, Albert gave his speech to the German University League titled "The Breach of Belgium [sic] Neutrality." Although the text of the speech has not been preserved, Albert likely used the arguments he listed in his diary entry quoted above. His notes clearly betray his knowledge that while enthusiastically welcomed by the German-American audience of the University League, these types of speeches would have very little convincing power with the general American public. Ordered from Germany,

Count Bernstorff issued the German version of what happened at Louvain a full week after the events: "[…] priests at Louvain gave arms and ammunition to the civilians, who began, at different places, suddenly to shoot out of windows at unsuspecting German troops, of whom many were wounded."[576] The razing of ancient towns and murdering of scores of civilians while transporting countless others to concentration camps overshadowed any attempt to blame priests and resistance fighters.

The decision was made on September 16th, after negotiations with George Sylvester Viereck and Bernhard Dernburg, to organize a press bureau in New York, aptly named the German Information Service.[577] Dernburg, who in the meantime had all but given up his hope to raise a large loan in the U.S., would become its head. The *Fatherland* editors, under the leadership of Viereck, took on most of the editing functions and moved into Dernburg's large office suite at 1123 Broadway. A supervisory board consisted of the HAPAG managers, Dr. Karl Buenz, Dr. Otto Ecker, Albert Polis, Julius P. Meyer, and German Red Cross representative Anton Meyer-Gerhard. Prince Hatzfeld represented the German embassy.[578] Heinrich Albert was in charge of finances. He immediately fired Heinrich Charles as head of German propaganda.

Charles did not leave voluntarily. He stuck around and free-lanced, disseminating German propaganda in South America after Albert fired him. Albert hinted at his relationship with Charles after September 1914 in a letter to Dernburg in 1915: "This [propaganda] is done through a private agency at whose head Ch. [Charles] stands with whom you are acquainted[,] whom I do not appreciate on account of his past and an attempt to blackmail me. He is carrying on the affair at his own expense. I do not think much of it. But we will let [sic] him alone, because we are convinced that no harm can be done […]"[579] In Charles's place, the group appointed Matthew B. Claussen, an employee of HAPAG. "Claussen had been an editor for *The New York Herald*, before he went into advertising."[580]

At HAPAG Claussen had worked in marketing, initiated creative publicity campaigns for the latest generation of super-luxury liners, and issued press releases. He had connections to the American press, had employed the well-known photographer and cinematographer, Albert Dawson, and was generally experienced in how to engage the American public. Another colleague of Claussen's at HAPAG, Alfred Cronemeyer, became his assistant. Cronemeyer was the former passenger agent of HAPAG without any publicity background. However, despite the experience, maybe as a result of the Germanic attitude of his superiors, Claussen did little to improve the German message.

Dernburg immediately immersed himself into his new task. From the pulpit of a *private* citizen and backed by the entire German staff, the former German colonial secretary bombarded the American public with a heavy barrage of articles and speeches. Within weeks of his arrival, articles penned by him (or his staff) appeared in *The New York Times*, *The Saturday Evening Post*, the *North American Review*, the *Review of Reviews*, the *Los Angeles Examiner*, and *The Independent*.[581] The themes ranged from defending militarism as a need for self-defense to promoting Germany as the bulwark against lower civilizations.[582] He made the case that treaties were not binding, and that Belgium was not neutral.[583] He espoused the historical ties between Germany and the United States.[584] He equated the German political system to that of the United States.[585] He warned "British greed would drag U.S. into war."[586] Finally, he declared the British goal to starve the German population through the naval blockade would never succeed because of Germany's technical superiority.[587] Only a few editors appreciated Dernburg's attempts to present the German case. The editor of the *Review of Reviews* introduced the German propagandist as a representative of the Red Cross and man with a distinct background:

> For some weeks Mr. Dernburg has been in New York, having come over in the interest of the German Red Cross. He typifies Germany's efficient men of affairs who have built up the empire's financial and industrial strength. He is one of the foremost of Berlin's bankers, is a member of the upper house of the Prussian parliament, was for four years the Emperor's Minister of Colonies, and is a man of an extraordinary range of information, not

only regarding the political, industrial, and military affairs of Germany, but also regarding the conflicts and rivalries of the great nations for foreign trade and colonial empire.[588]

Certainly, the flurry of activity of the Press Bureau made a huge impact if compared to the early attempts at propaganda with scholars and Heinrich Charles. However, Dernburg's message could never divorce itself from the pan-Germanism of his scholarly advisors and the fanatic attitudes of the *Fatherland* staff. The major themes contained in Dernburg's articles, the peace-loving empire forced into a struggle of survival against the greedy European nations, and the portrayal of Germany as the bulwark against Pan-Slavic *Untermenschen* (German for *sub humans*) simply did not synchronize with the American psyche. Another scholar, Irish-American history professor William Milligan Sloane defended German militarism on September 20th as defensive, and urged Americans to observe strict neutrality. His *New York Times Magazine* contribution, a huge two-page spread, earned him a sharp editorial rebuke and continued the string of arrogant, misplaced, and uncoordinated German intellectual propaganda.[589]

Count Bernstorff commented on Dernburg in his memoirs: "He had a gift for explaining the causes of the war in a quiet, interesting manner, and particularly for setting out the German standpoint in a conciliatory form [...] the whole New York Press [sic] readily printed all the articles he sent in to contradict the statements of the anti-Germans."[590] Dernburg's strategy scored initial successes. German-friendly publications such as the *New York Evening Mail*, *The Washington Post*, the *San Francisco Examiner*, the *Chicago Tribune*, *The Boston Globe*, and the Irish, Yiddish, and German language press such as the *Gaelic American*, *The Day*, and the *New Yorker Staats-Zeitung* published almost daily interviews with Count Bernstorff or articles that emanated from the press bureau. Hostile to the German cause were the majority of American dailies, especially *The New York Times* (although in comparison, quite fair in its presentation of both sides), the *New York World*, the *New York Evening Telegram*, and *The Providence Journal*. Dernburg and Count Bernstorff's efforts with the press also yielded regular published interviews in these papers.[591] The Dernburg office also contacted German-American, Irish-American or Jewish-American editors whom they hoped to influence, often with under-the-table payments.

Everyone related, even peripherally, to the Press Bureau floated articles. Krupp representative and German secret agent Hans Tauscher published a letter to the editor of the *New York Herald* on August 28th 1914, which earned him a rebuke from Karl Boy-Ed's office for forswearing his German nationality in order to travel on a neutral freighter.[592] The German naval attaché Boy-Ed and his colleague, von Papen, gagged by the German ambassador with respect to political utterances, engaged in daily rebuttals of stories they deemed not to be factual.[593] Boy-Ed's correspondence, which has been preserved in part, targeted mostly German-American editors at major press outlets in the defense of Germany's motives for starting the war.[594] He also readily chastised the *Associated Press*, *The New York Times*, the *New York Herald*, and the magazine *Luck* for articles that he considered misleading or factually false.[595] Competently, he laid out the facts as he knew them with respect to German casualties, navy strategy, and battle timelines. Thankfully, he did not act on all the advice he received. An undated letter signed 'Nietzsche' from a 'well-meaning' supporter of the German propaganda effort, advised Boy-Ed in the fall of 1914:

> Brother Boy-Ed,
>
> Your (New Sarajevo, alias Chicago) Press propaganda must be divided along scycological (sic!) [all original] Lines to reach the diverse ele-ments of America. A socialist must be in charge of the propaganda to reach the Socialist Liberals with the argument that Germany is the Cornerstone of Progress, hence the Alliance of the British and Yankee Ultra Capitalists and the French Bourgeoisie with the Cossacks. 2.) A Southerner must [be] shown in his leaflet [that] the Turks and Blacks

[were] being used to invade Germany to rape German womanhood. 3.) The Pacific coast leaflets must show the Judas ? [sic] of John Bulls [sic] alliance with the <u>Yellows</u> etc. It is no use to reach the Anglophile Church Hypocrite Yankees. Nietzsche.[596]

The Press Bureau published several hundred pro-German pamphlets between September 1914 and February 1917 through the *Fatherland* Press, the *German Publication Society*, and the publishing arm of the *German University League*.[597] The German-American scholars, Muensterberg, von Mach, Francke together with Dernburg, Viereck, and other prominent German-Americans served as authors.[598] The Bureau also translated and issued publications distributed directly from Berlin. However, the outlets almost exclusively targeted German-Americans in the various clubs and organizations that existed all across America. Obviously, the Dernburg organization wanted German-Americans to receive the arguments with which to convince their friends and neighbors.

One such pamphlet under the title, *The Truth about Germany: Facts about the War*, had been published in Germany in the middle of August and handed out to Americans stranded by the European war.[599] The first edition described German history, denied German responsibility for the war, and emphasized German commercial relations with the United States. The Press Bureau in New York reissued the pamphlet on September 20th. Edited by Professor Kuno Francke, among others, it added chapters on the "misrepresentation" of the facts in the international press, as well as a strong denial of the destruction of Louvain and the massacre of its residents.[600]

Clearly, Dernburg and the Secret War Council felt pressured by the events in late August. Hugo Muensterberg published a book on September 20th, named *The War and America*, in which he set forth the peaceful nature of Germany, denied the existence of militarism, and celebrated Germany as the bulwark against the Russian hordes.[601] Edmund von Mach published a treatise in October called, *What Germany Wants*, in part derived from his speeches and newspaper articles.[602] Von Mach argued that Germany was a commercially-oriented, democratically-governed empire that desired nothing more than peace. The prerequisite of peace was a pacification of Europe, a blatantly pan-German ideology. He blamed England for creating the arms race and causing the war. The common themes included the defensive nature of Germany's *citizen* army, the denial of Prussian militarism, and the role of Germany as a bulwark against *Slavish* and *Cossack* peoples. The assertion that the war was forced upon the empire, which threw her into a struggle of survival, rounded out the common themes in his book.

Heinrich Albert described in his diaries on September 16th, that the Secret War Council had organized a "[...] public meeting of German-Americans in the Terrace-Garden for the purpose of showing their patriotism; Dernberg [sic] made an address warranted from the viewpoint of the American press, skillfully delivered, but for the Germans not enthusiastic enough [...]"[603]

Albert's diary commentary went to the heart of the problems with the German information strategy. Dernburg, whose address would sound fanatic by today's standards, was not "enthusiastic" enough for the non-representative, intellectual elite assembled to hear him. Resulting from the pressure of the German-American leadership, German surrogates appeared extreme, arrogant, and even fanatical to the general public, even if Dernburg and Count Bernstorff indeed had more sensitivities vis-à-vis the American character. The demonstration in itself, following the scenes of flag-waiving German reservists on New York's streets did little to create sympathies in a general audience.

Episodes such as these emphasized the *differentness*, the foreign, disloyal character of the German minority groups. German propaganda continued to target the German-American community with a message that was wholly unfit for general consumption. After meeting the Austrian-American President of the Newspaper Association of Foreign Languages, a disgusted Albert noted in his diary: "[...] an uneducated man of Austrian descent, who speaks neither German nor English correctly; much bluffing, a self-made man."[604] While Albert did not, or probably could not, change the disastrous course German propaganda was taking in the United States, he remained an astute and accurate observer.

The Press Bureau received an important reinforcement Around September 25th. Dr. Karl Alexander Fuehr, a lawyer who acted as an interpreter for the German embassy in Japan, had been expelled with the declaration of war against Germany.[605] Ambassador von Bernstorff considered Fuehr an expert for the propaganda task, possessing "great experience in Press matters and[...] an intimate knowledge of American affairs."[606] According to historian David Hirst, Fuehr prepared "special propaganda directed toward the Chinese and Japanese with the objective of fostering hostility to the United States."[607]

Thirty-eight years old, Fuehr had been stationed in the diplomatic service in the Far East since 1905. An exception among the expatriate German officials in New York, Fuehr had arrived with his wife Maria, an American born in Savannah, Georgia, and their son Siegfried.[608] Highly educated, Alexander Fuehr was not only a *cultured* man in the German sense, but an American investigator considered him "one of the most intelligent of the outfit [German Information Service]."[609] Albert and Dernburg quickly introduced him to the social circles surrounding the German-American intellectuals, and the opera. Well versed in literature and music, he attended the coveted after-show parties at the Tauschers. Hans Tauscher's wife was the famous opera star, Madame Johanna Gadski. Fuehr translated German documents and press releases, at first. Within a few months, however, he became the operational heart of the Press Bureau with close links to the propaganda division of the Foreign Office in Berlin.

Fuehr joined Dernburg's team just a week after Sommerfeld had approached the former colonial secretary about a new direction for the propaganda work. Fuehr joining the group as well as the establishment of a press office indicated that a change of direction was well under way. Bureau of Investigation agent William Offley confirmed Sommerfeld's claim of having *changed* the German propaganda strategy in 1914. A newspaper reporter told Bureau of Investigation Agent William Offley,

Felix Summefeld [sic], agent here for Pancho Villa, Mexican Chief, lives in Hotel Astoria [sic]; is of German parentage and sympathies; shrewd, clear headed man, who knows U.S. and its people thoroughly and thinks German officialdom has blundered everywhere in seeking sympathy for German cause in America. He told Dernberg [sic] so and suggested, several months ago [memo was written in June 1915], to Dernberg [sic] and other German representatives here that they organize a regular press bureau taking the best American newspaper men [sic] they could get, paying them very highly and making no secret of the work of the bureau as an effort to educate American sentiment to a better understanding of Germany's real aims and ideals. His suggestion was not adopted.[610]

Agent Offley's last conclusion proved to be untrue. Though Dernburg already had established a press bureau, he did take Sommerfeld's advice for using a heavy hitter of the American press.

Sommerfeld suggested a longtime acquaintance and friend, the American newspaperman, William Bayard Hale, to Dernburg.[611] Born in 1869, Hale studied at Boston and Harvard universities. He graduated from Episcopal Theological Seminary in Cambridge, Massachussetts, and began his career as an ordained priest in Boston in 1893. The then thirty-one-year-old Hale decided to become a journalist in 1900. The retired clergyman signed on as managing editor of the Cosmopolitan Magazine as a first job. He switched to the Philadelphia Public Ledger after three years and ran the editorial board until 1906, when The New York Times hired him as foreign correspondent for Paris, France.[612]

Hale also wrote in 1908 for the New York American, a Hearst paper, as its Berlin correspondent. Widely acclaimed for his thoughtful political analysis, the journalist and author interviewed the German Kaiser. This interview was, according to some, the most insightful ever with the German monarch. The following year, 1909, Hale married Olga Unger, a German-American in London. Hale had written and published Woodrow Wilson's biography in 1911 as a personal friend and adviser of then-governor of New Jersey. He played a major role in the highly contested presidential election campaign of 1912. Hale went to Mexico and Central America on sensitive diplomatic missions in 1913 and 1914 as Wilson's friend and confidante. The first such mission resulted in the dismissal of the American ambassador to Mexico, Henry Lane Wilson, who had orchestrated the downfall of the Mexican president Francisco I. Madero.[613] Felix Sommerfeld, who supported Hale on his fact finding mission, had organized meetings between Hale and the First Chief of the Constitutionalists in Mexico, Venustiano Carranza. Before the war, the German agent had worked closely and successfully with the confidante of President Wilson.

To Sommerfeld, Hale was the perfect candidate for the job. Intimately familiar with the inner workings of the Wilson administration, well-liked and respected in Germany, especially by the Kaiser, and a successful and well-known author and journalist, he seemed like a perfect fit. Hale attended the first meeting of the Press Bureau in New York on October 2nd.[614] The American writer directed much of the output of the Press Bureau as a paid consultant by November. He also edited a book called, *Germany's Just Cause*, that appeared through the *Fatherland* Press in the fall of 1914.[615] Together with a host of American professors, such as his very good friend and fellow pacifist, Reverend Professor Thomas C. Hall, the book made the case for Germany being the victim in the international conflagration.

Thomas C. Hall, an avowed socialist married to a German, taught at the Union Theological Seminary in New York until 1916.[616] He attracted the ire of the American government not only because of his pro-German writings, but the reverend introduced the notorious sabotage agent Franz Rintelen to David Lamar and conspired with them to create strikes and labor unrest in the U.S.[617] He joined Hale as a pro-German propagandist in authoring numerous articles warning of the dire consequences of a U.S. involvement in the war.[618] The seminary fired him in 1916, which caused Hall to go to Germany. Just like his friend and colleague Hale, his reputation in the United States never recovered from these wartime activities. Sommerfeld seemed to have been unaware that President Wilson and Hale's relationship had soured by the fall of 1914. The expectation of the German officials in New York and Washington, that Hale still had access to the inner circle of the president and could somehow influence U.S. policy towards Germany proved to be an illusion. However, Hale's advice on mounting a wider-based German propaganda campaign in the U.S. changed the dynamic of the propaganda team in New York.

A clear division between the radical and more moderate forces in the German propaganda organization crystallized as a result: Count Bernstorff, Hale, Albert, Dernburg, Boy-Ed, and most likely Sommerfeld on one side, the *Fatherland* and pan-German scholars Muensterberg, von Mach, and Francke on the other. The latter group continued to pander to the German-American community. Mainstream America would never be convinced that the Prussian state was democratic, peaceful, victimized, and non-militaristic. The former, more moderate group tried its best to take German propaganda to the mainstream American public. Dernburg laid out a profound shift in his propaganda strategy, developed by the *moderate* group in a meeting of the propaganda chiefs at the Ritz-Carlton on November 5th, with Ambassador Count Bernstorff attending:

> Whatever action has originated in Germany in order to win for us public opinion here, has either made none or an unfavorable impression. The belief which apparently spread very recently, that American [sic] received only one-sided and colored news about the conditions in Europe, has not for eight weeks been true. The fact that from German sides it is still being emphasized, that this is the case, has called forth numerous unwilling protests in the local papers.
>
> In German press utterances and other means of news transmission, which should make an impression here, two subjects which must be strictly avoided are namely, the 'Kultur,' and secondly every criticism of the American sympathy. Those on the last subject with reference to the publications of the 'Kolnischen [sic] Zeitung' have unquestionably done us harm here [...]

> As to the extent of the propaganda spread in America, our guidance should be: No policy, which has as its object, to engage American in any way! We must avoid every appearance of mixing up in America's matters, but at the same time continue to demand 'fair play'.[619]

This statement clearly declared war on the radical and pan-German elements that had been running the propaganda show since the onset of the war. However, the continuation of demanding *fair play* did endorse the *Fatherland*. Viereck, so Dernburg and Count Bernstorff hoped, could be reined in. This meeting signaled the start of a last, desperate, and, as it turned out, futile attempt to turn the rudder of the propaganda ship.

Neither Alexander Fuehr's diary nor that of Heinrich Albert mentions Felix A. Sommerfeld as a member of the Press Bureau. However, the hiring of William Bayard Hale coincided with Sommerfeld's encounter of Bernhard Dernburg. The German agent would work closely with the propaganda chief in 1915. These facts suggest that Sommerfeld indeed became a propaganda advisor of Dernburg's in the fall of 1914. Count Bernstorff described in his memoirs, "For all questions of propaganda Dr. Dernburg had the assistance of a small committee nominated by himself and consisting, in addition to Herren Albert, Meyer, Gerhardt [sic] and Fuehr, of a few American journalists and business men."[620]

William Bayard Hale 1914[621]

The German message was unfocused, insensitive to the American public, without the proper use of surrogates, and uncoordinated from the start of the war. Hampered by the lack of intelligence support from Germany, the German Press Bureau did not cure these issues. The use of personnel like Charles, Claussen, and Fuehr virtually insured a failure in communication as Sommerfeld had told Dernburg. Dernburg's office was public and blatant. The worst mistake was the use of the *Fatherland* as the mouthpiece of the German government. The *World's Work*, one of the magazines leading the English propaganda attack on the German press bureau commented in 1915, "If the German press bureau backed this paper [which it did], it can be accused of something worse than poor taste; it has actively damaged its cause. Its pages are so vulgar, so indiscriminate in their abuse, so lacking in self-control and reasoned argument that it merits attention in this place only because of its apparent association with Dr. Dernburg's propaganda."[622]

The worst failure of the German effort had to do with timing. Wholly unprepared when the British cut the transatlantic cables, Germany did not have any expertise stationed in the United States, even missing the ambassador. The German officials in Washington and New York blundered the opportunity of a first impression without a means to receive up-to-date information from Germany and without any strategic guidance. Once opinions had formed, they proved hard to change. Historian Peterson characterized the early German propaganda effort as "blind, deaf, and dumb."[623] However, even if Haniel von Haimhausen had done a better job, the typical German traits of *Besserwisserei*, and the urge to impose a pre-formed opinion on others got in the way of effectively communicating the German message.[624]

Indeed, without help from the German embassy, newspapers in the south and the midwest independently railed against the British blockade. Labor unions decried the practices of taking ships into prize court on ever-increasing lists of *conditional contraband*. The American economy reeled from the interruption in international trade and the shortages of available commercial shipping since the very beginning of the war. Germany had the unique chance then to turn public opinion decidedly against the British government – and completely failed to recognize it. Even the Wilson administration found itself under pressure from the unions and the south.[625]

The prodding of southern politicians forced Wilson to accede to demands for curbing the British blockade and upholding international trade, if necessary, even with German ships. Just after Hale joined the Press Bureau in October, the American economy rebounded sharply. The price for cotton normalized in November; munitions and military supply demands from the allies all but eliminated unemployment and public discontent starting in January. It did not matter how much the American public was *dernburged* in the fall of 1914. The real and only opportunity to turn the German propaganda ship around had passed.

The British systematically disseminated messages among American papers through genuine journalists as surrogates, acknowledging the other side's argument to give the impression of impartiality.[626] Their intelligence services provided sensational news immediately when – sometimes even before – events occurred. The British operation combined restricting and controlling access to the news, and backed their reporting with thorough intelligence work. English propagandists exploited the realization that the American hunger for facts and sensation trumped any German efforts, even without a highly anglophile American press, public, and government.

Walter Nicolai, the head of the German Military Intelligence Service in World War I commented in his 1923 memoirs, that there was no intelligence link with the propaganda effort. "The 'Press Service,' which has often been, and still is, in Germany confused with the 'Intelligence Service,' first devolved on the General Staff after the outbreak of the War, because no government department had made any preparations for its establishment. The Imperial Government had not comprehended that without such a service even military operations were impossible [...] Unlike her opponents, Germany had not at her command a political, economic, and military service of information concocted in co-ordinated fashion by the Government. She did not [...] take any advantage of political conditions in enemy countries or influence the neutrals by means of propaganda [...]"[627]

Heinrich Albert seconded the spy chief's analysis. The German financial agent was certainly guilty of associating with the scholars and extremists of the New York organization. He likely failed to argue against their ideological pronouncements that proved so devastating. However, he spoke to the same issue as Nicolai, noting in his diary in the winter of 1914-15: "The English have systematically worked long before the war, and especially in the first few weeks when German news was not available here, in order to malign us, and to paint a fake picture of us. We neglected both to gain sufficient influence, and to win the entire American people; exchange professors influence but a small part of the nation; the only means [for us to counter the English propaganda would have been] English printed news papers [sic], which would give the readers, and impregnate them without their knowing or noticing it, German ideas. A great neglect, that we do not own one, just now when the newspapers play such a big part. Lectures are not nearly so far reaching an influence."[628]

The moderate wing of the German press bureau, Albert, Dernburg, Hale, Boy-Ed, and Count Bernstorff changed their propaganda strategy in November of 1914. The German government agreed to set aside one million dollars in order to buy American newspapers and *impregnate* the American public with *German ideas*. The radical wing of the German propaganda, the German University League and the pro-German minority publications continued to waste their resources and preach to the converted, thereby further alienating the general public and the U.S. government. The Entente had won all the battles in 1914, at least with respect to propaganda in the United States. These German losses on the battlefield of American public opinion laid the groundwork for the broad support President Wilson eventually received when in 1917 the U.S. joined the war on the side of the Entente.

CHAPTER 11:
THE ARMS OF THE ANNIE LARSEN

T HE PROPAGANDA EFFORTS OF THE German government coincided not only with the attempts to buy raw materials and to attack Canada, but also with coordinated efforts to prevent the Entente powers from sourcing arms and ammunition in the U.S. market. Intelligence from agents such as Sommerfeld and Tauscher gave the German military authorities a detailed picture of U.S. armament industries early into the conflict. Several strategies to prevent Germany's enemies from supplying themselves came under consideration.

The munitions industry only consisted of a handful of manufacturing plants at the beginning of the war. Von Papen (with Captain Tauscher and Felix Sommerfeld's help) evaluated whether the entire American munitions capacity could be cornered. The price of such an effort, as well as the question of what to do with these arms and ammunition once delivered to German agents, remained open. Sommerfeld offered to sell them off to revolutionary factions in Mexico. As a representative and chief arms buyer for Pancho Villa in the United States, absorbing the munitions through his contracts for the Division of the North was a given. Sommerfeld's thinking took the strategy of cornering the munitions market one step further. If the U.S. army saw a need to expand, for example as a result of border troubles with Mexico, American factories would be required to supply the U.S. military forces before they would be allowed to sell their production to any other customer. The question of how to create border troubles remained unanswered, but selling arms to the different factions in order to turn up the heat in the conflict would certainly create an even more volatile environment to the same end.

Von Papen, who worked diligently on gaining an overview of the American munitions industry as soon as had returned from Mexico in the first week of August 1914, did not work in a vacuum. He gathered a team of experts around him. The military attaché's main intelligence agent was Hans Tauscher, who provided von Papen with valuable information and contacts. In New York the Tauschers knew everyone. The German agent conversed as easily with high-level U.S. army commanders as he did with politicians, industrialists, and financiers. He brought a friend and customer who would play an important role in Germany's efforts to corner the American munitions market, George W. Hoadley.

Hoadley owned the American and British Manufacturing Company in Bridgeport, Connecticut. Incorporated in 1902, his company started out as an aluminum mill, and then turned to the lucrative task of making casings for artillery shells. During the decade before the war, Hoadley concluded large contracts with the U.S. army, large enough to double production capacity in 1906.[629] Tauscher not only was his friend, but he was intimately linked to Hoadley's business ventures.[630] Hoadley testified to agents of the Bureau of Investigation in 1918:

> I have known Captain Tauscher for a great many years. He represented the Erhard people in Germany who have an exclusive mode for making steel for making shells [...] our Government contemplated changing their artillery and they finally adopted the Erhard gun, but under our laws they cannot do business with a foreign concern so I arranged with the Erhard people through Captain Tauscher to represent them [...] we took the contract to build the Government's building and a portion of those guns, but the Navy could not buy the Erhard gun, so I arranged again with Tauscher to pay $750 royalty for each gun [...] I afterwards arranged through Captain Tauscher for the Erhard high explosive shell, and the Government made a contract with them whereby they got 10,000 shells [...][631]

Hoadley knew everyone, and most of everything going on in Connecticut, as a major industrial leader in the center of the American munitions industry. The largest manufacturer of munitions in Bridgeport was UMC Remington, a merger between Remington Arms Company and Union Metallic Cartridge Company. Since Hoadley's main customer was the U.S. government, the industrialist also had access to high-level military sources. Heinrich Albert first noted his participation in internal strategy meetings on September 10th 1914.[632]

Other members of the *munitions* team were Daniel Waetzoldt, the commercial attaché of the German consulate general in New York, and Heinrich Albert, who had the finger on German finances. Not listed in the meetings were the two highest German officials in the U.S., Bernhard Dernburg and Count Johann von Bernstorff. Clearly, both had knowledge of the team's efforts and, in the case of the ambassador, signed off on the team's recommendations. Boy-Ed did not seem to have joined the working meetings. However, the reports Felix Sommerfeld sent to him concerning Allied arms contracts found their way into von Papen's military reports to the War Department.[633] Boy-Ed also was intimately involved in the naval portion of the group's logistics efforts.

After assembling intelligence of armament production capacities and going market prices for munitions, the group around Military Attaché von Papen concluded that for twenty million dollars Germany could buy up the entire American munitions capacity for one year ($420 million in today's value).[634] Authored by Count Bernstorff, the military attaché dispatched a telegram to the Department of the Interior on September 10th.[635] The plan was sound. American exports of arms and ammunition in the nine months after the beginning of the war (August 1914 to April 1915) amounted to roughly twenty-two million dollars.[636] In case the War Department thought cornering the entire munitions industry was too expensive, von Papen estimated that, locking up just the artillery and shrapnel production in the U.S. would cost about twelve million dollars ($252 million in today's value).[637] These sums did not have to be paid outright. Typically, the supplier required a twenty-five percent down payment on a contract in order to activate it.

Albert approached the German Department of the Interior on September 10th with the same proposal: "Enemy trying to buy up American annual production of artillery ammunition. Can anticipate purchase. Amount required 20 million dollars [...] 25% down at conclusion of contract [...] first delivery in about 5 months [...] technical fulfillment possible through instructions to Tauscher. [...] urgent."[638]

Albert even worked out how the money could be sent: Edmee Busch Reisinger, whose millionaire husband had died in Germany in September and who was a very wealthy woman in her own right, was due to arrive back in the United States with her husband's coffin in the middle of October. Albert had known Hugo Reisinger personally from the time they both spent as German officials at the St. Louis world exhibition in 1904.[639] The funeral of the famous philanthropist was scheduled for the end of the month.[640] Albert proposed for Edmee Reisinger and her sister, Emilee Busch, to carry the funds declared as "Red Cross" contributions.[641]

The two sisters were daughters of the founder of a beer-brewing empire in the United States, the late Adolphus Busch.[642] Once deliveries left the factories, a balance for each call-off became due after five months. Von Papen and Albert envisioned selling off the artillery shells to the American government, Italy or "smaller neutral countries."[643] One of those "smaller neutral countries" was Mexico. The resulting payments for the arms sales to neutrals, von Papen and Albert believed, would offset the new delivery payments that became due.

The team in New York awaited an answer for more than a month. Meanwhile, Entente buyers scoured the market and concluded valuable, long-term contracts. Finally, the German government responded on October 15th: "Answer to telegram No. 219. For Albert: Purchase of munitions not considered here advisable. Imperial Department of the Interior Zimmermann."[644] German Ambassador Count Bernstorff transmitted the disappointing decision and informed the New York team two days later in a top-secret message, "[...] I am trying to prevent munitions purchasing of the allies by different means, since we are not getting an order to proceed with respect to the option."[645]

Count Bernstorff clearly was intimately involved in the scheme to corner the U.S. munitions market and supported the idea. After all, it was a perfectly legal approach to hurt the enemy. Lacking funding, he concentrated on lobbying pro-business and pro-German congressmen to apply pressure to the American government. The goal was to somehow restrict the Entente purchases, possibly even institute an arms embargo against all warring factions. However, the profits from these lucrative arms contracts in the middle of a recession proved too enticing to give up for the Wilson administration. It would have been political suicide to institute an embargo.

The decision of the Imperial Department of the Interior not to invest in locking up U.S. munitions capacities early in the war turned out to be a huge mistake. It is not clear what prompted the decision. England, in particular, needed the U.S. supplies badly since her domestic production capacities were woefully underdeveloped. Since only twenty-five percent of the contract prices had to be paid, the imperial government could have stifled the Entente supply lines for six months to a year for a trivial sum of three to five million dollars, less than one percent of the German annual pre-war expenditures. Simultaneously, the German investment would have generated huge amounts of goodwill since the American economy was in a slump.

The members of the Secret War Council considered the Imperial War Departments' procrastination and hesitancy to corner the U.S. munitions market for a relatively small sum a huge blunder. Yet justified objections existed. Opponents of the feasibility of such an investment within the German government questioned the chances for success of such a strategy in the medium and longer term. As indeed happened, a rapid increase of orders quickly resulted in added American capacities in a supply-and-demand economy. A logical conclusion to this argument even meant that capacities that would otherwise not have existed may have been created as a result of German money. The German investment under these considerations would not only evaporate without effect, but the increased size of U.S. production capacity would render any future attempts to corner the market useless and too expensive.

Both arguments certainly seemed powerful, since by 1915 the U.S. munitions industry ratcheted up production to the highest levels ever. However, the investment in plant and equipment, hiring and training of employees, and starting production could not be done that easily. The Western Cartridge Company, for example, required two years for the creation of 7mm cartridge capacities of any substantial size. This lengthy time frame existed despite Felix Sommerfeld dangling orders in front of Franklin Olin's eyes.

Considering that in October of 1914 the German government still hoped for a short war, gambling away the opportunity to disrupt the Entente supply lines even for only six months seems incomprehensible. Certainly, the German military attaché von Papen, Heinrich Albert, and Count Bernstorff thought so. However, despite the refusal of the Wilhelmstrasse to approve funding, the group in New York never gave up on their idea. Von Papen repeatedly warned the authorities in Berlin that procrastination on binding allied munitions purchases in the U.S. would only increase the price tag.[646] The huge demand indeed sent the market prices for munitions and related products soaring by the end of the year. As a result, Count Bernstorff, von Papen, Boy-Ed, and Albert decided to proceed with their strategy and skirt the orders of the German government.

The Foreign Office sent a telegram on October 11th 1914, asking Ambassador Count Bernstorff in Washington to purchase and ship arms and munitions for the resistance movements in British and French colonies.[647] The group used this request as their chance to try out their plan and prove its feasibility to the German government. Germany had maintained close contacts with several resistance groups fighting their colonial masters in Ireland, Palestine, India, Afghanistan, Persia, Indonesia, and North Africa.[648]

These groups only had one thing in common: Defeat England and France. That desire made them natural allies in Germany's efforts to "hurt the enemy." One of the most active and effective groups, an organization of Punjab Indians (Sikh not Hindu) was located in the United States. The group had formed the Ghadr party in 1913, under the leadership of Har Dayal, headquartered in San Francisco. The party grew quickly, mainly as a result of its leader's captivating personality. To his followers, Har Dayal incorporated the highest traits of wisdom and spiritualism. However, his success made him a target for the American authorities. They accused him of radical leanings and involvement with anarchist and socialist circles. Dayal's weekly paper, the *Hindustan Gadhar* promoted martyrdom, and recruited volunteers to fight against British rule. English, Canadian, and U.S. authorities tried their best to disperse and prosecute the Indian resistance leaders. After a brief arrest in April 1914 for "speeches so villainously offensive to common decency and order" Har Dayal decided to jump bail and move to Germany.[649] When the war started, he organized in the "Indian Independence Committee" in the German capital. The German government actively supported several Ghadr operations during the first months of the war in the Islamist areas of India, as well as in Afghanistan, and Singapore with money, transportation, and weapons.

The U.S. organization came under the control of writer and Ghadr paper editor Ram Chandra. "On August 5, 1914, party leaders gathered at Yugantar Ashram in San Francisco and declared war on Great Britain. Like their German counterparts in Latin America, many Indians in Canada and the U.S. liquidated their affairs in the Americas and boarded ships to go fight for independence. A group of 26 Indians left Vancouver on August 22, and another of 61 men left San Francisco a week later aboard the ship Korea. Like an agitated ant hill, Ghadr adherents the world over were scurrying about, tying up their worldly affairs and heeding the clarion to return home [India] for war."[650]

The war also interrupted the communications between the German and American members of India's resistance. Consequently, Count Bernstorff's embassy in Washington "[...] was turned into a kind of communication center for the messages between them [Indian groups in Germany and those in the United States], the General Staff, the Foreign Office in Berlin, and the agents located all over the Near and Far East."[651] The Ghadr activists planned to overthrow the colonial rule of India in the fall of 1914. The operation, a large-scale attack on several fronts, subversion, terrorism, and assassination were to occur simultaneously in February of 1915.

Admiral Paul von Hintze in Beijing and Dr. Franz von Zitelmann in Manila had charge of the missions to support the resistance movements in the Far East. In Washington, Ambassador von Bernstorff received orders to help in any way possible, hence the telegram of October 11th 1914.

Von Papen eagerly accepted the responsibility to organize the proposed military support of the Ghadr efforts. Not only could von Papen now buy military supplies in the U.S. market, he could also experiment with the logistics of selling arms and ammunition from the United States to third parties. The German embassy had close contacts to both the Villa and Carranza factions in Mexico through Sommerfeld and the pro-German envoy of the Constitutionalists in Washington, Rafael Zubaran Capmany.[652] Someone of the Carranza camp petitioned the German embassy for a supply of munitions on September 26th 1914.[653] The petitioner appears in the German correspondence log as "R. O. Fabricius, Progreso."[654] Whether the reference meant to describe the German businessman, Adolfo Fabricius, who indeed lived in Progreso, Yucatan, is not clear. Fabricius most likely was the German merchant to handle the order for Carranza's U.S. envoy, Rafael Zubaran Capmany. The request was approved on October 7th with the notation, "Forwarded to Tauscher. Not more than 100,000. Delivery in three months."[655] Albert noted in his diary on October 22nd 1914, "[...] give (Papen) check for $100,000 for arms Tauscher."[656]

Military Attaché von Papen, who was in charge of what the embassy correspondence log categorized as "Munitions Business," tasked Hans Tauscher to procure the required arms and ammunition for both the Indian resistance movement and the Mexican revolutionary forces.[657] The plan was to buy a large cache of rifles with corresponding cartridges. Von Papen made his first mistake of many in the execution of the operation by not telling Tauscher where the arms were destined. Tauscher submitted his invoice for the order on October 26th. He had found 10,890 rifles and 3.9 million cartridges through Robert vom Cleff, a small-time New York arms dealer and friend of Tauscher.[658] The rifles consisted mostly of Springfield 45/70s that had been designed in 1873 and not been used in the active U.S. military since 1897. The American government had been working on selling these weapons as surplus for a decade.

Archival documents show that vom Cleff was just a front. The arms had been sold through a Seattle arms dealer, W. Stokes Kirk, who in turn, had sourced them from the National Guard surplus depot in Kansas City.[659] The Stokes Kirk salesman testified to the Bureau of Investigation in 1917, "[...] in answer will say about the ammunition I sold Tauscher in New York I also sold him about 10,000 calibre 45 rifles, 10 Gatlin guns etc. Some of these goods were caught on the *Annie Larsen* [...]"[660] The *Annie Larson* was a three-mast, 326-ton lumber schooner. The sail ship had seen better days. It was built in 1881 and had been used to carry lumber from Oregon and Washington states down to San Francisco and other cities along the California coast.

A typical lumber schooner at anchor in Caspar Bay. Photo courtesy Tony Phillips.

Albert paid the remaining $59,049.48 of Tauscher's invoice totaling $159,049.48 ($3.3 million in today's value) the day he received it.[661] Tauscher gratefully remitted his *commissions* of approximately $2,200 he received from vom Cleff to the German

Military Attaché von Papen. However, the real profits for the two arms dealers consisted of the difference of what vom Cleff and Tauscher paid to W. Stokes Kirk, and what they, in turn, invoiced to von Papen. The price of $5 to $5.55 per rifle was a fraction of the cost of a modern 7mm Mauser that sold for $28 in December, 1914.[662] Given the German government's stinginess, the low price likely impressed the military attaché as a good deal.

The real value of the outdated guns seems to have been a fraction of the $5 von Papen paid. The same was true for the ancient black powder cartridges that may or may not have even worked (since the powder deteriorates over time). Such cartridges were hard to come by because no one used them anymore in the age of smokeless powder. Tauscher had a good reason to submit the fake invoice from vom Cleff to the military attaché and not a receipt from W. Stokes Kirk.

The story blew up in the German attaché's face in 1915, when The New York Times reported that four thousand rifles and one million cartridges were impounded.[663] The American customs official estimated the weapons and ammunition to have been worth around $25,000.[664] Calculating the cost for the impounded lot using the vom Cleff invoice, von Papen paid $43,750 for the seized shipment, which included about $3,630 in transportation costs.[665] The two arms dealers, therefore, pocketed a hefty profit of $15,120 ($317,520 in today's value). Von Papen blindly trusted Tauscher, which seems to have been a mistake. However, the military attaché should also have known the market value of these guns. Negligence on his part led to grossly overpaying his suppliers. Worse, by not telling Tauscher about the destination of the arms, the German government paid freight from the west coast to New York and back, an estimated $24,500 ($515,000 in today's value) plus $1,165 ($25,000 in today's value) for storage and insurance.[666]

Not all the weapons Tauscher sourced went to the west coast. Tauscher invoiced $159,049 to the German government, of which $6,360 consisted of an order for 250 automatic Mauser pistols. Tauscher sold these pistols to arms dealers in New York, Boston, and two Mexican agents at the direction of von Papen. Dr. Alfredo Caturegli received one of the pistols. He worked for the

Carranza government in New York and became heavily involved in sending German-financed arms to Mexico in 1916. The other, Ricardo Martinez, received two hundred pistols. He has yet to be identified. The broker in San Diego that handled the shipment was a company called Martinez and Co., which may have been the customer who received the two hundred pistols. Four more pistols were delivered to unspecified recipients on order of von Papen, free of charge. The sale of these 250 pistols, which as a sideline actually made the German government a twenty-five percent profit, led to a number of speculations.[667]

The side arms likely went to German agents, including Wachendorf and his group, on the order of the German military attaché. Some historians have speculated that von Papen organized German shock troops in the U.S. to attack Canada, and that these weapons had been part of a larger scheme to arm German reservists.[668] There is no archival evidence, either with respect to funding of such troops or sourcing of the necessary arms, to suggest that such a suicidal plan ever moved beyond mere brainstorming and wishful thinking. Two hundred fifty side arms certainly would not suffice in an attack on Canada.

On October 27th, the rifles and ammunition from the Kansas army surplus went to a storage facility at 521 West 20th Street in New York, a recently completed nine-story building in lower Manhattan. The project now became more complex. The arms had to be delivered to San Diego where, meanwhile, the German admiralty was to organize the transportation to Mexico and to a meeting point with Indian resistance fighters. Heinrich Albert booked space for the move to San Diego on the SS Nueces, a Mallory Line steamer, to take the shipment to Galveston, Texas. The Nueces was one of the ships Albert had leased for cotton shipments. The arms would then be transferred onto rail from Galveston and taken to San Diego, California. The Nueces left New York on January 9th 1915, with 561 cases of rifles (twenty per case), 3,759 cases of cartridges (1,000 per case), and ten bales of munitions belts.[669]

The shipment had been fully insured and consigned to Walter C. Hughes in San Diego. He was Tauscher's freight forwarder in New York with corresponding offices in Galveston and Los

Angeles. However, the real consignee, of course, was the German consulate in San Francisco. The shipment arrived in Galveston ten days later. This was a large order, even by the standards of the times when huge transfers of weapons from the United States to Mexico occurred almost daily. It took eleven freight cars to transport the shipment to San Diego.[670] The cost of the transfer from New York to San Diego amounted to $12,225.75 ($257,000 in today's value) plus $200 for insurance, a hefty price for transportation. The actual freight invoice from M. C. Hughes is not in the papers and receipts Tauscher submitted to von Papen. Given Tauscher's knack for skimming profits, the transportation invoice he received may have been quite a bit lower than what he charged to von Papen.

A front woman in San Francisco, probably employed by the Jebsen Shipping Line, sent a $14,000 payment ($294,000 in today's money) to a lawyer in San Diego on January 19th 1915, to lease the run-down, three-mast freighter *Annie Larsen*. The schooner's monthly lease, in addition to the down payment, was $1,250 ($26,250 in today's value).[671] The *Annie Larson* set sail from San Francisco on January 24th and took on the weapons in San Diego on February 3rd. The large amount of arms raised eyebrows with American customs officials in San Diego. The consignee of the shipment was "Juan Bernardo Bowen" in Topolobamba, Mexico. Topolobamba, Sinaloa, half-way between Guaymas and Mazatlan on the Gulf of Mexico, was under the control of Villistas at the time, but hotly contested.

Indications are that the shipment of arms, indeed, was destined for Villa's troops. *The New York Times* reported on February 19th, "Villa, who has just captured Guadalajara, is centring [sic] his attention now on his west coast campaign, and is doing so because he wants to make doubly sure of receiving a shipment of 9,000 rifles and 3,000,000 rounds of ammunition now being sent on a schooner from San Diego, Cal., to the Mexican west coast [...]"[672] It took until March 8th for the final clearance. The delay may have had to do with the difficulties Villa had in securing Mazatlan. The *Annie Larsen* had a crew of nine with German-born American citizen Captain Schlueter in command. The so-called super-cargo, the person who had authority over the movements of the ship, was the American-born, thirty-eight year-old German naval intelligence officer, Hermann Othmer. The agent arrived from the Marshal Islands in the United States on November 3rd 1914. The ship he traveled on was the four-masted German motorschooner, *Atlas*, which self-interned in San Francisco, California. Othmer is listed as a mate on the ship.[673]

Meanwhile, Frederick Jebsen, Karl Boy-Ed's agent in charge of supplying the German Pacific fleet, rigged an old oil tanker, the *SS Maverick*, to meet the *Annie Larsen* and take on the arms shipment for transfer to the Far East. He founded the American-Asiatic Oil Company under which he registered the 1,500-ton oil tanker. The front company led directly to Jebsen's office, which did not take the English secret service long to figure out. The *Maverick* previously sailed for the Standard Oil Company. She was cheap – and for a good reason.

Built in 1890 she had been salvaged after a fire and explosion sank her in Halifax in 1899.[674] Jebsen arranged the acquisition through the Craig Shipbuilding Company in Long Beach, California. Craig operated a large plant in the San Pedro harbor where, among other things, the company built submarines for the American government.[675] The *Maverick* went into dry-dock there to be refitted for transpacific runs. While in dry-dock, Jebsen bought the ship for $150,000 ($3.15 million in today's value). The low purchase price implies that the oil tanker had been virtually worthless when the Craig Shipbuilding Company took it over. Most of the purchase price must have gone into getting the old hull sea-worthy again. Whether there was a price difference between what Craig paid to Standard Oil on Jebsen's advice and what the German government paid to Jebsen is unknown.

The tanker took on a new crew after spending one month in dry-dock in the port of San Pedro outside of Los Angeles. American-born John B. Starr-Hunt boarded the *Maverick* as Germany's super-cargo to direct the American captain. Ram Chandra and his people also sent a group of five Indian resistance fighters with propaganda literature and orders on how to get the shipment to the revolutionaries in India. Finally, with eight thousand barrels of fuel oil in the hold (not for own consumption) she headed to the coast of Mexico, as well. Her papers listed the final destination as

"Anjer, Java." According to the pro-English account of the affair by historian French Strother, who quoted the testimony of super-cargo John B. Hunt-Starr, the *Maverick* had been scheduled to meet the *Annie Larsen* in San José del Cabo at the very tip of Baja California.[676] Starr-Hunt had orders to return to the U.S. with the schooner once the weapons were transferred. He testified about his mission in 1917:

> On the (?) of April, the *Maverick* finally sailed from Los Angeles. On the morning of that day Jebsen gave me a sealed letter, addressed to nobody, with verbal instructions to hand it over to Page on the *Annie Larsen* immediately after I met him [...] Jebsen also handed me a third letter, without address, for Page, and open. It contained typewrit-ten instructions as to how to stow the cargo to be transhipped [sic] from the *Annie Larsen* [...]. It said that the cases containing rifles were to be stowed in one of the two empty tanks of the Maverick and flooded with oil. The ammunition cases were to be stowed in the other empty tank which was not to be flooded except as a last resort[...] Five days after leaving Los Angeles we arrived at San José del Cabo, 27th April, I think [...] Jebsen had given me to understand that we might meet the *Annie Larsen* at San José del Cabo, but she was not there [...][677]

Starr-Hunt's account is highly suspicious. The British sub-sequently arrested him in 1915 in Singapore after the *Maverick* had reached Java but was impounded by the Dutch navy. It is not entirely clear, whether, indeed, Starr-Hunt was an English prisoner. Archival records from November 1915 show that he applied for and received an American passport supported by an affidavit certifying his U.S. cit-izenship. His uncle, Los Angeles attorney Lucien Gray, submitted the affidavit. The document had been sworn to before the English consul in Los Angeles, for which there is no reason other than Starr-Hunt's status was somehow related to the British government.

The young adventurer disappeared from public view (and archival records) for a year. After repeated attempts by American politicians from Texas and the State Department to *free* him, the British authorities transferred the "prisoner" to London on February 1st 1917 – first class, "c/o War Department."[678] Starr-Hunt showed up as a star witness for the prosecution in the trial against German consul Franz Bopp and two dozen conspirators. Similar to what seemed to have happened to Franz Wachendorf, alias Horst von der Goltz, while imprisoned in England, the British intelligence services turned the young adventurer Starr-Hunt into one of their own, as well. Amazingly, Starr-Hunt's, just like Wachendorf's account, has been taken as fact in virtually all historical analyses of the affair, with hardly any corroboration by either German or British sources.

John Brackenridge Starr-Hunt, from a 1915 U.S. passport[679]

John Brackenridge *Jack* Starr-Hunt was born on November 15th 1892 in San Antonio, Texas. His father's family came to the Texas town in the pioneer days and was highly regarded. His family moved to Mexico City when he was five.[680] His father, John Leander Starr-Hunt, worked for American businesses as an international lawyer.[681] According to the *San Antonio Light* newspaper, the six-foot two-inch Starr-Hunt joined the merchant marine at eighteen years old, shipping weapons from the United States to, among others,

Pancho Villa.[682] Working on behalf of the revolutionaries in Mexico had consequences. Starr-Hunt, who was on leave in the capital at the time, attempted to take himself and his wife Ruth to safety in the United States during the course of the American occupation of Veracruz. His father arranged for him to travel under protection of American Charge D'Affairs Nelson O'Shaughnessy. However, he and his wife were taken off the train before it left the capital and arrested.[683] How serious his predicament was is unknown. However, wallowing in war fever, sensationalist headlines in the United States told of an impending execution, some even reported that he had been killed.[684]

After an outcry that covered the entire U.S. press for days, the twenty-four year-old American and his family gained their freedom and left Mexico. Starr-Hunt settled back in San Antonio. It is likely that during his years in the commercial marine between Mexico and the United States, Starr-Hunt met, and possibly worked for, Frederick Jebsen. He was barely twenty-three years old when Jebsen hired him to be the supercargo on the *Maverick*. His obvious credentials were that he had an American passport, spoke Spanish without an accent, and had experience smuggling arms and ammunition in war-ravaged Mexico. Since the *Maverick* had business to conduct on the Mexican coast, Starr-Hunt seemed a good choice to oversee the transfer of the arms, and clearing the ship through Mexican ports.

Meanwhile, two months had passed since the *Annie Larsen* had arrived in San José del Cabo. British intelligence services were watching the movements of the old oil tanker when the *Maverick* was finally cleared to sail in the end of April 1915. The British agents suspected the identity of the *Maverick's* owners, the American-Asiatic Oil Company to be a cover. American customs officials boarded and searched the *Maverick* at the insistence of British intelligence, while still in harbor. However, her hold was empty. Still suspecting a German covert operation, the British cruiser HMS *Newcastle* shadowed the oil tanker when she finally sailed. The *Maverick's* captain decided to make a run to Socorro Island, about four hundred miles off the Mexican shore, with the British cruiser tailing. The Island was the agreed upon alternative meeting point with the weapons-laden schooner. The oil tanker shook the British cruiser, but did not find the *Anne Larsen* at the island.

The *Annie Larsen* indeed had sailed from the tip of the Baja California to Socorro Island, the secondary meeting point. However, the crew waited for one month, after which food and fresh water ran low. Then she sailed southeast to Acapulco in need of provisions to re-supply. Acapulco is one thousand miles south of the tip of Baja California and completely out of the way of her presumed final destination. However, the prevailing winds in the region did not allow the sail ship to go due east back to the Baja California. Instead, she had to tack south. It is not known if the *Annie Larsen* cleared any of her cargo while in San José del Cabo. If she did, it would have been the shipment Pancho Villa had been expecting.

When she arrived in Acapulco, which was in Carrancista territory, she cleared the majority of her cargo. Numerous accounts detailed how the Carrancista port authorities refused to let the ship continue on her voyage. According to author David Wilma, "Only through the intervention by U.S. Navy officers from the cruiser *U.S.S. Yorktown*, also at Acapulco at the time, was the *Annie Larsen* released."[685] In reality, the amount of cargo discharged at Acapulco matches almost exactly the $100,000 worth of arms, which the German embassy had approved on October 7th. Deducting the arms and munitions seized by American authorities as few months later, the remaining cargo amounted to $38,960 worth of rifles and $71,024 worth of cartridges and cartridge belts. It is very plausible that the Villistas at San José del Cabo took $10,000 worth of supplies, making the math match perfectly.

The *Annie Larsen* supposedly tried to return to Socorro Island after re-supplying in Acapulco. She never made it on account of *bad weather*. Indeed, it would be a tough trip to make against the strong headwinds, which prevail between the southern coast of Mexico and Socorro Island. Instead of heading out into the Pacific, the schooner headed up the U.S. coast to Washington State, her home base.

Finally, on June 29th 1915, the five-month odyssey of the *Annie Larsen* ended at Gray's Harbor in Hoquiam, Washington. The U.S. local customs collector impounded the ship, including what remained in her hold. He found 4,000 rifles and one million cartridges worth $25,000.[686] The German agent on board, who had directed the captain's movements, escaped. In a landmark trial in 1917 and 1918, German Consul General Bopp, his attachés Eckhard von Schack and Georg Wilhelm von Brincken, as well as two-dozen German and Indian conspirators involved in the plot were tried and convicted to hard time.[687] One of the Indian conspirators shot the leader of the Indian resistance movement, Ram Chandra, during the sensational end of the trial. The U.S. marshal in the courtroom, in turn, killed the attacker.

The *Maverick* returned from Socorro to San Diego in late May 1915 and remained anchored in international waters while Starr-Hunt and Captain Nelsen went ashore for new orders. They informed Jebsen that the *Annie Larsen* was nowhere to be found. Jebsen sent the *Maverick* on her way to the Far East via Hilo, Hawaii and the Johnston Atoll, 750 nautical miles west of Hawaii, where she was to attempt a rendezvous with the *Annie Larsen* one last time.[688] She arrived at Johnston Island in the Dutch West Indies on June 20th. The *Annie Larsen*, of course, was not there. The *Maverick* continued on to Batavia (Djakarta, Indonesia), part of the Dutch colonies in 1915, where she arrived a month later. She made several port calls in between, the details of which are not known. Rumor had it that the tanker picked up various shipments of supplies, maybe even arms, and distributed them among the extensive German naval intelligence network in the Pacific.

Since the *Maverick* never met up with the *Annie Larsen*, German naval intelligence now directed her to wait for the *Djember*, another merchant ship the German government had leased from the Holland Line. Hans Tauscher had purchased another batch of weapons for the Indian resistance in April 1915 and consigned it to Java, as well. This shipment consisted of 2.4 million cartridges, 7,300 old Springfield rifles with Bayonets (again from W. Stokes Kirk and Robert vom Cleff), one Gatlin gun, and 2,000 colt revolvers for $123,252 ($2.6 million in today's value).[689] However, the captain of the *Djember* refused to take the consigned weapons on board at the docks in New York. It turned out that British intelligence agents had found out about the shipment and forced the steam line to refuse the shipment.[690] The argument between Tauscher and the captain dragged into the night. The arms could not stay at the pier overnight. So Tauscher, without the required permit from the New York Fire Department, moved the arms back into his warehouse in lower Manhattan. Police stopped the trucks, and the entire circumstances of the shipment landed in the newspapers.

Hans Tauscher, his deputy Henry Muck, and Robert vom Cleff all faced trial. The arms remained in New York and never made it to Java as a result. Stuck in Batavia, the *Maverick* awaited instructions. By the end of July, with her owner Jebsen on the run and no apparent directions for her operation, the crew melted away. Starr-Hunt went on to Indonesia, where the British allegedly captured him. The five Ghadr representatives tried to make their way through Indonesia back to India. The fate of the tanker is unclear. There were numerous reports in 1916 that she had been sighted as a converted German raider. None of these reports could be verified.

Countless articles and scholarly treatises have been written about the "German-Hindu Conspiracy."[691] The affair resulted in one of the most widely publicized trials in World War I history. Similar to von Papen's passport affair, the Welland Canal sabotage, and the deplorable German propaganda efforts, this scandal added fuel to the fire of anti-German sentiment in the United States. English propaganda and historians who accepted publications, such as Strother's book, as fact painted the German officials as reckless agents trampling on American neutrality laws. This argument certainly held water in the case of von Papen's Canada excursions. However, while there was plenty of recklessness and bad planning in this case, the exportation of arms to Java was not a violation of American neutrality laws. Also, exportation of arms and ammunition to Mexico was perfectly legal.

The apparent American cooperation with British intelligence to dismantle the shipment of arms and ammunition to territories far from the American mainland became proof positive for German officials in the United States that American neutrality had become more than just one-sided. While American officials disrupted and tried the entire German diplomatic corps on the West Coast, the Entente shipped millions of dollars' worth of arms and ammunition to the European front. By the time the plot fell apart, German officials in the United States and Berlin had already decided to escalate their efforts to hit the United States directly as a presumed enemy. The whole operation not only aimed at hitting the Entente powers in their colonies, but also seemed to have been a trial run for buying U.S. munitions and selling them to third parties.

The fallout of the *German-Hindu* affair left German operations on the West Coast in shambles. The Tauscher trial and his now public link to von Papen hobbled his secret service missions on the east coast. The English goal was to use this affair to destroy the Indian resistance movement in the United States. This strategy succeeded splendidly following the death of its leader and the conviction of twelve top functionaries. In addition to the U.S. members of the Ghadr party, the English authorities were able to nab the five activists that had traveled on board of the *Maverick*, and executed them in October 1916.[692]

Frederick Jebsen, the flamboyant socialite and San Francisco shipping tycoon, escaped the dragnet of the American and British authorities in June of 1915. He had given up on his personal business. The destruction of Admiral Spee's squadron in the Falklands in December of 1914 also ended his supply efforts. He made his way to Germany in disguise and volunteered for service on the submarine U-36. She sank on July 24th 1915 off the Shetland Islands during Jebsen's first tour, shot to pieces by the English cruiser *HMS Baralong*.[693] Consul Bopp and his attachés remained in office but were rendered completely immobilized through a series of trials that lasted into 1918. The entire German naval intelligence operation on the west coast was gutted within six months. However, the secret service war also catapulted an important second-tier agent to the leadership cadre of German naval intelligence operations in California and later in Mexico. Kurt Jahnke, whose involvement in the Jebsen operations is unknown, became implicated in a host of sabotage missions both in the United States and in Mexico between 1915 and 1918.

The *Annie Larsen* saga has animated multiple accounts about the clumsiness of German secret service activities in the U.S. Perhaps this assessment is justifiable. However, it is important to note that this project served as a trial run for a larger German strategy, namely cornering the U.S. munitions market and selling arms and munitions to third parties. Equally significant is the evidence that the German embassy supported Venustiano Carranza militarily as early as the fall of 1914.

This shipment, a grant of $100,000, is the first proof of a deliberate strategy by German agents to add fuel to the conflict in Mexico and, thereby, tie American military resources at the border. The delivery of arms to Carranza coincided with the crisis at Naco, where two opposing Mexican forces battled right at the U.S.-Mexican border. The siege and constant engagements lasted for three months, and caused stray bullets as well as artillery shells to land on the American side on an almost daily basis. Unable to stop the hail of bullets the U.S. military decided to deploy thousands of troops in order to defend the border. Provoking a war between Mexico and the United States was within the realm of possibilities for the German officials in Washington and New York in the end of 1914.

Naval intelligence agent Felix Sommerfeld reported on the negotiations he brokered between the Mexican factions and the U.S. government as Pancho Villa's representative. He suggested to Bernhard Dernburg that American munitions production would go to the U.S. armed forces not to the Entente in the event of an American intervention in Mexico, which would require mobilization. Adding fuel to that fire in a perfectly legal way was a strategy even Ambassador Count Bernstorff could support.

The German ambassador judged the whole *Annie Larsen* affair to have been much ado about nothing in his memoirs. He reiterated his statements made to the U.S. Secretary of State that the weapons of the *Annie Larsen* were destined for German East Africa, not India or Mexico.[694] He did not speak to the badly botched logistics that caused the operation to blow up in Germany's face. He certainly did not mention Germany's meddling in Mexican affairs. Whether Villa received any weapons at this juncture or not cannot be confirmed. However, the information printed in *The New York Times* about Villa awaiting an important shipment for San Diego certainly had Sommerfeld's fingerprints all over. The chief arms buyer for the revolutionary either sent arms and ammunition paid for by the German government to his charge, or, at the very least, participated in a ruse on behalf of the German government to hide the fact that weapons were en route to India. The former suspicion seems more likely.

The *Annie Larsen* affair would not be the last effort to ship munitions to India's independence fighters. Neither would the Mexican revolutionaries have to wait long for more support from the German empire. However, the Annie Larsen conspiracy, as well as the severe American sanctioning of the people who had supplied the German naval assets in the Atlantic and Pacific theatres, changed the German attitude towards the United States. It appeared to German observers, and especially the officials of the Secret War Council in New York, that America had succumbed to the lure of profitable trade with the Entente powers on a large scale. Though formally, and in strictly legal terms, the Wilson administration argued that it was maintaining neutrality in the war, the U.S. had joined the Allies as a major supplier of war materials by the end of 1914. Munitions factories sprouted like mushrooms all over the country. Voices of moderation, such as that of William Jennings Bryan, drowned in a sea of exuberance with the new-found war profits.

EPILOGUE:
THE END OF CIVILITY

DESPITE THE INDEFENSIBLE GERMAN DECISION to be a driving force in starting this catastrophic world war, to execute it with a flawed and disastrous strategy, and to create carnage so massive that today's generation can still feel its impact, the German strategy towards the United States demonstrated undeniable consistency and logic. The Secret War Council refused to follow the letter of the law from the onset in its attacks on Canada, in its dispatch of military personnel to the front, and in its efforts to supply the imperial navy. The Wilson administration also clearly chose early in the war to side implicitly with the Entente for economic reasons. This decision precipitated a change in the German policy towards the United States. It is not possible, nor is it intellectually consistent, to decouple the American supply of Germany's enemies on a grand scale from the German decision to see the U.S. as a combatant in the war starting in January of 1915.

It would be too easy to define the German activities as hostile to American neutrality in a purely black-and-white analysis. Clearly, Germany broke American laws. However, the target of German clandestine missions was not the United States, but rather involved issues related to the conduct of the war in Europe. Without question, the American government had to assert its status as a neutral power that was open to business for anyone. Knowingly breaking the law, German officials expected repercussions for their illegal actions should they be discovered. However, the severity of the American reaction, when some of the clandestine missions indeed came to light, surprised the German government. It also surprised segments of American society, such as pro-German minorities, the peace movement, a host of moderate politicians, and prominent members of the American intelligentsia.

An ever-widening schism between German and American interests developed over the course of the first year of the war, egged on by effective British propaganda and an increasing economic dependence on trade with the Entente powers. Officials in the Secret War Council and hard-line war planners in Germany moved from directing their efforts on American soil against Britain, France, and Russia, to targeting the United States outright as a vital piece in the Entente supply lines. American government officials willingly accepted the repercussions of supplying the Entente. Councilor of the State Department Frank L. Polk wrote in 1916: "When you have a horse and a wagon you then go to the market, when you have no horse you might as well grow flowers in the wagon."[695]

America had wagons and British, French, and Russian supply needs provided the horses. A trade boycott of the warring factions, or limited trade with Germany in the face of an effective British sea blockade, would have equated to growing flowers in the underutilized U.S. factories. Germany and the United States lost their ability to coexist following an American economic boom that resulted from trade with Germany's enemies, as well as German disrespect and miscalculation of the American legal, political, and economic system.

The German secret service organization directed by the Secret War Council was by no means an amateurish and ridiculous affair. Despite many shortcomings, none the least lacking a thorough understanding of the American democracy, the German officials managed to set afoot a host of important projects, often against the odds of lackluster finances and untrained personnel. Despite increasing pressure from U.S. officials and a war effort favoring the Allies in the long run, the Secret War Council gained experience, efficiency, and effectiveness over the first year of the war. Law enforcement also had to learn how to combat a secret war fought on its soil. Although hot on the heels of many of the conspirators from the beginning of the war, the German spies proved hard to prosecute. Local and federal police, as well as clandestine services had few legal tools to stop various foreign agencies from operating on American soil until the passing of the Espionage Act on June 15th 1917. Laws to prosecute criminal acts, such as destruction of property, existed, of course. These covered the acts of sabotage German agents had committed between 1914 and 1916. Along the Mexican border, agents of the Justice Department prosecuted arms smugglers, recruiters, propagandists, revolutionaries, and filibusters of all shades and backgrounds using the Neutrality Act of 1794. However, none of these legal frameworks netted the masterminds of the German secret service.

The *Annie Larsen* affair and the seizing of the SS *Wilhelmina* in the spring of 1915 triggered a significant shift in the attitude of German officials towards the United States.[696] Shipping weapons from the United States to Mexico was not illegal. Neither was the transshipment to India or any other place. The seizing of the *Wilhelmina*, which Albert had purchased in October through a dummy firm to ship foodstuffs and cotton, underscored the fact that even that would not be tolerated. The British government added foodstuffs to their contraband lists, which became the legal foundation for seizing the freighter. The German attempts to respect U.S. neutrality and expend huge efforts in organizing and financing the export operations to avoid violating U.S. laws did not result in any tangible appreciation or acceptance by the U.S. government.

The Wilson administration made the conscious decision to extract the maximum economic benefit from the European conflict. Neutrality in a strictly legal sense — since the Central Powers could purchase American goods, just not be able to transport them to Europe — allowed the United States to permit J.P. Morgan and other U.S.-based banks to finance Entente purchases and American manufacturers to ship goods on a grand scale. This one-sided approach to trading with the warring factions in Europe brought with it the threat of repercussions.

In addition to the American trade policy that disadvantaged the Central Powers, the United States was unwilling to permit any German efforts against the Entente from American soil. Undoubtedly, von Papen's passport scheme, the attack on Canadian installations, the supply of German cruisers from the U.S. were illegal

activities. However, German officials initially thought these operations were all peccadilloes that, at worst, would trigger a slap on
the wrist from the American government. However, the severe
reactions of the American public, the decision of the U.S. government to become the crucial link in the Entente's supply chain, and
an increasingly effective English propaganda, forced the Wilson
administration to severely sanction the German covert operations.
In landmark trials, courts imposed harsh sentences on the former
German Minister to Mexico and HAPAG director in New York Karl
Buenz and a whole host of his employees in the fall of 1915. Dernburg left voluntarily in the summer of 1915, while the Wilson administration evicted von Papen and Boy-Ed in end of that year.

Contemporaries of the World War as well as scores of historians thereafter lamented the German sabotage war of 1915.
German clandestine operations were reckless, to be sure, but also
were the direct result of the American government's decision to
profit from the European war. No matter the argument that the
United States had every right to trade with the Entente powers,
including military supplies, the United States did become a major, if
not the main source supplying the enemies of Germany as a result.
From a military strategy standpoint it should not have been a surprise, that the German government regarded the United States'
trade with England, France and Russia a threat to its war effort and
initiated activities to combat that threat. German government officials certainly could have, and in hindsight for the sake of American
public opinion should have, made the decision to interrupt American trade with the enemies of Germany on the high seas, not on
U.S. soil. However, those capabilities, mainly the German submarine force, had not reached a level where the impact would have
amounted to more than creating fear, increasing insurance premiums, and interrupting oceanic travel. The sheer amount of supplies
floating to British and French coasts were unstoppable in the fall of
1914 and spring of 1915.

Indeed, Albert, Dernburg, Boy-Ed, and von Papen's efforts
up to the end of 1914 had had virtually no impact on the war effort.
Berlin appreciated the efforts to send reservists, scare the Canadians, and supply the remnants of Germany's navy. Yet, the lack

of financial support for the Secret War Council in that time speaks volumes. In the first months of the war, when the Secret War Council could have made a large impact on the developing role of the U.S. in the war by buying up arms and munitions capacities, engaging in effective propaganda, and pushing the Wilson administration through political pressure, the German government left the agents stationed in the U.S. starved of funding. This lack of financial means, in part, resulted in the amateurish perception of German operations in the United States. There was no strategic plan underlying these disconnected efforts.

In response to the American policy towards Germany, the Foreign Office, Interior Ministry, the German General Staff of the Army, and the Admiralty, initiated a coordinated campaign in the spring of 1915 directed squarely at the United States of America. The strategic goal was the disruption of munitions exports to the Entente powers by any means. Orders to the effect went to the German officials in New York on January 24th, authorizing sabotage against factories and ships.[697] Germany announced unrestricted submarine warfare against commercial shipping on February 4th. March and April saw the arrival of proper funding of clandestine and public operations in the U.S., as well as the arrival of teams of sabotage agents.[698]

The Imperial Foreign Office had the thankless task of maintaining a diplomatic effort to keep the United States neutral as long as possible. This balancing act of mounting operations against the United States, retreating slightly, only to push the limits of American patience again, took into consideration the calculated risk of an eventual entry of the United States into the war on the side of the Entente. The challenge of American resolve never was a question of chance, or trial and error. Heinrich Albert wrote on May 10th 1915 to his superior, Interior Secretary Clemens von Delbrück,

> Imagine the extreme case that the United States would resort to rigorous measures, such as either declaring war on their own initiative or force us to declare war because of their extreme actions such as impounding all our ships in these harbors, what

would be the result? First, a huge relieve, because the government would use all its power to fill up stocks of munitions here, would therefore make the exportation of weapons and ammunition impossible because it would need the total domestic production or at least a majority of it. I certainly do not have to point out that militarily or from a naval perspective the United States would have any impact. The situation would be one of standing at attention, which we can calmly sit out, because everything the United States can do against Germany, it is practically already doing: Financing our enemies, arms and ammunition transports, compliance in all matters concerning England [...][699]

When the United States finally entered the war on the side of the Entente in the spring of 1917, the German government, including all her military and most of her political leaders, had decided that American neutrality had outlived its usefulness. Much has been made of the apparent resistance of Chancellor von Bethmann-Hollweg and Ambassador Count Bernstorff to a more aggressive demeanor against the United States. However, all archival sources in the decision-making process on the German actions against the United States clearly showed not only knowledge of, but an integral participation of the Foreign Office in the planning, financing, and execution of German operations in the U.S. The friction within the German government and the military leadership focused on how far to bend the bow. The definitions of risk and reward remained the undefined and hotly debated issues. War planners and politicians, hardliners, and accommodators disagreed about the point at which an American entry into the war had little or no impact on the German execution of its war strategy.

This secret war against the largest neutral power in the world proved to be disastrous. The American public, which voted for President Wilson in 1916 "because he kept us out of war," finally supported the U.S. to go to war in 1917.[700] This was the result of the actions of the Secret War Council to a large degree. Dozens of American factories had exploded, ships were fire-bombed, and workers in critical industries struck with secret German funding and agitation.

By the summer of 1916, the New York harbor lay in shambles, and virtually the entire regular U.S. army was busy settling German-caused troubles inside Mexico and along the Mexican-American border. The national security of the United States was under threat. Indeed, the country had briefly lost its ability to enter the European conflict on the side of the Entente. The hardliners' inability to sway Kaiser Wilhelm II and Chancellor von Bethmann-Hollweg to institute unrestricted submarine warfare in the summer of 1916 ended the last, albeit faint, chance to garner any positive result from the secret war against the United States.

In the end, the time-consuming submarine debate within the German government and Germany's miscalculation of American military and economic resolve would tip the balance on the stagnant fronts of Europe. The German Kaiser had loaded the *Maquina Loca*, a *crazy train*, with the awesome firepower of the entire Prussian war machine. He set it on its tracks, only to see it lose steam before it reached the enemy, roll back, and devastate the Fatherland. Another, smaller and lesser known *Maquina Loca* did the same in the United States. Loaded with the awesome financial and economic power of the entire nation, it steamed towards Europe. The last railcar broke lose, rolled back and left American factories in flames, the Mexican-American border unsettled, and workers on strike.

— The end —

ENDNOTES

1   NA RG 131 Alien Property Custodian, Entry 199, Box 28 file 654, Statement of Frederick A. Borgemeister. The flat was owned by HAPAG director William Sickels

2   *The Milwaukee Journal*, July 20, 1942, "The Man Who Revealed German Plan in First War Leaves Secret Service." Another version of the disappearance of Albert's briefcase exists by Emanuel Victor Voska, and Will Irwin, *Spy and Counter-Spy* (London: George G. Harrap and Co. Ltd., 1941), p. 90 ff; however, his version has not been acknowledged as accurate in most of the historiography.

3   Definition used for this purpose: The Secret War Council describes an empowered group of decision-makers who decide on important questions of strategy and tactics under the pressure of adverse conditions in a series of organized and documented meetings. NA RG 65 Albert Papers, Box 5, Memorandum of Carl Heynen, September 30, 1915. The actual term was coined by Carl Heynen, who referred to regular meetings at Heinrich Albert's office as "war council meetings." "[...] we will have to conduct a 'war council meeting' with B. [Albert] to discuss [...]"

4   Rodolfo Fierro, the Mexican revolutionary and Pancho Villa's henchman known for his murderous appetite, fitted out locomotives with dynamite, then ran them down the track at full speed into the defensive lines of his enemies. The resulting chaos and destruction received the name, *Maquina Loca*, crazy train.

5   *New York Herald*, June 28, 1914; also Johann Heinrich Count von Bernstorff, *My Three Years in America* (London: Skeffington and Son, unknown date, approximately 1920), p. 30.

6   Count Bernstorff, *My Three Years in America*, p. 30.

7   See Heribert von Feilitzsch, *In Plain Sight: Felix A. Sommerfeld, Spymaster in Mexico, 1908-1914* (Amissville: Henselstone Verlag LLC., 2012), chapter 23.

8   Ibid., chapter 19.

9   Immanuel Geiss, Ed., *July 1914: The Outbreak of the First World War: Selected Documents* (New York: Charles Scribner's and Sons, 1967), p. 10.

10   See Alfred Count von Schlieffen, "The Schlieffen Plan" (1905), printed in Gerhard Ritter, *Der Schlieffenplan: Kritik eines Mythos* (München: Verlag R. Oldenbourg, 1956).

11   See Paul Dehn and various editors, *The Truth about Germany: Facts about the War* (New York: The Trow Press, 1914), p. 19. This propaganda publication dated 1914 was issued in the United States to counteract British propaganda, in which the unknown authors claim that "nearly four million men had to be transported [...]"

12   Heinrich Albert, the Commercial Attaché, directed the German secret service in the U.S. but reported to the Department of Interior not War, as a result.

13   Michael L. Hadley, Roger Flynn Sarty, *Tin-Pots and Pirate Ships: Canadian Naval Forces and German Sea Raiders 1880 – 1918* (Montreal, Quebec: McGill-Queens University Press, 1991), p. 83.

14   Ulrich Cartarius ed., *Deutschland im Ersten Weltkrieg: Texte und Dokumente* (München: DTV, 1982), p. 57, Aufruf an die deutsche Industrie, nach August 1914.

15   Department of Commerce, Bureau of Foreign and Domestic Commerce, Miscellaneous Series, No. 57, *German Foreign Trade Organization* (Washington D.C.: Government Printing Office, 1917), p. 114.

16   http://www.history.com/this-day-in-history/walter-rathenau-of-aeg-takes-charge-of-german-war-production, viewed 12-1-2011; for a deeper discussion of the K.R.A. (*Kriegsrohstoffabteilung*) see Gerald D. Feldman, *Army, Industry, and Labor in Germany, 1914-1918*, (Providence: Berg Publishers Inc., 1992), pp. 45-52.

17   Ibid.

18   Reichsgesetzblatt 1914, p. 327, reprinted in Wolfdieter Bihl, Ed., *Deutsche Quellen zur Geschichte des Ersten Weltkrieges* (Darmstadt: Wissenschaftliche Buchgesellschaft, 1991), p. 52.

19   Gerd Hardach, *The First World War, 1914-1918* (Berkley and Los Angeles: University of California Press, 1977), p. 62.

20   See Hardach, *The First World War*, pp. 11-34, for a more exhaustive discussion of the efficiency of the sea blockade.

21   Frederic William Wile, *Men around the Kaiser: The Makers of Modern Germany* (Toronto: MacLean Publishing Company, 1913), p. 159.

22   Ibid.

23   Department of Commerce, *German Foreign Trade Organization*, p. 9.

24   Ibid., p. 8.

25   Wile, *Men around the Kaiser*, p. 12.

26   Ibid., p. 6.

27   Ibid., p. 13. The Commerce Department figures count 192 ships and 1.2 million tons.

28   Department of Commerce, *German Foreign Trade Organization*, p. 48.

29   Ibid., p. 49.

30   Ibid., p. 50.

31   The *Mauretania* held the speed record with 26.06 Knots from 1909 until 1929.

32   Count Bernstorff, *My Three Years in America*, p. 30.

33   http://www.history.navy.mil/photos/images/h43000/h43553.jpg,   viewed 10-2011. Technical data: Length: 950 feet (*Titanic* 882 feet, *Lusitania* 787 feet); Width: 100 feet (*Titanic* 92 feet, *Lusitania* 87 feet); Draught: 36 feet (*Titanic* 35 feet, *Lusitania* 34 feet); Gross Registered Tons: 54,282 (*Titanic* 46,328, *Lusitania* 31,550); Crew: 1,234 (*Titanic* 885, *Lusitania* 850); Passengers: 3,909 (*Titanic* 3,547, *Lusitania* 2,198); Engines: 4 Blohm and Voss Steam Turbines, 100,000 hp (*Titanic* 59,000 hp, *Lusitania* 76,000 hp); Max Speed 26.3 Knots (*Titanic* 23 Knots, *Lusitania* 26.7 Knots).

34   Count Bernstorff, *My Three Years in America*, p. 32.

35   Wile, *Men around the Kaiser*, p. 190.

36   There have been numerous conspiracy theories that the ambassador had been recalled after the assassination of Duke Ferdinand on June 28th. However, Count Bernstorff applied for his vacation weeks before. See, for example, NA RG 65 FBI Case Files, M1085, File 8000-174, Telegram from Count Bernstorff to Count Wedel, June 25, 1914, "Wäre dankbar, ob Urlaub bewilligt wird [...]"

37   Count Bernstorff, *My Three Years in America*, p. 30. No record of his actual travel on the *Vaterland* in July 1914 can be found. According to the Staatsarchiv Hamburg, the *Vaterland* left from New York on May 14, June 6, June 27, and July 22 1914. It is possible that Bernstorff sailed on a different ship and mentioned the HAPAG liner only to pay tribute to his late friend, Albert Ballin.

38   Reinhard R. Doerries, *Imperial Challenge: Ambassador Count Bernstorff and*

German-American Relations, 1908-1917 (Chapel Hill: University of North Carolina Press, 1989), p. 39. Many scholars have alleged that Bernstorff was 're-called,' which is not factual given his preoccupation with the Mexican situation as the only burning issue in June 1914.

39   *The Fatherland*, Volume II, Number 16 (May 26, 1915). Copyright expired.

40   Johann Heinrich Count von Bernstorff, *Memoirs of Count Bernstorff* (New York: Random House, 1936), p. 122, Bernstorff to von dem Busche, June 6, 1914.

41   Doerries, *Imperial Challenge*, p. 40. Refer to von Feilitzsch, *In Plain Sight*, chapter 16 for a short biography and analysis of Bernstorff's time as an ambassador before the war.

42   David Wayne Hirst, *German Propaganda in the United States, 1914-1917* (Evanston: Northwestern University PhD. Dissertation, 1962), p. 22.

43   Werner Schieffel, *Bernhard Dernburg 1865 - 1937: Kolonialpolitiker und Bankier im wilhelminischen Deutschland* (Zürich: Atlantis Verlag, 1974), p. 29.

44   Wile, *Men around the Kaiser*, p. 180.

45   Schieffel, *Bernhard Dernburg,* pp. 146-147.

46   NA RG 65 Papers of Dr. Heinrich F. Albert, Numbered Correspondence 1914 to 1917, Box 22, "III. Kapitel, die Geldbeschaffung."

47   As quoted in Schieffel, *Bernhard Dernburg*, p. 143.

48   It turns out that despite the legal possibility to keep and use the money in the U.S. while crediting the Red Cross in Germany, Dernburg sent an estimated $7 to $8 million of Red Cross proceeds to Germany between 1914 and 1916. See NA RG 65 Albert Papers, Box 22, Chapter III, page 5.

49   Schieffel, *Bernhard Dernburg*, p. 17. Also, The National Archives of the UK, Kew, Surrey, England, Board of Trade, Commercial and Statistical Department and successors, arriving Passenger Lists, Series BT26, part 397, article 35. Arrival of "His Excellency B. Dernburg in England, November 1, 1909."

50   Library of Congress, Prints and Photographs Division, LC-B2- 3458-4 [P&P], Bain collection, copyright expired.

51   NA RG 36 Passenger and Crew Lists of Vessels Arriving at New York, New York, 1914, T715, Roll 2364, page 47, line 20. Also NA RG 65 Albert Papers, Box 23, diary entry for August 26, 1914. The Allied Property Custodian determined on August 13, 1918 that Albert arrived on the SS *Oskar* on August 11, 1914, and listed visiting a "friend" Mr. Reisinger. Neither the diary nor the arriving vessel documentation

corroborates that claim. See NA RG 131 Alien Property Custodian, Entry 199 Box 38 File 907. An historical irony, *Oskar II* not only carried the most powerful German spymaster to the U.S. to command the German clandestine operations there, but it also became Henry Ford's peace expedition ship in 1915.

52   Baccalaureate in Germany is the so-called *Abitur*, which allows a graduating student to be admitted to college.

53   Johannes Reiling, *Deutschland: Safe for Democracy?* (Stuttgart: Franz Steiner Verlag, 1997), pp. 15-16. Reiling could not find any evidence of Albert having finished a PhD. However, he mistakenly argues that only Americans accorded him an academic title. His passport issued in Hamburg August 1914 read: "Bearer of this identification, Dr. Heinrich F. Albert goes as private secretary to the director of the Hamburg-America Line Mr. Ecker via Copenhagen to the United States of America." NA RG 65 Albert Papers, Box 23. It is not clear whether Albert did or did not earn the academic title.

54   *Geheimrat* is a title that was bestowed upon bureaucrats in the German and Austro-Hungarian empires before 1918. It has nothing to do with "secret" (literal translation), or even an allusion to secret agent as some writers have alleged. Rather, the word *geheim* can be translated to 'trusted,' in this case. The *Geheimrat*, therefore, has the meaning of trusted advisor to the court, a purely bureaucratic title.

55   Clemens Delbrück was a cousin of Hans Delbrück, the accomplished scholar. The Emperor accorded Clemens the status of Baron in 1916.

56   NA RG 65 Albert Papers, Box 23, Letter to Ida, January 17, 1916.

57   NA RG 65 Albert Papers Box 23.

58   Historian Barbara Tuchman, for example.

59   NA RG 85, Immigration and Naturalization Service, T715, Roll 2364, page 47, line 20.

60   NA RG 131 Records of the Alien Property Custodian, Entry 199, Box 48, file 1123, Statement of Karl Neumond.

61   NA RG 131 Alien Property Custodian, Entry 199 Box 38 file 907, Alien Property Custodian to Francis B. Garvan, October 6, 1918.

62   NA RG 65 Albert Papers, Box 23, diary entry August 29, 1914, for example.

63   NA RG 65 Albert Papers, Box 23, diary entry September 1, 1914, for example.

64   Ibid., diary entry September 18, 1914.

65   Count Bernstorff, *My Three Years in America*, p. 31.

66   John Price Jones, *The German Spy in America: The Secret Plotting of German Spies in the United States and the Inside Story of the Sinking of the Lusitania* (London: Hutchinson and Co., 1917), p. 205. Jones was reporter for the *New York Sun* newspaper during the war.

67   NA RG 65 Albert Papers, Box 22, personal expenses 1914 to 1917.

68   Library of Congress, Prints and Photographs Division Washington, D.C., LC-G432-1381, 1916, public domain.

69   NA RG 65 Albert Papers, Box 22, chapter 3.

70   Ibid., chapter 7.

71   Ibid., Box 18, chapter 5.

72   Ibid., Box 5, Ballin to Albert, 11-10-1914.

73   Ibid., Box 22, chapter 2.

74   Boy-Ed far outranked von Papen. Both are accorded the rank *Captain* in the English-speaking historiography, which led to serious mistakes especially with respect to determining for whom Felix Sommerfeld actually worked. Captain von Papen had the rank *Rittmeister* since he served in the *Husaren* or cavalry which is the army rank of Captain. Captain Boy-Ed had the military rank of *Korvettenkapitän*, which is the navy rank of *Commander* equivalent to the army rank of colonel. Hans Tauscher, who worked for von Papen in the war, was also an army Captain of the reserve, in German *Hauptmann der Reserve*; however, not *Rittmeister* because he earned his rank in the *Landwehr* (National Guard).

75   See for example, Barbara Tuchman, *The Zimmermann Telegram* (New York: Macmillan Company, 1958), p. 68; Frank J. Rafalko, Ed., *A Counterintelligence Reader*, Volume I, Chapter 3 "Post Civil War to World War I," www.fas.org/irp/ops/ci/docs/ci1, viewed 9-22-2011.

76   John Price Jones (1917) and Reinhard Doerries (1989) are two examples of historians who correctly traced the command and control to Albert.

77   NA RG 65 Albert Papers, Box 22, accounting of personal expenses 1914-1917.

78   NA RG 65 Albert Papers, Box 25, for example. *Abteilung IIIB* did not have responsibility for naval assets. Those reported via Karl Boy-Ed to the *Nachrichtenabteilung N* (Office of Naval Intelligence).

79   NA RG 65 Albert Papers, Box 24, Diary entry for August 10, 1914. It is unclear, but virtually certain, that Albert meant U.S. Dollars not Reichsmark.

80   Jones, *The German Spy in America*, p. 206, "upon him [Albert] has rested the task of spending between $2,000,000 and $3,000,000 a week [...]" for example.

81   NA RG 65, Albert Papers, Box 24, Deposits 1914; also NA RG 65, Albert Papers, Box 22, Chapter III, page 6.

82   NA RG 65 Albert Papers, Box 22, "Kapitel 3." The exchange rate between USD and Reichsmark was fixed at 4.18RM/USD before the war. As the war broke out, the fixed rate could no longer be supported by the German government. Albert seems to be quoting the variation from the fixed rate (100) as the "exchange rate."

83   NA RG 65 Albert Papers, Box 22, Draft of chapter 3.

84   Marine Crew Chronik, Marineschule Mürwik, Flensburg, Deutschland, MIM620/CREW, 1891, pp. 159-160, autobiographic article by Karl Boy-Ed.

85   Ibid.

86   Ibid.

87   Ibid. Paul von Hintze later served as imperial minister to Mexico and witnessed the coup d'etat against President Francisco Madero. In that time period von Hintze was Felix Sommerfeld's superior and directed the German naval intelligence organization in North America. When von Hintze went to China for his was assignment there, Boy-Ed took over the naval intelligence responsibilities for North America. Von Hintze briefly served as the Foreign Secretary at the end of the war.

88   Ibid. The short biography of Karl Boy-Ed also appeared in Heribert von Feilitzsch, *The Secret War on the United States in 1915: A Tale of Sabotage, Labor Unrest and Border Troubles* (Amissville: Henselstone Verlag LLC, 2015), pp. 6-10.

89   NA RG 76 Mixed Claims Commission, Box 12, Memorandum on the Activities of Franz von Papen, June 7, 1931.

90   Picture of unknown origin, approximately 1873, public domain.

91   Library of Congress Prints and Photographs Division Washington, D.C., public domain.

92   Library of Congress Prints and Photographs Division, LC-B2- 3707-5 [P&P]

93   Bundesarchiv für Militärgeschichte, Freiburg, RM 3, file 7934, War Financing.

Rintelen's rank is described as *Oberleutnant* (first Lieutenant), an army rank. He likely held the rank of *Oberleutnant zur See* (Lieutenant Commander), a navy rank.

94   *The New York Times Current History: The European War, Volume 17, October, November, December 1918* (New York: New York Times Company, 1919), p. 167; also BAMG, Freiburg, RM 3, file 7934, Rintelen to HAPAG, August 10, 1914.

95   NA RG 65 FBI Case Files, Old German Files, Roll 877, File 8000-925, Statement of Walter T. Scheele, 1918.

96   Kuhlenkampf had been in the U.S. for years. One of his business partners was Edmund Pavenstedt, the brother of the Amsinck director and business connection of Heinrich Albert. See *The Trow: Copartnership and Corporation Directory of the Boroughs of Manhattan and the Bronx,* (New York: Association of American Directory Publishers, March 1908), p. 764.

97   NA RG 65 Old German files, M1085, Roll 264, file 156.

98   *The Day* (London, Ct), November 23, 1915, "Boy-Ed Activity Alleged in Court."

99   *Hawera and Normanby Star*, January 18, 1916, "Boy-Ed the Spy."

100 NA RG 65 Old German files, M1085, Roll 264, file 156.

101 Ibid.

102 J. Castell Hopkins, editor, *The Canadian annual review of public affairs, 1915* (Toronto: The Annual Review Publishing Company, 1916), p. 455.

103 NA RG 65 Albert Papers, Box 7, Boy-Ed Accounts, Boy-Ed to HAPAG Generalbevollmächtigter, October 23, 1914.

104 Ibid.

105 Earl Evelyn Sperry, Willis Mason West, *German Plots and Intrigues in the United Stated during the Period of our Neutrality* (Washington D.C.: Committee on Public Information, July 1918), pp. 38-39.

106 NA RG 65 Albert Papers, Box 7, Boy-Ed Accounts

107 Ibid.

108 Ibid., Boy-Ed to Generalbevollmächtigter HAPAG, November 3 ($125,000), and on November 7 ($35,000) 1915.

109 *St. Petersburg Times*, May 25, 1940, "Former German Spy Chief Arrested in England."

110   Franz Rintelen von Kleist, *The Dark Invader: Wartime Reminiscences of a German Naval Intelligence Officer* (London: Lovat Dickson Limited, 1933), p. 88.

111   *The New York Times*, August 17, 1915, "Says German Spies Reveal Our Secrets." The article quotes an intercepted wireless in which Boy-Ed gives his address. Also Jones, *The German Spy in America*, p. 25. Jones gave Room 801 as Boy-Ed's address which could have been part of a suite.

112   NA RG 65 Albert Papers, Box 24, financials.

113   Ibid., Box 3, folder 10, Bernstorff to Albert and Dernburg, October 17, 1914.

114   Ibid., Box 23, Diary entry for August 26, 1914.

115   Ibid.

116   Ibid.

117   Ibid.

118   See, for example, the guest list in the *New York Times*, January 13, 1909, "Honor Karl Buenz." Also, *The New York Times*, October 30, 1912, "Karl Buenz gives a Dinner."

119   NA RG 65 Albert Papers, Box 23, Diary entry for August 26, 1914.

120   Ibid.

121   NA RG 131 Records of the Alien Property Custodian, Entry 199, Box 28, file 654, Statement of Frederick Borgemeister.

122   NA RG 65 Albert Papers, Box 23, Diary entry for August 26, 1914.

123   Ibid..

124   Ibid., Box 29, Miscellaneous images.

125   Ibid., Box 24, Diary entry for August 30 and 31, 1914.

126   Many books mentioning Albert accorded him the title of Commercial Attaché. He only received this position in August 1915 from the German ambassador to prevent his impending arrest for conspiracy.

127   NA RG 65 Albert Papers, Box 23, Albert to Lewald, December 6, 1915.

128   Ibid., Albert to Ida, August 24, 1915.

129   Count Bernstorff, *My Three Years in America*, pp. 90-92.

130   See Doerries, *Imperial Challenge*, pp. 175-176; Doerries discusses the likelihood that Count Bernstorff knew a lot of what was going as a result of his position. However, there is no evidence that Bernstorff actively authorized or participated in any sabotage conspiracies or even arms purchases. This information would have exposed the ambassador to immediate expulsion. Count Bernstorff's post war claims of ignorance are probably untrue, but his claims of non-involvement seem to be accurate.

131   NA RG 65 Albert Papers, Box 24, Diary entry for August 31, 1914.

132   Ibid., Diary entry for September 2, 1914.

133   Ibid., Diary entry for August 28, and August 30 1914, *"English White Book for Dernburg."*

134   Ibid., Diary entry for September 15, 1914.

135   Ibid., Box 22, Chapter III.

136   Ibid., page 6. Also NA RG 131, Alien Property Custodian, Entry 199, Box 28, file 654, Statement of Frederick A. Borgemeister. For exchange rate see Harold Marcuse, August 19, 2005, http://www.history.ucsb.edu/faculty/marcuse/projects/currency.htm viewed 10-11-2011; 4.23 German Reichsmark to 1 US Dollar in 1914. In today's value, a 1914 USD is worth 21.88 USD in 2011. See www.dollartimes.com viewed 04-2010.

137   NA RG 65 Albert Papers, Box 22, Chapter III, page 7.

138   Ibid., Box 6, Replay to official notice, document 73. Also, Schieffel, *Bernhard Dernburg*, p. 150. Schieffel quotes Dernburg claiming that, by 25 of November, the German Red Cross in New York had collected $576,000.

139   Schieffel, *Bernhard Dernburg*, p. 150.

140   NA RG 65 Albert Papers, Box 23, Albert diary, August 31, 1914. The fact that the German government, not private concerns, ordered the meat made the shipments liable for seizure by Britain.

141   *The New York Times*, August 16, 1914, "Armour's offer to France."

142   NA RG 65 Albert Papers, Box 23, Albert diary, September 1, 1914.

143   Ibid., September 25, 1914, *"T. yield half of his commission (2 ½%)."*

144   Ibid., Box 9, Chapter IV, page 2.

145   Ibid., Box 23, Albert diary, September 9, 1914, "Arrangement with HAPAG[...]"

146   Ibid., Box 8, list of Neumond shipments, undated (1916).

147   Ibid.

148   Ibid., Box 3, folder 16, Balance Sheets 1916, 1917.

149   Ibid., Balance Sheets 1916, 1917; NA RG 65. Albert Papers, Box 24, Balance Sheets 1915.

150   Ibid., Box 22, Chapter III.

151   Ibid., Box 23, Albert diary, September 10, and 15, 1914.

152   NA RG 65 Albert Papers, Box 24, Albert diary, September 22, 1914. Von Falkenhausen became a towering giant in German military and political history in later years. He served in the German army in Palestine and Turkey, and then taught at the Infantry School in Dresden. Von Falkenhausen became Chiang Kai-Shek's military advisor in the 1930s. He served as an infantry general on the western front during World War II. He was implicated in the attempt on Hitler in 1944, and spent the rest of the war in various concentration camps. He survived Hitler's wrath but had to serve three years for war crimes. He died in 1966.

153   Richard B. Spence, "K. A. Jahnke and the German Sabotage Campaign in the United States and Mexico, 1914-1918," *The Historian*, Volume 59, Issue 1 (September 1996), pp. 94-95.

154   Ibid., p. 94.

155   Ibid., p. 95.

156   Bundesarchiv für Militärgeschichte, Deutsche Dienststelle (WASt), Deutsche Verlustlisten 1914 bis 1917, Berlin, Deutschland, October 18, 1914.

157   NA RG 65 Albert Papers, Box 24, Albert diary, September 20, 1914.

158   Ibid., September 2, 1914.

159   Ibid., August 31, 1914.

160   Ibid., September 9, 1914.

161   Ibid., Box 23, Albert diary, September 20 to 23, 1914.

162 Ibid., Box 24, Albert diary, September 14, 1914, *"Train nothing special (Limited), no parlor car; saving $2."*

163 Ibid., September 22, 1914.

164 Ibid., September 28, 1914.

165 Ibid., September 25, 1914.

166 Ibid., September 3, 1914.

167 United States Senate, *Brewing and Liquor interests and German and Bolshevik Propaganda*, Report and Hearings of the Subcommittee on the Judiciary of the United States Senate, Government Printing Office 1919, p. 1372.

168 United States Senate, *Brewing and Liquor interests and German and Bolshevik Propaganda*, p. 1399.

169 NA RG 65 Albert Papers, Box 24, Albert diary, September 11-14, 1914.

170 Ibid.

171 Ibid., September 19, 1914.

172 Hirst, *German Propaganda in the United States, 1914-1917*, p. 67.

173 NA RG 65 FBI Case Files, File 8000-174, anonymous fall 1915.

174 NA RG 65, Albert Papers, Box 29, subject files.

175 Ibid., miscellaneous pictures.

176 Ray Stannard Baker, *Woodrow Wilson, Life and Letters: Neutrality 194 –1915*, Volume 5 (New York: Doubleday, Doran and Company, 1938), p. 195.

177 Graf Harry Kessler, *Walther Rathenau: His Life and Work* (New York: Harcourt, Brace and Company, 1930), pp. 171-176.

178 See Nicholas A. Lambert, *Planning Armageddon: British Economic Warfare and the First World War* (Cambridge: Harvard University Press, 2012).

179 Ibid., p. 211.

180 Ibid., pp. 210-211.

181 Ibid., 210.

182   Baker, *Woodrow Wilson, Life and Letters: Neutrality 194 –1915*, Volume 5, p. 152.

183   Ibid., p. 151.

184   James Brown Scott, editor, *The Declaration of London: A Collection of Official Papers and Documents relating to the International Naval Conference held in London December, 1908 to February, 1909* (New York: Oxford University Press, 1919), p. 27.

185   Scott, editor, *The Declaration of London*, p. 31.

186   Ibid.

187   Prize Court was an international body of judges that heard and decided upon cases of seizure. The court was established as a result of an international conference and agreement in The Hague in 1907. Great Britain did not ratify this agreement, either. See Scott, editor, *The Declaration of London*, p. 9.

188   It consisted of the armored cruisers *SMS Scharnhorst* and *SMS Gneisenau* and the light cruisers *Emden, Leipzig*, and *Nürnberg*. The *SMS Koenigsberg* patrolled the African coast and the Indian Ocean in East Africa. The cruisers, *Dresden* and *Karlsruhe*, raided English merchant shipping, soon aided by the *Leipzig* on Mexico's west coast in the Caribbean theatre. The *Dresden* continued on to the Pacific Ocean, while the *Karlsruhe*, under Captain Köhler, outfitted the German liner, *Kronprinz Wilhelm*, as an auxiliary cruiser. The two commercial steamers, *Kronprinz Wilhelm* and *Prinz Eitel Friedrich*, had been en route to the U.S. when the war started. The *Kronprinz Wilhelm* re-supplied in New York and snuck out of the harbor on August 3rd, provoking a storm of protest from England (*The New York Times*, August 18, 1914, "Many German Ships are for Sale here."). These two ships became feared raiders as auxiliary cruisers in the waters of South and Central America. Needing repairs and worn out from the continuous war duty, they both sought refuge in Newport News, Virginia in March and April of 1915. (*The New York Times*, March 11, 1915, "Sea Rover Prinz Eitel Friedrich takes refuge at Hampton Roads.") See http://www.worldwar1.co.uk.) for more detailed information on naval battles in World War I.

189   Reinhard Scheer, *Germany's High Sea Fleet in the World War* (London: Cassell and Company, 1920), pp. 34-35.

190   Scott, editor, *The Declaration of London*, p. 57.

191   *The New York Times*, August 3, 1914, "The Financial Situation in America and Europe."

192   Stanley Lebergott, *The Measurement and Behavior of Unemployment, Annual Estimates of Unemployment in the United States1900-1954* (Washinton, D.C.: National Bureau of Economic Research, 1957), p. 215.

193   NA RG 65 Albert Papers, Box 9, Chapter IV, p. 19.

194   Ibid. Albert wrote the 6-cent number, *The New York Times* on September 20th substantiates Albert's number. See *The New York Times*, September 20, 1914, "Costs South 700,000,000."

195   Woodrow Wilson, Message to Congress, 63rd Cong., 2d Sess., Senate Doc. No. 566 (Washington, 1914), pp. 3-4.

196   United States, Senate Hearings, 74th Cong, 2d Sess., "Munitions Industry Hearings," Part 25, January 7, 8, 1936, (Washington, 1937), pp. 7665-6.

197   Reiling, *Deutschland: Safe for Democracy?*, p. 92.

198   NA RG 65 Albert Papers, Box 22, Chapter 2, p. 22.

199   Ibid., Chapter IV, p. 6.

200   *The New York Times*, October 17, 1915, "Germans get Cotton Cargo."

201   *The New York Times*, October 20, 1915, "A Protest by Norway."

202   NA RG 65 Albert Papers, Box 22, Chapter IV, p. 6.

203   Count Bernstorff, *My Three Years in America*, p. 73.

204   Reiling, *Deutschland: Safe for Democracy?*, p. 416.

205   NA RG 65 Albert Papers, Box 29.

206   Ibid., Box 8, "food shipments."

207   NA RG 131 Alien Property Custodian, Entry 199, Box 48, file 1123.

208   NA RG 65 Albert Papers, Box 9, Chapter IV, p. 7. The 'Office' was Albert's Central Purchasing Agency.

209   Ibid., Box 23, diary entry September 28, 1914. *See also The New York Times*, June 20, 1915 as quoted in Reiling, *Deutschland: Safe for Democracy?*, p. 123, Germany received $825,000 for seized cotton.

210   *The World's Work*, Volume 30, Number 4 (August 1915), p. 444.

211   NA RG 65 Albert Papers, Box 9, Chapter IV, p. 20.

212   *The World's Work*, Volume 30, Number 4 (August 1915), p. 444.

213   Douglas T. Hamilton, *Shrapnel Shell Manufacture* (New York: The New Industrial Press, 1915), p.17.

214   Scott, *The Declaration of London,* p. 119.

215   *The New York Times*, August 3, 1914, "Say We Can Get Plenty of Ships."

216   *The New York Times*, August 19, 1914, "New Shipping Law Signed by Wilson."

217   NA RG 65 Albert Papers, Box 18, chapter V, p. 1.

218   Charles Ranlett Flint had important investments in rubber pantations in Mexico. Thus he played an important role in the development of railroads. Together with oil tycoon Henry Clay Pierce he had supported various revolutionary factions in Mexico, including the government of Francisco I. Madero, Pancho Villa, and Venustiano Carranza. Flint owned the US Rubber Corporation, American Chicle, American Woolen, and became the founder of the Computing-Tabulating-Recording Company that later turned into IBM.

219   *The New York Times*, August 17, 1914, "England Disturbed over Ship Sales."

220   NA RG 65 Albert Papers, Box 29, "Cotton Shipments."

221   NA RG 65 Albert Papers, Box 9, Chapter IV, p. 20.

222   Ibid., p. 21.

223   See von Feilitzsch, *In Plain Sight*, chapter 15.

224   NA RG 65 Albert Papers, Box 24, Amsinck Accounts.

225   NA RG 65 Albert Papers, Box 33, Tauscher to von Papen, Expenses 1914.

226   NA RG 65 Albert Papers, Box 23, Memorandum for Albert, June 15, 1915.

227   NA RG 65 Albert Papers, Box 9, Chapter IV, p. 1.

228   NA RG 65 Albert Papers, Box 23, Diary entry October 21, 1914.

229   NA RG 65 Albert Papers, Box 23, Diary entry September 19, 1914.

230   The HAPAG steamer *Ypiranga* from Germany to Veracruz had weapons for Huerta on board. It caused the American occupation of Veracruz in April 1914. See von Feilitzsch, *In Plain Sight*, chapter 20, "The Arms of the *Ypiranga*."

231   *The New York Times*, November 26, 1915, "Gans Company got Ships for Packers."

232 Reports of International Arbitral Awards, Volume VIII, United Nations, 2007, pp. 21-24, Gans Steamship Line (United States) v. Germany (31 August 1926).

233 NA RG 65 Albert Papers, Box 24, Diary entry October 2, 1914.

234 Simon operated the Southern Product Trading Company, another dummy firm under Albert's control. Simon and his company litigated the suit against Great Britain.

235 NA RG 65 Albert Papers, Box 30, accounts January 21, 1916.

236 Ibid.

237 *The New York Times*, October 17, 1915, "Germans get Cotton Cargo."

238 NA RG 65 Albert Papers, Box 30, accounts January 21, 1916.

239 United States Census, *Cotton Production and Distribution* (Washington D.C.: Government Printing Office, 1915), p. 19.

240 United States Department of Agriculture, *Monthly Crop Reporter, May 10, 1915* (Washington, D.C.: Government Printing Office, 1915), p. 49.

241 United States Department of Commerce, *Commerce Reports, Part 3, July, August, September, 1918* (Washington, D.C.: Government Printing Office, 1918), p. 762.

242 United States Senate, *Brewing and Liquor interests and German and Bolshevik Propaganda*, p. 2013.

243 NA RG 131 Alien Property Custodian, Entry 199, Box 28, file 654.

244 Reiling, *Deutschland: Safe for Democracy?*, p. 118.

245 NA RG 65 Albert Papers Box 21, Letter to Ida, July 21, 1915.

246 NA RG 65 Albert Papers, Box 23, Diary entry September 2, 1914. "With Polis and Ecker about report (11 O'clock) to R.A.D.I. [Reichsamt des Inneren]". These entries disappear later in his diary, which does not mean that he was no longer sending reports to Germany.

247 Ten million dollars for food and supply shipments, four million dollars for ships and transportation, two to three million dollars for insurance and legal expenses.

248 Franz von Papen, *Memoirs* (New York: E. P. Dutton and Company Inc., 1953), p. 33.

249 Thoms J. Tunney, *Throttled: The Detection of the German and Anarchist Bomb Plotters in the United States* (Boston: Small Maynard and Company, 1919), p. 127. Tunney estimated 80 ships in New York alone. The true number is far below that. A total of fifty-four ships sought refuge in all U.S. harbors on August 4. A good portion of those were the North German Lloyd liners moored in Baltimore. *The New York Times*, August 6, 1914, "Ships Dodge into Port," reported 23 ships to be moored in New York with another 30 expected in the following week.

250 *The New York Times*, November 23, 1915, "Accept ten Jurors in Ship Plot Case."

251 NA RG 45 M2089, Naval Records, Volume 1 through 16, Logbooks of unarmored cruiser *SMS Geier*.

252 NA RG 131 Alien Property Custodian, Entry 199, Box 131 file 3221. Also *The Ogden Standard*, October 16, 1914, "German Gunboat Geier Interned."

253 NA RG 65 Albert Papers, Box 7, Boy-Ed Accounts. Boy Ed lists expenses for the *Patagonia, Spreewald, Praesident, Stadt Schleswig*, all HAPAG supply ships for the German raiders in the Atlantic. See http://www.worldwar1.co.uk/karlsruhe.html detailing the rendezvous of the supply ships with the German armed cruiser, *SMS Karlsruhe*. Also, *The New York Times*, November 23, 1915, "Accept ten Jurors in Ship Plot Case," the article lists another supply ship, the *Berwind*. This ship was owned by the Gans Steamship Line. *The New York Times*, August 19, 1914, "British Protest to Cuba." The British government warned Cuba not to support the supply operation since the *SS Bavaria* and *SS Praesident* had supplied the *SMS Karlsruhe* from there multiple times. *See also, The New York Times*, August 16, 1914, "Cubans hear firing at Sea."

254 NA RG 65 Albert Papers, Box 7, Boy-Ed Accounts, November 7, 1914.

255 *Alexandria (Sacramento), Bangor, Bering, Berwind, Fanny Moll, Fram, Gladstone, Greacia, Guita, Heina, Lorenzo, Macedonia, Mahoney, Mazatlan (Jason/Edna), Mowinckle, Navarra, Nepos, Nordpol, Olsen, Patagonia, Praesident, Retriever, Somerstad, Spreewald, Stadt Schleswig, Thor,* and *Unita.* Sources are NA RG 65 Albert Papers, RG 131 Alien Property Custodian, Entry 199, Box 131 file 3221, Poverty Bay Herald, Volume XLII, Issue 13875, December 24, 1915, "Conspirators rode rough-shod over laws and treaties;" *The New York Times*, November 25, 1915, "Boy-Ed Managed Ship Plot Details;" Jones, *The German Spy in America*, pp. 120-129.

256 NA RG 131 Alien Property Custodian, Entry 199, Box 131, file 3221.

257 *The New York Times*, August 22, 1914, "German Ship Ready to Sail."

258 *The New York Times*, August 24, 1914, "Coals German Cruiser." Also *The New York Times*, August 23, 1914, "German Liner puts to Sea."

259   *The New York Times*, February 9, 1916, "Consul of Germany and his Aid Indicted." Also *The Spokane Daily Chronicle*, October 5, 1914, "Hold German Ship at San Francisco."

260   Marine Crew Chronik MIM620/CREW, Marineschule Mürwik, Flensburg, Deutschland, p. 45.

261   *The San Francisco Call and Post*, April 14, 1909, "Control Coffee Trade by Rebates." Also February 23, 1912, "The Smart Set." Also December 2, 1912, "Ferry Tales."

262   *The San Francisco Call and Post*, December 8, 1913, "Jebsen tells of Jail Experience."

263   *The San Francisco Call and Post*, August 22, 1913, "Ferry Tales."

264   *The San Francisco Call and Post*, May 30, 1913, "Ferry Tales."

265   *The San Francisco Call and Post*, October 6, 1913, "Rich S. F. Ship Owner in Mexican Jail."

266   *The San Francisco Call and Post*, October 7, 1913, "Germany's Fiat sets Jebsen Free."

267   *The San Francisco Call and Post*, December 8, 1913, "Jebsen tells of Jail Experience."

268   *The Los Angeles Herald*, May 29, 1908, "Freight Rates on Grain Products Cut to Orient."

269   *The San Francisco Call and Post*, October 6, 1913.

270   Marine Crew Chronik MIM620/CREW, Marineschule Mürwik, Flensburg, Deutschland, p. 45.

271   *The New York Times*, August 18, 1914, "The Leipzig Gets Coal."

272   Jamie Bisher, *World War I Intelligence in Latin America* (unpublished manuscript, 2008), p. 66.

273   *The Hartford Courant*, October 6, 1914, "How German Cruiser Leipzig Got Coal." Also, United Nations, *Reports of International Arbitral Awards, S. S. 'Edna.' Disposal of pecuniary claims arising out of the recent war (1914-1918)*, United States, Great Britain, Volume III (December 1934), pp. 1592-1596.

274   Friedrich Katz, *Secret War in Mexico: Europe, the United States, and the*

Mexican Revolution (Chicago: University of Chicago Press, 1981), p. 414. Also Bisher, *World War I Intelligence in Latin America*, p. 66. Katz cites no source for the white slavery story.

275 It originated in Katz's book and has floated through the Internet ever since.

276 NA RG 65 Old German files, M1085, roll 264, file 156.

277 NA RG 65 Albert Papers, Box 7, Boy-Ed accounting, November 7, 1914.

278 NA RG 65 Old German files, M1085, roll 264, file 156. The American prosecutor at Kuhlenkampf's trial traced a $135,000 payment to HAPAG in the beginning of the war for the purpose of buying a ship.

279 *The San Francisco Call and Post*, March 13, 1913, "Fire in Lumber Cargo Delays Big Freighter."

280 United Nations, *Reports of International Arbitral Awards, S. S. 'Edna.' Disposal of pecuniary claims arising out of the recent war (1914-1918)*, United States, Great Britain, Volume III (December 1934), p. 1592.

281 Ibid., p. 1594.

282 Ibid., p. 1595.

283 *The New York Times*, November 23, 1915, "Accept ten Jurors in Ship Plot Case."

284 *The New York Times*, September 16, 1918, "Karl Buenz dies in Atlanta Prison;" Also Count Bernstorff, *My Three Years in America*, p. 86.

285 Karl Boy-Ed, *Verschwörer?* (Berlin: Verlag August Scherl, 1920), p. 5.

286 *The New York Times*, August 1, 1914, "May Charter Ships to Carry Reserves."

287 *The New York Times*, August 4, 1914, "Reservists Throng to Answer Calls." "Die Wacht am Rhein" is a patriotic German anthem by Max Schneckenburger (1840).

288 Jones, *The German Spy in America*, p. 72.

289 Library of Congress, Prints and Photographs Division Washington, D.C., LC-B2- 3707-6, public domain.

290 *The New York Times*, April 19, 1914, "Von Papen's Aid Arrested."

291 NA RG 65 FBI Case Files, M1085, Roll 877, File 8000-229, Statement of Carl

Ruerode, Fulton County Jail, undated.

292 NA RG 65 Albert Papers, Box 10, Papen Memorandum, Berlin, November 23, 1916. Also, *The New York Times*, December 19, 1918, "Papen's Letters, seized by British, go to Senators."

293 Sperry, West, *German Plots and Intrigues in the United Stated during the Period of our Neutrality*, p. 36.

294 NA RG 65 Albert Papers, Box 46, Falmouth Papers, pp. 19-20.

295 United States Senate, *Brewing and Liquor interests and German and Bolshevik Propaganda*, p. 1690.

296 William H. Skaggs, *German Conspiracies in America*, (London: T. Fisher Unwin Ltd., approximately 1916), p. 49.

297 Jones, *The German Spy in America*, p. 76.

298 Skaggs, *German Conspiracies in America*, p. 50.

299 Jones, *The German Spy in America*, p. 74.

300 *The New York Times*, January 3, 1915, "Get 4 Reservists in Passport Plot."

301 Von Papen, *Memoirs*, p. 33.

302 NA RG 65 FBI Case Files, M1085, Roll 877, File 8000-229, Statement of Carl Ruerode, Fulton County Jail, undated. Urquidi's mother had children with Stallforth's uncle Friedrich. Juan Urquidi, therefore, was Stallforth's cousin.

303 NA RG 65 FBI Case Files, M1085, Roll 877, File 8000-229, Statement of Carl Ruerode, Fulton County Jail, undated.

304 NA RG 65 Albert Papers, Box 45, Falmouth Papers, p. 20, Checks #66 and #71.

305 *The New York Times*, January 3, 1915, "Get 4 Reservists in Passport Plot."

306 http://h-net.msu.edu, posted by Dr. Simon Fielding, September 24, 2008.

307 Sperry, West, *German Plots and Intrigues in the United Stated during the Period of our Neutrality*, pp. 35-36.

308 NA RG 65 Albert Papers, Box 45, Falmouth Papers, p. 20.

309 NA RG 65 FBI Case Files, M1085, Roll 877, File 8000-229, Statement of Carl Ruerode, Fulton County Jail, undated. Oelrichs and Company shipped artificial

fertilizer from the New Jersey Agricultural and Chemical Company owned by Walter T. Scheele to Germany via Sweden. The fertilizer, indeed, was lubricating oil that had been solidified to pass through the British blockade.

310   *The New York Times*, January 3, 1915, "Get 4 Reservists in Passport Plot."

311   *The New York Times*, March 9, 1915, "Passport Plotter to Serve Three Years."

312   NA RG 242 T141 Roll 19, von Papen to Auswärtiges Amt, July 30, 1914.

313   NA RG 242 T141, von Papen to Abteilung IIIb, No. 1610, March 31, 1914. Salary data is contained in NA RG 65 Albert Papers, Box 45, Selection from Papers found in the Possession of Captain von Papen, Falmouth, January 2 and 3, 1916, check No. 41, November 2, "W. von Igel (salary for October.)"

314   It is unclear from the archival sources when von Igel was hired. *The New York Times* mentioned in an article on von Igel's arrest that "the crime for which von Igel is under indictment was committed in the first two months of the war [...]" See *The New York Times*, April 19, 1916, "Von Papen's Aid Arrested."

315   Reiling, *Deutschland: Safe for Democracy?*, p. 127.

316   NA RG 242 T141 Roll 19, von Papen to Auswärtiges Amt, July 30, 1914.

317   Horst von der Goltz, *My Adventures as a German Secret Agent* (New York: Robert M. McBride and Company, 1917), p. 56.

318   Von Papen, *Memoirs*, p. 30.

319   NA RG 76 Mixed Claims Commission, Box 12, memorandum, June 7, 1932.

320   Tunney, *Throttled*, p. 20.

321   NA RG 76 Mixed Claims Commission, Box 10, immigration form, May 6, 1929. Also NA RG 65 Old German Files, Roll 264, file 119.

322   Jones, *German Spy in America*, pp. 95-96.

323   NA RG 131 Alien Property Custodian, Entry 199, Box 129, File 3199. The file lists him to have worked on the *Manchuria* in 1909. However, immigration records show him traveling to New York in November 1908. He listed his residence as San Francisco. See Staatsarchiv Hamburg, 373-7 I, VIII A 1 Vol. 205, page 1618. Also www.Ancestry.com, Passenger- and crew lists California, 1882-1957, Provo, UT, USA, June 30, 1907 SS *City of Para* from Arcon and Way Ports to San Francisco.

324   NA RG 36 Passenger and Crew Lists of Vessels Arriving at New York, New York, 1897-1957, T 715, Roll 1170, page 70.

325   NA RG 131 Alien Property Custodian, Entry 199, Box 129, File 3199. Also www.Ancestry.com, Passenger- and crew lists California, 1882-1957, Provo, UT, USA, August 14, 1910 *SS Radames* from Salina Cruz, *Nanaimo* via San Francisco to Seattle, WA.

326   U.S. Census 1930, Brooklyn, Kings, New York; Roll 1538; Page 9A; The census form showed that both of Martha's parents were Norwegian. The largest group of Thorstedts in North America is found around Quebec.

327   NA RG 65 Old German Files, M1085, Roll 264, file 119. Also NA RG 76 Mixed Claims Commission, Box 10, Certificate of Admission May 16, 1929 lists "Martha E. Koenig, wife." Also U.S. Census 1930, Brooklyn, Kings, New York; Roll 1538; Page 9A. See Tunney, *Throttled*, p. 18, for his moving date to New York.

328   NA RG 65 Old German files, M1085, roll 264, file 119, Statement of Frederick J. Metzler, undated. Koenig actually moved into that office on December 31, 1913, as evidenced by his P.O. Box application.

329   NA RG 131 Alien Property Custodian, Entry 199, Box 239, file 3199. Also, The Day, December 20, 1915, "Say Koenig had 25 German Agents Working in Big City."

330   U.S. Census 1930, Brooklyn, Kings, New York; Roll 1538; Page 9A.

331   NA RG 76 Mixed Claims Commission, Box 10, Martin to Peasley, March 23, 1934.

332   NA RG 36 Passenger and Crew Lists of Vessels Arriving at New York, New York, 1897-1957, T 715, Roll 1668, page 187; also NA RG 36 Passenger and Crew Lists of Vessels Arriving at New York, New York, 1897-1957, T 715, Roll 1170, page 70.

333   Tunney, *Throttled*, p. 10.

334   Koenig's jobs as auditor, superintendent of police, secret service chief, and finally statistician (on 1930 census) all point to his knack for collecting and correlating details, a prerequisite for a good intelligence analyst.

335   Jones, *German Spy in America*, p. 96.

336   *The New York Times*, December 22, 1915, "Metzler lays bare Koenig's activities."

337   Tunney, *Throttled*, p. 21.

338   Ibid., pp. 24-25.

339   Von Papen, *Memoirs*, p. 36.

340 Ibid.

341 Tunney, *Throttled*, pp. 10-11.

342 1910 Federal Population Census, T624, Roll 892, Page 2, Jersey City Ward 11, Hudson, New Jersey.

343 NA RG 65 Old German Files, M1085, Roll 264, file 119, Examination of Frederick J. Metzler.

344 NA RG 65 Old German Files, M1085, Roll, 264, file 119, Agent Adams to Department, December 18, 1915.

345 Historian Reiling mistakenly identified Wilkens as "Albert's personal servant," rather than a high-level Koenig agent. See Reiling, *Deutschland: Safe for Democracy?*, p. 248.

346 NA RG 65 Old German files, M1085, roll 264, file 119. Chief Bielaski to Warren, December 22, 1916. Also Assistant Attorney General to Secretary of State, December 23, 1915.

347 NA RG 65 Old German Files, M1085, Roll 264, file 119, Examination of Frederick J. Metzler.

348 Reinhard R. Doerries, *Diplomaten und Agenten: Nachrichtendienste in der Geschichte der deutsch-amerikanischen Beziehungen* (Heidelberg: Universitätsverlag C. Winter, 2001), p. 12. Doerries cites an agreement from May 1912 made between the German army and navy to share intelligence. Boy-Ed's reports that are shared with von Papen show that this cooperation seemed to work, at least as far as these two officials were concerned.

349 NA RG 65 Albert Papers, Box 19, Sommerfeld to Boy-Ed, November 11, 1914.

350 Ibid., Sommerfeld to Boy-Ed, November 11, 1914, Sommerfeld to Boy-Ed, November 29, 1914.

351 Ibid. Notice in the first letter that Sommerfeld wrote, "Herrn Kapitän K. Boy-Ed." He wrote, "Geehrter Herr Kapitän," clearly referring to the same person in the second.

352 NA RG 60, Department of Justice, file 9-16-12-5305, Statement F. A. Sommerfeld, June 21, 1918.

353 NA RG 76 Mixed Claims Commission, Box 9, Statement of Friedrich Hinsch. Hinsch testified that immediately after mooring the SS *Neckar* in September 1914 in Baltimore, he went to see Boy-Ed, presumably to receive instructions.

354 United States Senate, *Brewing and Liquor interests and German and Bolshevik Propaganda*, p. 1561.

355 NA RG 65 Albert Papers, Box 19, reports from Theodore Otto to von Papen.

356 NA RG 65 Albert Papers Box 23, reports from Otto Heins to Albert.

357 United States Senate, *Brewing and Liquor interests and German and Bolshevik Propaganda*, p. 1544.

358 Ibid.

359 NA RG 65 Albert Papers Box 23, reports from Otto Heins to Albert.

360 Von Papen, *Memoirs*, p. 37.

361 NA RG 65, Old German Files, M1085, Roll 264, file 119, Agent Adams to Department, April 21, 1916.

362 Ibid.

363 NA RG 65 Old German Files, M1085, Roll 264, file 119, Examination of Frederick J. Metzler.

364 *The New York Times*, December 25, 1915, "Schleindl in Court." Also, *Fort Wayne News*, December 18, 1915, "German Bank Clerk held for Conspiracy."

365 NA RG 65 Old German Files, M1085, Roll 264, file 119, Offley to Bielaski, February 5, 1916.

366 NA RG 65 Old German Files, M1085, Roll 264, file 119, Agent Adams to Department, April 24, 1916.

367 NA RG 65 Albert Papers, Box 19, von Papen to General Staff, undated; Von Papen quoted Count Bernstorff's telegram and added more details for his superiors. Also, Box 23, Diary of Heinrich Albert, entry for September 10, 1914.

368 Von Papen, *Memoirs*, p. 37.

369 NA RG 65 Albert Papers, Box 19, von Papen to General Staff, undated; von Papen quoted Count Bernstorff's telegram and added more details for his superiors.

370 NA RG 242 Captured German Documents, Roll 377, Document 735, Dernburg to Admiral Henning von Holtzendorff, May 10, 1915.

NA RG 65 Albert Papers, Box 3, Folder 10, Count Bernstorff to Dernburg and Albert, October 17, 1914.

372 NA RG 65 Albert Papers, Box 19, Prinz Hatzfeld to Albert, October 27, 1914.

373 NA RG 65 Albert Papers, Box 19, von Papen to von Falkenhayn, April 9, 1915, "The first proposal made by me[...]met very naturally with no consideration[...]"

374 NA RG 65 Albert Papers Box 8, "Massregeln zur Schädigung des Feindes." Quoted in Reiling, *Deutschland: Safe for Democracy?*, p. 125.

375 Von Papen, *Memoirs*, p. 36.

376 Ministry of National Defense, Commonwealth of Canada, Colonel G. W. L. Nicholson, C.D., Army Historical Section, Roger Duhamel, F.R.S.C.*The Official History of the Canadian Army: The Canadian E`xpeditionary Force, 1914-1919* (Ottawa: Queen's Printer and Controller of Stationary, 1962), p. 12.

377 Ibid., pp. 29-31.

378 "The Peopling of Canada: 1891-1921" (Calgary: The University of Calgary Applied Research Group, 1997). Also www.ancestry.de, 1911 Canadian Census data.

379 Alexandra Bailey, "German Internment During the First and Second World Wars," *Centre for Constitutional Studies*, University of Alberta, http://www.law.ualberta.ca/centres/ccs/issues/germaninternment.php, viewed 12-2011.

380 NA RG 76 Mixed Claims Commission, Box 12, Memorandum, June 7, 1938.

381 Reiling, *Deutschland: Safe for Democracy?* p. 156. Reiling devotes one paragraph to the Canadian missions, calls them "smaller actions," and concludes that the missions "failed miserably." Case in point for ignoring the effort stop the Canadian expeditionary force from deploying in Europe is Barbara Tuchman, *The Zimmermann Telegram*.

382 For example Reiling, *Deutschland: Safe for Democracy?* p. 156. Also Howard Blum, *Dark Invasion, 1915: Germany's Secret War and the Hunt for the First Terrorist Cell in America* (New York: HarperCollins Publishers, 2014), p. 83. The author of this popolar history, with very scant research and lot's of embellishments in the tradition of Tuchman, calls the von der Goltz mission to blow up the Wellland Canal "pathetic."

383 *The Frederick Post*, December 28, 1915, "Koenig Spy in Quebec Fall of 1914."

384 *The New York Times*, December 25, 1915, "Recalls Koenig in Quebec." *The Reading Eagle*, December 25, 1915, "Tracing his Movements," reported Koenig's associate's name as Siegfried Lundheim, which is mistaken. Canadian National

Archives document a S. H. Mundheim as an internee in Ontario in 1915.

385 *The Frederick Post*, December 28, 1915, "Koenig Spy in Quebec Fall of 1914."

386 *The New York Times*, December 25, 1915, "Recalls Koenig in Quebec."

387 Library and Archives Canada, Department of Militia and Defence, RG13-A-2, file 1915 959, "Internment of S. H. Mundheim, manager of the Cement Products Co." Also *The Frederick Post*, December 28, 1915, "Koenig Spy in Quebec Fall of 1914."

388 *The Frederick Post*, December 28, 1915, "Koenig Spy in Quebec Fall of 1914."

389 Ibid.

390 *Fort Wayne News*, December 23, 1915, "Paul Koenig Said to be Conspiracy's Brains."

391 *The New York Times*, April 28, 1916.

392 *The New York Times*, October 16, 1915, "Louden indicted on bigamy charge."

393 *The New York Times*, October 18, 1915, "Berlin now wants 'versatile' Count."

394 *The New York Times*, August 13, 1914, "Arrest Germans as Spies."

395 See copy of appointment letter in von der Goltz, *My Adventures as a German Secret Agent*, p. 153.

396 Wachendorf gave his name as Franz Hobart Wachendorf from Koblenz, Germany. However, the only record of his exists as Frank R. Wachendorf, enlisted at the 19th Infantry Regiment in 1912 as a private. See NA RG 94 Records of the Adjutant General's Office, M665, Roll 210. Also, NA RG 65 Old German Files, M1085, Roll 96, card for Horst von der Goltz. The FBI records show that Frank R. Wachendorf and Horst von der Goltz were the same person.

397 NA RG 163 Records of the Selective Service System, M1509, Roll 1786851, Registration 159. No record has been found on his birth. There are Wachendorf families in both countries.

398 Horst von der Goltz, *My Adventures as a German Secret Service Agent*, p. 111. Von der Goltz claimed to have come to the U.S. after he quit the German army in April 1912. However, he never was in the German army, which could still allow for him to have come to the U.S. in May 1912.

399 NA RG 94 Records of the Adjutant General's Office, M665, Roll 210, Condition of the Regiment on the last day of July 1912.

400 Ibid., Condition of the Regiment on the last day of April 1913.

401 Horst von der Goltz, *My Adventures as a German Secret Service Agent*, p. 115.

402 See picture of him next to Sommerfeld in his memoirs, page 43.

403 Von der Goltz, *My Adventures as a German Secret Agent*, p. 48.

404 Ibid., pp. 117 ff.

405 Ibid., p. 48.

406 See von Feilitzsch, *In Plain Sight*, chapter 7, "Apprenticeship in Spy Craft."

407 AA Mexiko II, Paket 5, Kueck to German Ambassador, August 10, 1914.

408 Von der Goltz, *My Adventures as a German Secret Agent*, p. 149.

409 Stallforth Papers, Interview Frank L. Polk with Frederico Stallforth, Washington D.C., March 15-16, 1916.

410 NA RG 131 Alien Property Custodian, Entry 199, Box 95, file 1955.

411 *The New York Times*, April 21, 1916, "Dynamite Plots bared in Detail by von der Goltz."

412 *The New York Times*, May 4, 1916, "Name editor Devoy in plot indictment."

413 NA RG 29 Federal Population Census 1910, T624, Brooklyn Ward 26, Kings, New York, Roll 979.

414 NA RG 65 Albert Papers Box 45, E. Gonzales to von Papen, October 19, 1914.

415 United States Senate, *Brewing and Liquor interests and German and Bolshevik Propaganda*, p. 1927.

416 *The New York Times*, April 21, 1916, "Dynamite Plots bared in Detail by von der Goltz."

417 *The New York Times*, June 17, 1915, "Seek Light on Meyer-Gerhard."

418 NA RG 36 Passenger and Crew Lists of Vessels Arriving at New York, 1897-1957, T715, Roll 2319, Page 15, May 19, 1914.

419 *The New York Times*, June 28, 1916, "Says von der Goltz made him join Plot."

420 Von der Goltz, *My Adventures as a German Secret Agent*, p. 161.

421 *The New York Times*, June 28, 1916, "Says von der Goltz made him join plot."

422 *The New York Times*, June 27, 1916, "Von der Goltz Bares Plot Against Canal."

423 Von der Goltz, *My Adventures as a German Secret Agent*, p. 167.

424 Miscellaneous No, 13 (1916), *Sworn Statement by Horst von der Goltz alias Bridgeman Taylor* (London: Harrison and Sons, 1916), p. 2.

425 NA RG 59 Records of the Department of State, M1490, Roll 222.

426 Ibid.

427 http://www.ancestry.de, *Rang- und Quartierliste der Königlich Preußischen Armee und des XIII Königlich Württembergischen Armee 1905*, p. 664.

428 NA RG 36 Records of the Immigration and Naturalization Service, T715, Roll 2360, page 20.

429 Doerries, *Imperial Challenge*, p. 336, note 238.

430 NA RG 65 Albert Papers, Box 45, Busse to von Papen, August 19, 1915.

431 Ibid., Busse to von Papen, August 2, 1915; It says "secret agent," in the heading of the letter besides Busse's name and address.

432 NA RG 65 Albert Papers, Box 45, Falmouth Papers, p. 22.

433 NA RG 65 FBI Case Files, M1085, Roll 163, file 5994, Memo to Chief of Bureau, undated.

434 NA RG 36 Records of the Immigration and Naturalization Service, T715, Roll 809, page 117; also, NA RG 36 Records of the Immigration and Naturalization Service, T715, Roll 2247, page 109.

435 Miscellaneous No, 13 (1916), *Sworn Statement by Horst von der Goltz alias Bridgeman Taylor*, p. 4. Also NA RG 65 FBI Case Files, M1085, Roll 163, file 5994.

436 Ibid.

437 *The New York Times*, April 21, 1916, "Dynamite Plots bared in Detail by von der Goltz."

438 Miscellaneous No, 13 (1916), *Sworn Statement by Horst von der Goltz alias Bridgeman Taylor*, p. 3.

439   A thorough search of the Records of the FBI shows amazingly little information on von der Goltz. No surveillance reports on him, either, in El Paso or New York exist for 1914.

440   NA RG 76 Mixed Claims Commission, Box 12, Memorandum on the Activities of Franz von Papen, June 7, 1931, p. 8.

441   NA RG 131 Alien Property Custodian, Entry 199 Box 95 file 1955.

442   Von der Goltz, My Adventures as a German Secret Agent, p. 181.

443   NA RG 131 Alien Property Custodian, Entry 199 Box 95 file 1955.

444   Ibid., Memorandum undated.

445   Von der Goltz, My Adventures as a German Secret Agent, 167.

446   NA RG 131 Alien Property Custodian, Entry 199, Box 95, file 1955, Memorandum undated.

447   The Fort Wayne News, December 22, 1915, "Another Man Arrested in Alleged Teuton Plot."

448   NA RG 76 Mixed Claims Commission, Box 12, Memorandum on the Activities of Franz von Papen, June 7, 1931, p. 8. Also, Miscellaneous No, 13 (1916), Sworn Statement by Horst von der Goltz alias Bridgeman Taylor, p. 4.

449   Nigel West, Historical Dictionary of Sexspionage (Plymouth: Scarecrow Press Inc., 2009), pp. 75-76.

450   NA RG 65 Albert Papers, Box 24, Diary entry October 25, 1914.

451   Von Papen, Memoirs, p. 56.

452   The New York Times, June 28, 1916, "Says von der Goltz made him Join Plot."

453   The New York Times, June 28, 1916, "Says von der Goltz made him Join Plot."

454   The New York Times, June 28, 1916, "Says von der Goltz made him Join Plot."

455   The Buffalo New York Morning Express, April 22, 1916, "John T. Ryan not Saying Anything."

456   NA RG 131 Alien Property Custodian, Entry 199, Box 95, file 1955.

457   The Buffalo New York Morning Express, April 22, 1916, "John T. Ryan not Saying

Anything."

458 The New York Times, May 4, 1916, "Name editor Devoy in plot indictment."

459 The New York Times, June 28, 1916, "Says von der Goltz made him join plot."

460 NA RG 131 Alien Property Custodian, Entry 199, Box 95, file 1955.

461 Ibid.

462 Ibid.

463 NA RG 65 Albert Papers, Box 45, Falmouth Papers, p. 19, Check No. 37, October 14, 1914, "for Fritzen and Busse, Buffalo." Historians have taken von Papen's financial support of $40 to the two stranded agents in Buffalo in October 1914 as evidence that the two agents were left on their own. However, Paul Koenig's accounting shows A. Fritzen working for him as late as March 28, 1916. Busse wrote a letter to von Papen headed "secret agent" on August 2, 1915. See NA RG 65 Albert Papers, Box 45, F. J. Busse to von Papen, August 2, 1915. Busse also received "compensation" from Paul Koenig on July 16, 1915. See NA RG 65 Albert Papers, Box 13, Koenig accounting; also, Sperry, West, German Plots and Intrigues in the United Stated during the Period of our Neutrality, p. 29.

464 Grant W. Grams, Journal of Military and Strategic Studies, Vol. 8, Issue 1 (Fall 2005), p. 2. "Karl Respa and German Espionage in Canada during World War One,"

465 Miscellaneous No, 13 (1916), Sworn Statement by Horst von der Goltz alias Bridgeman Taylor, p. 3.

466 Von der Goltz, My Adventures as a German Secret Agent, p. 168.

467 NA RG 131 Alien Property Custodian, Entry 199, Box 95, file 1955.

468 Miscellaneous No, 13 (1916), Sworn Statement by Horst von der Goltz alias Bridgeman Taylor, p. 4.

469 Brian Lee Massey, "A Brief History of the Canadian Expeditionary Force," http://www.rootsweb.ancestry.com/~ww1can/cef14_15.htm, 1997 - 2007.

470 Hermann Bauer, Als Führer der U-Boote im Weltkriege (Leipzig: Koehler and Amelang, 1941), p. 100.

471 NA RG 65 Albert Papers, Box 10, Memorandum, Berlin, November 3, 1916.

472 Reiling, Deutschland: Safe for Democracy?, p. 157.

473 NA RG 36 Records of the Immigration and Naturalization Service, T715, Roll

2459, p. 42.

474 Ibid., p. 34.

475 Reiling, *Deutschland: Safe for Democracy?*, p. 157.

476 Miscellaneous No, 13 (1916), *Sworn Statement by Horst von der Goltz alias Bridgeman Taylor*, p. 4.

477 Horst von der Goltz, *My Adventures as a German Secret Agent*, p. 168.

478 Ibid., p. 190.

479 NA RG 65 Albert Papers, Box 45, Falmouth Papers, p. 17. Some historians have taken the notations as made by von Papen, and concluded that the quoted explanation of von der Goltz was proof that Germany sent him to England as a spy. The opposite is true.

480 NA RG 65 Albert Papers, Box 13, Folder 69. Tucker re-appeared in Koenig's accounting on in May and June 1916, referring to the cipher name "Dikcal," which the American investigators traced to "Tucker."

481 NA RG 65 Albert Papers, Box 45, E. Gonzales [sic] to von Papen, October 19, 1914.

482 Ibid.

483 Von Papen, *Memoirs*, p. 34.

484 Sperry, West, *German Plots and Intrigues in the United States during the Period of our Neutrality*, p. 25. Zimmermann to Count Bernstorff, mistakenly described as January 3, 1916.

485 United Nations, *Reports of International Arbitral Awards*, "S. S. 'Edna'," p. 260.

486 NA RG 131 Allied Property Custodian, Entry 199, Box 129, File 3209.

487 Ibid.

488 NA RG 85 Passenger Lists of Vessels Arriving at New Orleans, Louisiana, 1910-1945, T905, Roll 53.

489 NA RG 65 FBI Case Files, M1085, Roll 877, File 8000-229, Agent Tucker to Department, February 4, 1915.

490 NA RG 65 FBI Case Files, M1085, Roll 877, File 8000-229, Memo to Frank Burke, August 1, 1919.

491 Ibid.

492 NA RG 65 FBI Case Files, M1085, Roll 877, File 8000-229, Bielaski to Attorney General, Interview with Werner Horn, February 13, 1915.

493 Ibid. Virtually all historical accounts of the Horn mission report him having carried dynamite to Vanceboro. However, Horn clearly testified that his suitcase contained sixty small vials of nitroglycerin, describing their diameter and the fact that they were made of glass. If Koenig sent him on his way with nitroglycerin using multiple passenger trains, Horn's mission was indeed a huge threat to public safety, even if he only ended up damaging the bridge.

494 NA RG 65 Albert Papers, Box 45, papers taken from Franz von Papen at Falmouth, check stub 87, January 19, 1915.

495 Tunney, *Throttled*, p. 32.

496 NA RG 65 FBI Case Files, M1085, Roll 877, File 8000-229, Statement of Aubrey Take, undated.

497 NA RG 131 Allied Property Custodian, Entry 199, Box 129, File 3209.

498 Ibid.

499 NA RG 65 FBI Case Files, M1085, Roll 877, File 8000-229, Bielaski to Attorney General, January 1918. Horn was finally extradited to Canada in 1918 where he served another sentence.

500 As quoted in Erhard Geissler, *Biologische Waffen – Nicht in Hitlers Arsenalen: Biologische and Toxin-Kampfmittel von 1915 bis 1945* (Münster: LIT Verlag, 1999), p. 91.

501 NA RG 131 Alien Property Custodian, Entry 199, File 3221, Boy-Ed Accounts.

502   http://www.irishbrigade.eu/other-men/germans/boehm/boehm.html, viewed February 2013. This site contains the most complete biography of this German agent.

503 University College Dublin, Ireland, Boehm/Casement Papers.

504   http://www.irishbrigade.eu/other-men/germans/boehm/boehm.html, viewed February 2013.

505 Vanceborohs.tripod.com/id52.htm, viewed 1-24-2013, public domain.

506 NA RG 65 Albert Papers, Box 45, Von Papen checkbook stub 110.

507   NA RG 65 FBI Case Files, M1085, File 8000-174, Telegram from von Reiswitz to von Papen May 3, 1915 acknowledging receipt of $24,400.

508   Grams, "Karl Respa and German Espionage in Canada during World War One," p. 10.

509   NA RG 65 Albert Papers, Box 45, von Papen checkbook stub 92.

510   NA RG 76 Mixed Claims Commission, Box 12, Memorandum on Activities of Franz von Papen, June 7, 1932.

511   Stallforth Papers, Interview Frank L. Polk with Frederico Stallforth, Washington D.C., March 15-16, 1916. Stallforth deducted $30 to $35, according to his statement to the Bureau of Investigations in 1917.

512   NA RG 76 Mixed Claims Commission, Box 14, Frederico Stallforth file, October 10, 1936.

513   Stallforth Papers, Interview Frank L. Polk with Frederico Stallforth, Washington D.C., March 15-16, 1916.

514   NA RG 76 Mixed Claims Commission, Box 12, Memorandum on the Activities of Franz von Papen, June 7, 1932.

515   NA RG 65 Albert Papers, Box 45, Falmouth Papers.

516   NA RG 165 Military Intelligence, 9140-878, Statement of Frederico Stallforth, February 23, 1918.

517   NA RG 65 FBI Case Files, M1085, File 8000-3089, Statement of Melville S. Forrester.

518   NA RG 165 Military Intelligence, 9140-878, Statement of Frederico Stallforth, February 23, 1918.

519   NA RG 65 Albert Papers, Box 24, Diary 1914 to 1915. Albert kept two diaries. One of them listed him leaving for Chicago on the 3rd at 2pm; the other, giving the lecture in the evening on the 3rd. He might have mistaken the day or the transcriber made a mistake and the lecture indeed occurred on the 2nd in the evening.

520   Stallforth Papers, Financials for Stallforth Inc., 1921.

521   The New York Times, April 7, 1917, "7 German Plotters are sent to Prison," Fritzen received a 18 month prison term.

522   Horace Cornelius Peterson, Propaganda for War: The Campaign against American Neutrality, 1914-1917 (Norman: University of Oklahoma Press, 1939),

p. 137.

523   Karl Boy-Ed, *Verschwoerer?*, p. 26.

524   NA RG 60 Department of Justice, File 9-16-12-5305, Statement F. A. Sommerfeld, June 24, 1918.

525   NA RD 65 Albert Papers, Box 23, Diary entry for September 18, 1914. The timing matches the assumption of September 16 as the day of the original meeting. Dernburg, Albert, and the HAPAG managers met on September 18, "about the unification of the Press Bureau." Sommerfeld is not listed as a participant, but does not preclude the possibility that he attended, given he was a secret agent.

526   NA RG 60 Department of Justice, File 9-16-12-5305, Statement F. A. Sommerfeld, June 24, 1918.

527   See von Feilitzsch, *In Plain Sight,* chapter 12.

528   Ibid., chapter 23.

529   To be clear, the author formulated these rules after a thorough analysis of Sommerfeld's publicity campaigns for Madero, Carranza, and Villa.

530   *The New York Times*, August 5, 1914, "Multitudes Cheer at Bulletin Boards."

531   *The New York Times*, August 5, 1914, "New York Press Reviews."

532   Ibid.

533   Ibid.

534   Ibid.

535   *The New York Times*, August 10, 1914, "Consuls in Touch with Bryan Again."

536   See, for example, *The London Times*, August 9, 1914, "Legion of Honour for Liege."

537   *The Worlds Work*, Volume 30, Number 2 (June 1915), (New York: Doubleday, Page and Co.), "The March of Events," p. 134.

538   Frederick C. Luebke, *Bonds of Loyalty: German Americans and World War I* (DeKalb: Northern Illinois University Press, 1974), preface.

539   Carl Wittke, *The German-Language Press in America* (Louisville: University of Kentucky Press, 1957), p. 235.

540 Doerries, *Imperial Challenge*, p. 68.

541 *The New York Times*, August 9, 1914, "German Envoy Tells of British Demands."

542 *The New York Times*, August 10, 1914, "German Envoy's Plans." Also *The New York Times*, August 17, 1914, "German Embassy in Dark."

543 *The New York Times*, September 25, 1914, "A Barbarous Land; This to Mr. Charles." The other members were Herman A. Metz, Edwin R. A. Seligman, and Hugo Cillis.

544 *The New York Times*, September 29, 1914, "Hugo Reisinger Dies in Germany."

545 *The New York Times*, June 18, 1910, "Says America was named by a German."

546 Heinrich Charles, *The Electro-Individualistic Manifesto: The Anti-Thesis of the Communistic Manifesto by Karl Marx and Friedrich Engels, and the Synthesis of Social-Individualism* (, New York: published by the author, 1913).

547 *The New York Times*, September 25, 1914, "A barbarous land – this to Mr. Charles." The original quote is in *The New York Times*, June 18, 1910, "Says America was named by a German."

548 *The New York Times*, August 16, 1914, "Aid to the Kaiser Reviews the War."

549 *Ibid.*

550 *Ibid.*

551 *The New York Times*, August 22, 1914, "Accuse the British of Double Dealing."

552 NA RG 65 Albert Papers, Box 20, Fatherland financials. Also ibid., Box 23, Diary entry for September 16.

553 See *Gedichte*, 1904, *A Game at Love, and Other Plays*, 1906, *Niniveh, and Other Poems*, 1907, *The House of the Vampire*, 1907, *Confessions of a Barbarian*, 1910, *The Candle and the Flame*, 1912.

554 Phyllis Keller, *The Journal of Interdisciplinary History*, Vol. 2, No. 1 (Summer 1971), "George Sylvester Viereck: The Psychology of a German-American Militant."

555 *The Fatherland*, Volume 1, Number 1 (August 10, 1914), "Wilhelm II., Prince of Peace."

556 *The New York Times*, August 8, 1914, "Germany, Says the Kaiser, Will Fight to the End."

557 *The Fatherland*, Volume 1, Number 1 (August 10, 1914), "The Germanophobe

Press."

558 *The New York Times*, August 6, 1914, "Germany's Motive."

559 *The Fatherland*, Volume 1, Number 1 (August 10, 1914), "Fair Play."

560 *The New York Times*, August 8, 1914, "Crime is Russia's, Dr. Bonn Asserts."

561 Isaac Strauss and Arthur Meyrowitz arrived on September 8th 1914 on the *SS Rotterdam*. Both were agents of the Reichsmarineamt (Imperial Navy). See Doerries, *Imperial Challenge*, p. 62.

562 NA RG 65 Albert Papers, Box 5, Propaganda account "von Papen III."

563 *The Fatherland*, Volume 1, Number 2 (August 17, 1914), "Where the Crowd Stands."

564 *The New York Times*, August 24, 1914, "Full Text of the German 'White Paper' on the War."

565 *The New York Times*, August 23, 1914, "Complete Correspondence that Led up to England's Declaration of War Against Germany."

566 *The New York Times*, August 23, 1914, "Justice on German Side, Says Prof. Kuno Francke."

567 *The New York Times*, August 24, 1914, "Germany Presents her Case."

568 *The New York Times*, August 23, 1914, "Germany Warns World Against Falsehoods."

569 *The New York Tribune*, August 31, 1914, "Germans Sack Louvain; Women and Children Shot."

570 *The Fatherland*, Volume 1, Number 3 (August 31, 1914), "Secret of the American Attitude to Germany."

571 NA RG 65 Albert Papers, Box 24, Diary entry for August 27, 1914.

572 Karl Boy-Ed, *Verschwoerer?* p. 34.

573 NA RG 65 Albert Papers, Box 24, Diary entry for September 2, 1914.

574 Karl Boy-Ed, *Verschwoerer?* p. 35.

575 NA RG 65 Albert Papers, Box 24, Diary entry September 14, 1914.

576　*The New York Times Current History: The European War*, Volume 1, Number 2 (New York: The New York Times Company, 1915). Official Dispatch from Berlin to German Embassy at Washington, August 29, 1914.

577　NA RG 65 Albert Papers, Box 23, Diary entry, September 16, 1914. "Transaction with Fatherland group."

578　NA RG 65 Albert Papers, Box 23, Diary entry, September 18, 1914.

579　NA RG 65 Albert Papers, Box 5, Folder 20, Albert to Dernburg, November 25, 1915.

580　Ron Van Dopperen, Cooper C. Graham, *Shooting the Great War: Albert Dawson and the American Correspondent Film Company, 1914-1918* (Charleston: CreateSpace, 2013), p. 31.

581　These articles are collected in Dernburg's publication *Search-Lights on the War* (New York: Fatherland Press, 1915).

582　Dernburg, *Search-Lights on the War*, p. 6, "I do not say that Germany's civilization is superior to that of England and France;
it certainly is superior to the civilization of any of the other warring nations."

583　Ibid., p. 7.

584　Ibid., p. 46.

585　*The New York Times*, September 20, 1914. "The German Constitution."

586　*The Los Angeles Examiner*, September 23, 1914, "'British Greed Would Drag U.S. Into War,' German View."

587　Dernburg, *Search-Lights on the War*, pp. 53 ff.

588　*The American Review of Reviews*, Volume L (November 1914), (New York: Review of Review Companies, 1914), pp. 64 ff.

589　*The New York Times*, September 20, 1914, "Another Defense of Germany."

590　Count Bernstorff, *My Three Years in America*, p. 35.

591　See, for example, *The New York Times*, September 1, 1914, "Ambassador Happy Over German News."

592　NA RG 65 Albert Papers, Box 5, Gierkowski to Tauscher, August 28, 1914.

593　NA RG 65 Albert Papers, Bernstorff to Boy-Ed, December 18, 1914; "[...] that

I now, since the situation has changed, have no more objections to you writing letters to the American Press, as long as you concentrate of naval issues."

594 See, for example, NA RG 65 Albert Papers, Box 32, Boy-Ed to Miles, September 16, 1914; also Boy-Ed to Melville Stone (General Manager of AP News), September 25, 1914.

595 NA RG 65 Albert Papers, Box 32, Boy-Ed to AP editor Klaessig, August 28, 1914; also Boy-Ed to Editor of *Luck*, October 17, 1914; also, Boy-Ed to the Editor of the *New York Times*, November 27, 1914; also, Boy-Ed to the Editor of the *New York Herald*, December 18, 1914;

596 NA RG 65 Albert Papers, Box 32, undated letter. All underlined sections as in original.

597 See Unites States Senate, *Brewing and Liquor Interests and German Propaganda*, Subcommittee of the Committee of the Judiciary, Volume 2 (Washington D.C.: Government Printing Office, 1919), pp. 1410-11. Also, footnote in H.C. Peterson, *Propaganda for War*, p. 137; *The War Plotters of Wall Street, Thou Shalt Not Kill, The Truth About Germany, Germany's Just Cause, Germany's Hour of Destiny, The Catechism of Balaam Jr.* are just some examples quoted in George Sylvester Viereck, *Spreading Germs of Hate* (London: Duckworth, 1931), p. 82 ff.

598 There were dozens of additional authors writing on behalf of Germany. See George William Hau, *War Echoes or Germany and Austria in the Crisis* (Chicago: Morton M. Malone, 1915), p. 3, "List of Representative Articles with the Names of the Authors." Hau's collection feature 20 authors (other than the ones mentioned above) as contributors to his collection. The most complete analysis of the German propaganda in the United States in WW I is contained in David Hirst, *German Propaganda in the United States, 1914-1917*.

599 *The New York Times*, August 22, 1914, "Work to Aid German Trade."

600 *The Truth about Germany: Facts about the War*, September 20, 1914.

601 Hugo Muensterberg, *The War and America* (New York: D. Appleton and Co., 1914).

602 Edmund von Mach, *What Germany Wants* (Boston: Little, Brown and Company, 1914).

603 NA RG 65 Albert Papers, Box 23, Diary entry September 16, 1914.

604 NA RG 65 Albert Papers, Box 23, Diary entry September 23, 1914.

605 He is first mentioned as part of the Press Bureau team on September 25th. See NA RG 65 Albert Papers, Box 23, Diary entry September 25, 1914.

606 Count Bernstorff, *My Three Years in America*, p. 41.

607 Hirst, *German Propaganda in the United States, 1914 – 1917*, p. 25.

608 Van Dopperen, Graham, *Shooting the Great War*, p. 38.

609 As quoted in Hirst, *German Propaganda in the United States, 1914 – 1917*, p. 26.

610 NA RG 76 Mixed Claims Commission, Box 13, William M. Offley to Department, June 29, 1915.

611 NA RG 65 Albert Papers, Box 3, Folder 10, Count Bernstorff to Dernburg and Albert, October 17, 1914. Bernstorff suggests in this letter that he "sent one of the best American journalists Hill, who had been laid off by the *Tribune* for money reasons, to privy counselor Albert, since Hill want to help us." The possibility that Hale and Hill are the same has been considered but discarded, since Bernstorff certainly knew Hale and would not have misspelled his name. Hale also never worked for the *Tribune* and had already met with Dernburg and Albert on October 2.

612 *The New York Times*, October 6, 1909, "Dr. Wm. Bayard Hale Weds."

613 Arthur S. Link, *Wilson: The New Freedom* (New Jersey: Princeton University Press, 1956), p. 356.

614 NA RG 65 Albert Papers, Box 23, Diary entry for October 2, 1914.

615 William Bayard Hale, *Germany's Just Cause* (New York: The Fatherland Press, 1914).

616 William J. Weston, *Presbyterian Pluralism: Competition in a Protestant House* (Knoxville: University of Tennessee Press, 1997), p .99.

617 United States Senate, *Brewing and Liquor interests and German and Bolshevik Propaganda*, p. 2783.

618 See for example William Bayard Hale, *The Case Against Armed Merchantmen* (New York: unknown publisher, timely reprints from the New York Press, 1914), pp. 6-9, "The Real Issue in Washington."

619 Unites States Senate, *Brewing and Liquor Interests and German Propaganda, Subcommittee of the Committee of the Judiciary*, pp. 1391-1392.

620 Count Bernstorff, *My Three Years in America*, p. 42.

621 *The World's Work*, Volume 28 (May to October 1914), (New York: Doubleday,

Page and Co., May 1914), p. 9.

622 *The World's Work*, Vol. 30 (New York 1915), (New York: Doubleday, Page and Co., 1915), p. 135.

623 Peterson, *Propaganda for War*, p. 137.

624 Literally translated, it means to know better. However, it is not only to know better; *Besserwisserei* is to show off one's *Allgemeinbildung* (*common knowledge*) and arrogantly, without *allowing* a contrary argument, insist upon the acceptance of one's *educated* opinion. This trait is especially pronounced in intellectual circles, that are generally accepted as people who *know better*. This authoritarian urge to preach is foreign to a society based on individualism and equality.

625 *The Christian Science Monitor*, September 4, 1914, "Protection of Cotton Sought." Also September 12, 1914, "Cotton Industry Leader Urges The Need Of Action."

626 One of the most thorough treatments of the English propaganda in the U.S. is Peterson, *Propaganda for War*.

627 Walter Nicolai, *The German Secret Service*, translated with an additional chapter by George Renwick (London: Stanley Paul and Co., 1924), pp. 9-10.

628 NA RG 65 Albert Papers, Box 5, Private Correspondence, undated letter (estimated November or December 1914).

629 *The New York Times*, April 24, 1903, "The United Service;" also, *American Machinist*, Volume 29 (New York 1906), p. 170.

630 NA RG 65 FBI Case File, M1085, File 8000-174, von Papen to War Department, Military Report March 30, 1915. Tauscher vouched completely for Hoadley.

631 NA RG 65 Albert Papers, Box 5, Statement of George W. Hoadley, October 30, 1918.

632 NA RG 65 Albert Papers, Box 23, Diary entry, September 10, 1914.

633 NA RG 65 Albert Papers, Box 19, Sommerfeld to Boy-Ed, November 11, 1914 and November 19, 1914. Both of these intelligence reports show that Boy-Ed copied von Papen. Von Papen reports the information on munitions contracts and U.S. firms mentioned in Sommerfeld's reports to the War Department in his military reports; see, for example, the one dated February 11, 1915. See NA RG 65 Albert Papers, Box 19, von Papen to General Staff, February 11, 1915.

634 NA RG 65 Albert Papers, Box 19, Albert to Imperial office of the Interior, September 10, 1914.

635 NA RG 65 Albert Papers, Box 23, Diary entry, September 10, 1914. "Bernstorff, Waetzold, Tauscher; draft. a telegram[...]"

636 Hardach, *The First World War, 1914-1918*, p. 150.

637 NA RG 65 Albert Papers, Box 19, von Papen to unknown recipient, copy to Albert, undated (estimated September 1914).

638 NA RG 65 Albert Papers, Box 19, Albert to Imperial Department of Interior, September 10, 1914

639 *The New York Times*, September 29, 1914, "Hugo Reisinger Dies in Germany."

640 *The New York Times*, October 29, 1914, "Hugo Reisinger's Funeral."

641 NA RG 65 Albert Papers, Box 19, Folder 104, Albert memorandum, undated. Mrs. Reisinger and Mrs. Busch were supposed to transmit the money.

642 NA RG 76 Mixed Claims Commission, Box 5, William M. Flynn to William H. Kiler, June 5, 1931.

643 NA RG 65 Albert Papers, Box 19, von Papen to unknown recipient, copy to Albert, undated (estimated September 1914).

644 NA RG 65 Albert Papers, Box 19, Zimmerman to Albert, October 15, 1914.

645 NA RG 65 Albert Papers, Box 3, Folder 10, Bernstorff to Albert and Dernburg, top secret, October 17, 1914.

646 For example NA RG 65 Albert Papers, Box 19, von Papen to War Department, February 11, 1915.

647 Doerries, *Imperial Challenge*, p. 151, relating an order from the Foreign Office to Count Bernstorff dated October 11, 1914.

648 Doerries, *Imperial Challenge*, p. 148, decribes the German-Indian connection and alludes to "agents located all over the Near and Far East."

649 French Strother, *Fighting Germany's Spies* (Garden City: Doubleday Page and Company, 1918), p. 228.

650 Bisher, *World War I Intelligence in Latin America*, p. 64.

651 Doerries, *Imperial Challenge*, p. 148.

652 Zubaran would become Mexican Ambassador to Germany later in the war.

653 NA RG 65 Albert Papers, Box 25, Correspondence Log.

654 Ibid.

655 Ibid.

656 Ibid., Box 23, Albert Diary, Entry for October 22, 1914.

657 NA RG 65 Albert Papers, Box 25, Correspondence Log.

658 NA RG 65 Albert Papers, Box 33, Invoice from Robert vom Cleff, October 26, 1914.

659 David Wilma, "U.S. Customs at Grays Harbor seizes the schooner *Annie Larsen* loaded with arms and ammunition on June 29, 1915," (www.HistoryLink.org, May 18, 2006); Also, *The Tacoma Times*, July 24, 1915, "Uncle Sam Wants to Know."

660 NA RG 65 M1085, Roll 855 file 232-37, Agent Wright to Department, January 12, 1917.

661 NA RG 65 Albert Papers, Box 33, Tauscher to von Papen, October 26, 1914.

662 NA RG 65 Albert Papers, Box 14, offer of rifles, cartridges, Gatlin guns, and trucks, December 1, 1914.

663 *The New York Times*, June 30, 1915, "Seize Ship with Arms."

664 Ibid.

665 NA RG 65 Albert Papers, Box 33, Tauscher accounts for munitions sales 1914 to 1915. The total transportation cost is divided into the arms that were impounded.

666 Ibid.

667 NA RG 65 Albert Papers, Box 33, Tauscher to von Papen, July 26, 1915.

668 Doerries, *Imperial Challenge*, p. 179.

669 NA RG 65 Albert Papers, Box 33, Memorandum of Load by Mallory Steamship Company, January 8, 1915.

670 NA RG 65 Albert Papers, Box 33, Tauscher to von Papen, January 26, 1915.

671 NA RG 131 Alien Property Custodian Entry 199, Box 129, file 3208. Strother mentions $19,000 as a one-time payment, which is atypical for a lease agreement. This author could not substantiate either number with independent sources.

672 *The New York Times*, February 19, 1915, "Mexico City Still Held by Carranza."

673 http://www. Ancestry.com, California Passenger and Crew Lists, 1882-1957, Roll 1416, Page 15.

674 *St. John Daily Sun*, July 18, 1899, "A Big Blaze."

675 *The Washington Herald*, January 1, 1913, "Awards Contracts for 8 Submarines."

676 Strother, *Fighting Germany's Spies*, p. 236.

677 Ibid., pp. 236-242.

678 The National Archives of the UK, Board of Trade, Commercial and Statistical Department and successors, Inwards Passenger Lists, Kew, Surrey, England, BT26, Part 639, Element 78.

679 NA RG 59 Passport Applications Argentina thru Venezuela, 1906-1925, M1372, ARC Identifier 1244183 / MLR Number A1 544, public domain.

680 NA RG 36 Records of the Immigration and Naturalization Service, T175, Roll 998, page 63.

681 *The San Antonio Light*, July 19, 1951, "Adventurer's Funeral Pends."

682 Ibid.

683 *The Day Book*, April 25, 1914, "Volunteer Guards at Embassy Surrender U.S. Guns without Resistance." Also, *The Washington Times*, April 25, 1914, "Consul Reports Arrest of Americans in Mexico City."

684 *The Washington Times, The New York Sun, The Day Book, The San Antonio Light*, between April 25 and April 26, 1914.

685 Wilma, "U.S. Customs at Grays Harbor seizes the schooner *Annie Larsen* loaded with arms and ammunition on June 29, 1915."

686 *The New York Times*, June 30, 1915, "Seize Ship with Arms."

687 The Southern Division of the United States District Court for the Northern District of California, First Division, United States of America vs. Franz Bopp, et al., April 23, 1918.

688 Strother, *Fighting Germany's Spies*, p. 246. He is quoting from Starr-Hunt's testimony and mentioned "Johnson Island." The island he is actually referring to is Johnston Atoll in the East Indies.

689 NA RG 65 Albert Papers, Box 33, Tauscher to von Papen, May 12, 1915.

690 NA RG 65 Albert Papers, Box 33, Tauscher to von Papen, July 30, 1915.

691 See, for example, Giles Brown, "The Hindu Conspiracy, 1914-1917," *The Pacific Historical Review*, Vol. 17, No. 3. (Aug., 1948), (Oakland: University of California Press), pp. 299-310; Don Dignan, "The Hindu Conspiracy in Anglo-American Relations during World War I," *The Pacific Historical Review*, volume 40 (Oakland: University of California Press), pp. 57–76; Karl Hoover, "The Hindu Conspiracy in California, 1913-1918," *German Studies Review*, Volume 8 (May 1985), (Los Angeles: German Studies Association, 1985), pp. 245–261.

692 *The Tacoma Times*, October 28, 1916, "Hindus Reach Home; Are Hung."

693 *The Ogden Standard*, December 10, 1915; Also Marine Crew Chronik MIM620/CREW, Marineschule Mürwik, Flensburg, Deutschland, p. 46.

694 Count Bernstorff, *My Three Years in America*, p. 102.

695 Stallforth Papers, miscellaneous correspondence 1916.

696 See Jules Whitcover, *Sabotage at Black Tom: Imperial Germany's Secret War in America, 1914-1917* (Chapel Hill: Algonquin Books of Chapel Hill, 1989), p. 54.

697 NA RG 76 Mixed Claims Commission, Box 14, Generalstab der Armee, Abt. IIIB to Foreign Office, January 24, 1915.

698 The sabotage teams will be discussed in great detail later in the book.

699 NA RG 65 Albert Papers, Box 24, Albert to Delbrück, May 10, 1915.

700 www.whitehouse.gov/1600/presidents/woodrowwilson. This was Wilson's campaign slogan for the 1916 election.

BIBLIOGRAPHY:
SECONDARY LITERATURE

Ackermann, Carl W., *Mexico's Dilemma* (New York: George H. Doran Company, 1918).

Albertini, Luigi, *The Origins of the War of 1914*, vols. 1-3, (New York: Enigma Books, 2005).

Baecker, Thomas, *Die deutsche Mexikopolitik 1913/14*, (Berlin: Colloquium Verlag, 1971).

Bailey, Thomas A., Ryan, Paul B., *The Lusitania Disaster: The Real Answers behind the World's most controversial Sea Tragedy* (New York: The Free Press, 1975).

Baker, Ray Stannard, *Woodrow Wilson, Life and Letters*, seven volumes (New York: Doubleday, Doran and Company, 1938).

Bernstein, Herman, *Celebrities of our time: Interviews* (New York: Joseph Lawren, 1924).

Bihl, Wolf Dieter, ed., *Deutsche Quellen zur Geschichte des Ersten Weltkrieges* (Darmstadt: Wissenschaftliche Buchgesellschaft, 1991).

Bisher, Jamie, *World War I Intelligence in Latin America* (unpublished manuscript, 2008).

Blum, Howard, *Dark Invasion, 1915: Germany's Secret War and the Hunt for the First Terrorist Cell in America* (New York: Harper Collins Publishers, 2014).

Bonsor, N. R. P., *North Atlantic Seaway: An Illustrated History of the Passenger Services Linking the Old World with the New*, four volumes (Wheat Ridge: Brookside Publications, 1978).

Calvert, Peter, *The Mexican Revolution 1910-1914: The Diplomacy of Anglo-American Conflict* (New York: Cambridge University Press, 1968).

Carlisle, Rodney P., *World War I* (New York: Facts on File Inc., 2007).

Carosso, Vincent P., Carosso, Rose C., *The Morgans: Private International Bankers, 1854-1913* (Cambridge: Harvard Studies in Business History, Harvard University Press, 1987).

Cartarius, Ulrich ed., *Deutschland im Ersten Weltkrieg: Texte und Dokumente* (München: DTV, 1982).

Cecil, Lamar, *Albert Ballin: Wirtschaft und Politik im Deutschen Kaiserreich* (Hamburg: Hoffmann und Campe, 1969).

Chalkley, John F., *Zach Lamar Cobb: El Paso Collector of Customs and Intelligence During the Mexican Revolution, 1913-1918*, Southwestern Studies, No. 103 (El Paso: University of Texas Press, 1998).

Colby, Frank Moore, Williams, Talcott, eds., *The New International Encyclopedia*, Volume 24 (New York: Dodd, Mead, and Company, 1918).

Collier, Peter and Horowitz, David, *The Rockefellers, An American Dynasty* (New York: Summit Books, 1989).

Cooper, John Milton Jr., *Woodrow Wilson: A Biography* (New York: Alfred A. Knopf, 2009).

Clendenen, Clarence, *The United States and Pancho Villa: A study in unconventional diplomacy* (Ithaca: Cornell University Press, 1961).

Cumberland, Charles C., *The Mexican Revolution: The Constitutionalist Years* (Austin: University of Texas Press, 1974).

Daniels, Josephus, *The Life of Woodrow Wilson* (Chicago, Philadelphia: John C. Winston Company, 1924).

De Bekker, Leander Jan, *The Plot Against Mexico* New York: Alfred A. Knopf Publishers, 1919).

Doenecke, Justus D., *Nothing Less Than War: A New History of America's Entry into World War I* (Lexington: The University Press of Kentucky, 2011).

Doerries, Reinhard R., *Imperial Challenge: Ambassador Count Bernstorff and German-American Relations, 1908-1917* (Chapel Hill: University of North Carolina Press, 1989).

Doerries, Reinhard R., Editor, *Diplomaten und Agenten: Nachrichtendienste in der Geschichte der deutsch-amerikanischen Beziehungen* (Heidelberg: Universitätsverlag C. Winter, 2001).

Doerries, Reinhard R., *Prelude to the Easter Rising: Sir Roger Casement in Imperial Germany* (Portland: Frank Cass Publishers, 2000).

Ecke, Heinz, *Four Spies Speak* (London: John Hamilton Limited, 1933).

Eisenhower, John S. D., *Intervention! The United States and the Mexican Revolution, 1913-1917* (New York: W.W. Norton and Company Inc., 1993).

Fabela, Isidro, *Historia diplomática de la Revolución Mexicana*, vol I. (1912-1917) (México Ciudad: Fondo de Cultura Económica, 1958).

Feldman, Gerald D., *Army, Industry, and Labor in Germany, 1914-1918*, (Providence: Berg Publishers Inc., 1992).

Fischer, Fritz, *Griff nach der Weltmacht: Die Kriegszielpolitik des kaiserlichen Deutschland 1914/18* (Düsseldorf: Droste Verlag, 1961).

French, David, *British Economic and Strategic Planning 1905 to 1915* (Abingdon: Routledge Library Editions, 2006).

Geiss, Immanuel, Ed., *July 1914: The Outbreak of the First World War: Selected Documents* (New York: Charles Scribner's and Sons, 1967).

Geissler, Erhard, *Biologische Waffen – Nicht in Hitlers Arsenalen: Biologische and Toxin-Kampfmittel von 1915 bis 1945* (Münster: LIT Verlag, 1999).

Gerhardt, Johannes, *Albert Ballin* (Hamburg: Hamburg University Press, 2010).

Hadley, Michael L., Sarty, Roger Flynn, *Tin-Pots and Pirate Ships: Canadian Naval Forces and German Sea Raiders 1880 – 1918* (Quebec: McGill-Queens University Press, 1991).

Haley, Edward P., *Revolution and Intervention: The Diplomacy of Taft and Wilson with Mexico, 1910-1917* (Cambridge: The MIT Press, 1970).

Hamilton, Douglas T., *Shrapnel Shell Manufacture* (New York: The New Industrial Press, 1915).

Hardach, Gerd, *The First World War, 1914-1918* (Berkeley and Los Angeles: University of California Press, 1977).

Harris, Charles H., III and Sadler, Louis R., *The Secret War in El Paso: Mexican Revolutionary Intrigue, 1906-1920* (Albuquerque: University of New Mexico Press, 2009).

Harris, Charles H., III and Sadler, Louis R., *The Texas Rangers and the Mexican Revolution: The Bloodiest Decade, 1910-1920* (Albuquerque: University of New Mexico Press, 2004).

Harris, Charles H., III and Sadler, Louis R., *The Plan de San Diego: Tejano Rebellion, Mexican Intrigues*, (Lincoln: University of Nebraska Press, 2013).

Hau, George William, *War Echoes or Germany and Austria in the Crisis* (Chicago: Morton M. Malone, 1915).

Hirst, David Wayne, *German Propaganda in the United States, 1914-1917* (Evanston: Northwestern University PhD. Dissertation, 1962).

Hopkins, J. Castell, editor, *The Canadian annual review of public affairs, 1915* (Toronto: The Annual Review Publishing Company, 1916).

Huertner, Johannes, editor, *Paul von Hintze: Marineoffizier, Diplomat, Staatssekretär, Dokumente einer Karriere zwischen Militär und Politik, 1903-1918* (München: Harald Boldt Verlag, 1998).

Huldermann, Bernhard, *Albert Ballin* (New York: Cassell and Company Ltd., 1922).

Jeffreys, Diarmuid, *Aspirin: The Remarkable Story of a Wonder Drug* (New York: Bloomsbury Publishing, 2005).

Jeffreys-Jones, Rhodri, *Cloak and Dollar: A History of American Secret Intelligence* (New Haven: Yale University Press, 2002).

Jensen, Joan M., *The Price of Vigilance* (Chicago and New York: Rand McNally and Company, 1968).

Katz, Friedrich, *The Secret War in Mexico: Europe, the United States, and the Mexican Revolution* (Chicago: The University of Chicago Press, 1981).

Katz, Friedrich, *The Life and Times of Pancho Villa* (Stanford: Stanford University Press, 1998).

Keegan, John, *The First World War* (New York: Alfred A. Knopf, Inc., 1999).

Kelly, Patrick J., *Tirpitz and the Imperial German Navy* (Bloomington: Indiana University Press, 2011).

Kessler, Graf Harry, *Walther Rathenau: His Life and Work* (New York: Harcourt, Brace and Company, 1930).

Knight, Alan, *The Mexican Revolution: Volume 2: Counter-revolution and Reconstruction* (Cambridge: Cambridge University Press, 1986).

Koenig, Louis W., *Bryan: A Political Biography of William Jennings Bryan* (New York: G.P. Putnam's Sons, 1971).

Koenig, Robert L., *The Fourth Horseman: One Man's Mission to Wage the Great War in America* (New York: Public Affairs, 2006).

Landau, Henry, *The Enemy Within: The Inside Story of German Sabotage in America* (New York: G.P. Putnam's Sons, 1937).

Link, Arthur S., editor, *Woodrow Wilson: Revolution, War, and Peace* (Hoboken: John Wiley and Sons, 1979).

Link, Arthur S., editor, *Woodrow Wilson and a Revolutionary World, 1913-1921* (Chapel Hill: University of North Carolina Press, 1982).

Link, Arthur S., *Wilson and the Progressive Era 1910 to 1917* (New York: Harper and Brothers, 1954).

Link, Arthur S., *The Papers of Woodrow Wilson*, vols. 23-26 (Princeton: Princeton University Press, 1966).

Link, Arthur S., *Wilson: The New Freedom* (New Jersey: Princeton University Press, 1956)

Link, Arthur S., Wilson, vol. 3, *The Struggle for Neutrality, 1914–1915* (Princeton: Princeton University Press, 1960).

Löwer, Thomas, *American Jews in World War I - German Propaganda Courting the American Jewry* (München: GRIN Publishing GmbH, 2004).

Ludwig, Emil, *Wilhelm Hohenzollern: The Last of the Kaisers* (New York: G. P. Putnam's Sons, 1927).

Luebke, Frederick C., *Bonds of Loyalty: German-Americans and World War I* (DeKalb: Northern Illinois University Press, 1974).

Luff, Jennifer, *Commonsense Anticommunism: Labor and Civil Liberties between the World Wars* (Raleigh: University of North Carolina Press, 2012).

Machado, Manuel A. Jr., *Centaur of the North: Francisco Villa, the Mexican Revolution, and Northern Mexico* (Austin: Eakin Press, 1988).

Mauch, Christoff, *The Shadow War Against Hitler: The Covert Operations of America's Wartime Secret Intelligence Service* (New York: Columbia University Press, 1999).

McKenna, Marthe, *My Master Spy: A Narrative of the Secret Service* (London: Jarrolds Publishers Ltd., 1936).

McLynn, Frank, *Villa and Zapata: A History of the Mexican Revolution* (New York: Basic Books, 2000).

McMaster, John Bach, *The United States in the World War* (New York: D. Appleton and Company, 1918).

Millman, Chad, *The Detonators: The Secret Plot to Destroy America and an Epic Hunt for Justice* (New York: Little, Brown and Company, 2006).

Nasaw, David, *The Chief: The Life of William Randolph Hearst* (New York: Houghton Mifflin Company, 2000).

Newman, Bernard, *Secrets of German Espionage* (London: The Right Book Club, 1940).

Peterson, Horace Cornelius, *Propaganda for War: The Campaign against American Neutrality, 1914-1917* (Norman: University of Oklahoma Press, 1939).

Preston, Diana, *Lusitania: An Epic Tragedy* (New York: Walker and Company, 2002).

Quirk, Robert E., *The Mexican Revolution, 1914-1915: The Convention of Aguascalientes* (Bloomington: University of Indiana Press, 1960).

Raat, W. Dirk and Beezley, William H., editors, *Twentieth Century Mexico* (Lincoln: University of Nebraska Press, 1986).

Reiling, Johannes, *Deutschland: Safe for Democracy?* (Stuttgart: Franz Steiner Verlag, 1997).

Ritter, Gerhard, *Der Schlieffenplan: Kritik eines Mythos* (München: Verlag R. Oldenbourg, 1956).

Ritter, Gerhard, *Staatskunst und Kriegshandwerk* (München: Verlag R. Oldenbourg, 1954).

Roessler, Eberhard, *Die Unterseeboote der Kaiserlichen Marine* (Bonn: Bernard und Graefe Verlag, 1997).

Scheina, Robert L., *Villa, Soldier of the Mexican Revolution* (Washington D.C.: Potomac Books, 2004).

Schieffel, Werner, *Bernhard Dernburg 1865 - 1937: Kolonialpolitiker und Bankier im wilhelminischen Deutschland* (Zürich: Atlantis Verlag, 1974).

Schroeder, Joachim, *Die U-Boote des Kaisers: Die Geschichte des deutschen U-Boot-Krieges gegen Grossbritannien im Ersten Weltkrieg* (Lauf a. d. Pegnitz: Bernard und Graefe, 2003).

Scott, James Brown, editor, *The Declaration of London: A Collection of Official Papers and Documents relating to the International Naval Conference held in London December, 1908 to February, 1909* (New York: Oxford University Press, 1919).

Shrapnel and other War Material: A Reprint of Important Articles Presented in the American Machinist from January to June 1915 (New York: McGraw-Hill Book Company, 1915).

Skaggs, William H., *German Conspiracies in America* (London: T. Fisher Unwin Ltd., approximately 1916).

Small, Michael, *The Forgotten Peace: Mediation at Niagara Falls, 1914* (Ottawa: University of Ottawa Press, 2009).

Smith, Arthur D. Howden, *Mr. House of Texas* (New York: Funk and Wagnalls Company, 1940).

Smith, Arthur D. Howden, *The Real Mr. House* (New York: George H. Doran Company, 1918).

Smith, Leonard V., Audoin-Rousseau, Stephanie, Becker, Annette, *France and the Great War, 1914-1918* (Cambridge: Cambridge University Press, 2003).

Strother, French, *Fighting Germany's Spies* (Garden City: Doubleday Page and Company, 1918).

Stubmann, Peter Franz, *Ballin: Leben und Werk eines deutschen Reeders* (Berlin: Hermann Klemm AG, 1926).

Synon, Mary, *McAdoo: The Man and his Times, A Panorama in Democracy* (Indianapolis: The Bobbs-Merrill Company, 1924).

Teitelbaum, Louis M., *Woodrow Wilson and the Mexican Revolution, 1913-1916* (New York: Exposition Press, 1967).

Thomas, William H. Jr., *Unsafe for Democracy: World War I and the U.S. Justice Department's Covert Campaign to Suppress Dissent* (Madison: The University of Wisconsin Press, 2008).

Tuchman, Barbara, *The Zimmermann Telegram* (New York: Macmillan Company, 1958).

Turner, John Kenneth, *Hands off Mexico* (New York: Rand School of Social Science, NY, 1920).

Volkman, Ernest, *Espionage: The Greatest Spy Operations of the 20th Century* (New York: John Wiley and Sons Inc., 1995).

Volkman, Ernest and Baggett, Blaine, *Secret Intelligence: The Inside Story of America's Espionage Empire* (New York: Doubleday, 1989).

Von Feilitzsch, Heribert, *In Plain Sight: Felix A. Sommerfeld, Spymaster in Mexico, 1908 to 1914* (Amissville: Henselstone Verlag LLC., 2012).

Von Feilitzsch, Heribert, *Felix A. Sommerfeld and the Mexican Front in the Great War* (Amissville: Henselstone Verlag LLC., 2015).

Von Feilitzsch, Heribert, *The Secret War on the United States in 1915: A Tale of sabotage, Labor Unrest and Border Troubles* (Amissville: Henselstone Verlag LLC., 2015).

West, Nigel, *Historical Dictionary of Sexspionage* (Plymouth: Scarecrow Press Inc., 2009).

Weston, William J., *Presbyterian Pluralism: Competition in a Protestant House* (Knoxville: University of Tennessee Press, 1997).

Wile, Frederic William, *Men around the Kaiser: The Makers of Modern Germany* (Toronto: The MacLean Publishing Company, 1913).

Wilkins, Mira, *The History of Foreign Investment in the United States,*

1914-1945 (Cambridge: Harvard University Press, 2004).

Witcover, Jules, *Sabotage at Black Tom* (Chapel Hill: Algonquin Books of Chapel Hill, 1989).

Wittke, Carl, *The German-Language Press in America* (Louisville: University of Kentucky Press, 1957).

Young, William, *German Diplomatic Relations, 1871-1945* (New York: iUniverse, Inc., 2006).

Zuber, Terence, *Inventing the Schlieffen Plan: German War Planning 1871-1914* (New York: Oxford University Press, 2002).

NEWSPAPERS, BULLETINS, DIRECTORIES, AND MAGAZINES

American Machinist, Volume 29 (1906).

Baecker, Thomas, "The Arms of the Ypiranga: The German Side," *The Americas*, Vol. 30, No. 1 (Jul., 1973): pp. 1-17.

Bailey, Alexandra, "German Internment During the First and Second World Wars," *Centre for Constitutional Studies*, (University of Alberta, http://www.law.ualberta.ca/centres/ccs/issues/germaninternment. php, viewed 12-2011).

Baptista, Robert J., "Spies and Dies," *http://www.ColorantsHistory. Org* (updated March 4, 2010).

Brenner, Anita, "The Wind that Swept Mexico," Part I, II, and III, *Harper's Magazine* (November 1942).

Broadberry, Stephen, Howlett, Peter, "The United Kingdom during World War I: Business as usual?" http://www2.warwick.ac.uk/fac/soc/ economics /staff/.../wp/wwipap4.pdf (June 2003).

Brown, Giles, "The Hindu Conspiracy, 1914-1917," *The Pacific Historical Review*, Vol. 17, No. 3 (April 1948): pp. 299-310.

Carlisle, Rodney, "The Attacks on U.S. Shipping that Precipitated American Entry into World War I," *The Northern Mariner/Le marin du nord*, XVII, No. 3 (July, 2007): pp. 41-66.

Day Book, Chicago, IL, 1914.

Day, New London, CT, 1914-1916.

Dignan, Don, "The Hindu Conspiracy in Anglo-American Relations during World War I," *The Pacific Historical Review*, volume 40 (Feb., 1971): pp. 57-76.

Doerries, Reinhard R., "Aspects of World War II German Intelligence," *Journal of Intelligence History*, Volume 4, Number 1 (Summer 2004).

El Paso Herald, El Paso, TX, 1910-1920.

Evening Herald, Albuquerque, NM, 1914-1916.

Fatherland, Volumes I and II (New York: The Fatherland Cooperation, 1914 to 1917).

Financier, Volume 114, New York, August 1, 1919.

Finley, James P., "The Buffalo Soldiers at Fort Huachuca," *Huachuca Illustrated, Volumes 1, 2, 3* (1993).

Fort Wayne News, Fort Wayne, TX, 1914 to 1918.

Grams, Grant W., "Karl Respa and German Espionage in Canada during World War One," *Journal of Military and Strategic Studies*, Vol. 8, Issue 1 (Fall 2005).

Harris, Charles H. III, Sadler, Louis R. "The Underside of the Mexican Revolution: El Paso, 1912," *The Americas*, Vol. 39, No. 1 (July, 1982): pp. 69-83.
Hoover, Karl, "The Hindu Conspiracy in California, 1913-1918," *German Studies Review, Volume 8 (May 1985), (Los Angeles: German Studies Association, 1985)*: pp. 245-261.

Katz, Friedrich, "Pancho Villa and the Attack on Columbus, New Mexico,"*The American Historical Review*, Vol. 83, No. 1 (Feb., 1978): pp. 101-130.

Keller, Phyllis, "George Sylvester Viereck: The Psychology of a German-American Militant," *The Journal of Interdisciplinary History*, Vol. 2, No. 1 (Summer 1971).

Kerig, Dorothy Pierson, "Luther T. Ellsworth: U.S. Consul on the Border During the Mexican Revolution," *Southwestern Studies*, Monograph number 47 (El Paso: Texas Western Press, 1975).

Law Notes, Volume 7 (April 1903 to March 1904), (Northport: Edward Thompson Company, 1904).

Lerner, Victoria, "Exiliados de la revolución mexicana: El caso de los villistas (1915-1921)," *Mexican Studies*, Vol. 17, No.1 (Winter, 2001).

Lewiston Evening Journal, 1915.

Massey, Brian Lee, "A Brief History of the Canadian Expeditionary Force," *http://www.rootsweb.ancestry.com/~ww1can/cef14_15.htm*, (1997-2007).

Metal Industry Magazine, Volume 13 (January to December 1915), (New York: The Metal Industry Publishing Company, 1916).
Metal Industry, Vol. 13 (January to December 1915), (New York: The Metal Industry Publishing Company, 1916).

Mexican Yearbook 1912 (London: McCorqudale and Company Limited, 1912).

Milwaukee Journal, Milwaukee, WI, 1942.

Morning Call, November 1, 2010, "Forging America: The Story of Bethlehem Steel."

Mumme, Stephen P., "The Battle of Naco, Factionalism and Conflict in Sonora: 1914-1915," *Arizona and the West*, Volume 21, No. 2 (Summer, 1979): pp. 157-186.

Nation, volume 109 (July 1, 1919 to December 31, 1919), (New York: The Nation Press, 1919).

New York Times Current History: The European War, Volume 1 (New York: The New York Times Company, 1915).

New York Times Current History: The European War, Volume 17 (October, November, December 1918), (New York: New York Times Company, 1919).

New York Times, New York, NY, Archives 1896-1942.

New York Tribune, New York, NY, 1910-1918.

O'Shaughnessy, Edith, "Diplomatic Days in Mexico, First, Second, Third Papers," *Harpers Magazine* (September, October, November 1917).

Oakland Tribune, April 18, 1915.

Rafalko, Frank J., Ed., "Post Civil War to World War I," A *Counterintelligence Reader*, volume I, Chapter 3 www.fas.org/irp/ops/ci/docs/ci1, viewed 9-22-2011.

Sabazius, "The Invisible Basilica: Dr. Arnoldo Krumm-Heller (1876 -1949 e.v.)" (United States: Ordo Templi Orientis, 1997).

San Francisco Call and Post, San Francisco, CA, 1908-1917.

Skirius, John, "Railroad, Oil and Other Foreign Interests in the Mexican Revolution, 1911 to 1914," *Journal of Latin American Studies*, Vol. 35, No. 1 (Feb. 2003).

Spence, Richard B., "K. A. Jahnke and the German Sabotage Campaign in the United States and Mexico, 1914-1918," *The Historian*, Volume 59, Issue 1 (Sep., 1996): pages 89–112.

St. John Daily Sun, St. John, Newfoundland, Canada, 1899.

Stapleton, F.G., "The unpredictable dynamo: Germany's Economy, 1870-1918," *History Review* (December 2002).

The Bankers Magazine, Volume 77 (July to December 1908), (New York: Bankers Publishing Company, 1908).

The Massey-Gilbert Blue Book of Mexico for 1903: A Directory in English of the City of Mexico (Mexico D.F.: The Massey-Qilbert Company, Sucs., 1903).

The Trow: Copartnership and Corporation Directory of the Boroughs of Manhattan and the Bronx (New York: Association of American Directory Publishers, March 1908).

Times-Picayune, New Orleans, LA, July 1 to July 6, 1914.

University of Calgary, "The Peopling of Canada: 1891-1921," (Calgary: The Applied Research Group, 1997).

Van Dopperen, Ron, "Shooting the Great War: Albert Dawson and the American Correspondent Film Company, 1914-1918," *Film History*, Volume 4, No. 2 (1990): pp. 123-129.

Von Feilitzsch, Heribert, "Operation 'Perez': The German Attempt to Own American Newspapers in World War I," Journal of the Florida Conference of Historians, Volume 22 (June 2015): pp. 87-102.

Washington Herald, Washington, D.C., 1910-1922

Washington Post, Washington, D.C., 1911-1922.

Washington Times, Washington D.C., 1910-1914.

While, E. Bruce, "The Muddied Waters of Columbus, New Mexico," *The Americas*, Vol. 32, No. 1 (Jul., 1975): pp. 72-98.

Wilma, David, "U.S. Customs at Grays Harbor seizes the schooner *Annie Larsen* loaded with arms and ammunition on June 29, 1915," *http://www.HistoryLink.org* (May 18, 2006).

World's Work, Volume 28 (May to October 1914), (New York: Doubleday, Page and Co., 1914).

World's Work, Volume 30 (May to October 1918), (New York: Doubleday, Page and Co., 1915).

World's Work, Volume 36 (May to October 1918), (New York: Doubleday, Page and Co., 1918).

ORIGINAL, ARCHIVAL, AND GOVERNMENT SOURCES

Auswärtiges Amt, Politisches Archiv Berlin, Mexiko Band I bis X.

Bundesarchiv fuer Militärgeschichte, Freiburg; Record Groups RM 2, RM 3, RM 5.

Die Österreichisch-Ungarischen Dokumente zum Kriegsausbruch (Berlin: National-Verlag, Staatsamt für Äußeres in Wien, 1923).

Gooch, G.P., Litt, D., Temperley, Harold, editors, British Documents on the Origins of the War, 1898-1914, Vol. XI: The Outbreak of War: Foreign Office Documents (June 28th-August 4th, 1914), (London: His Majesty's Stationery Office, 1926).

Department of Commerce, Bureau of Foreign and Domestic Commerce, Miscellaneous Series, No. 57, German Foreign Trade Organization, Government Printing Office, 1917.

Ministry of National Defense, Commonwealth of Canada, The Official History of the Canadian Army: The Canadian Expeditionary Force, 1914-1919, by Colonel G. W. L. Nicholson, C.D., Army Historical Section, Roger Duhamel, F.R.S.C. (Ottawa: Queen's Printer and Controller of Stationary, 1962).

Holmdahl Papers, University of California at Berkley, Bancroft Library, C-B-921.

German Diplomatic Papers, University of California at Berkley, Bancroft Library, M-B 12.

Horne, Charles F., editor, *Source Records of the Great War*, Volumes I to VII (New York: National Alumni, 1923).

Koerver, Joachim, ed., *German Submarine Warfare 1914-1918 in the Eyes of British Intelligence: Selected Sources from the British National Archives, Kew* (Berlin: Schaltungsdienst Lange, 2010).

Silvestre Terrazas Papers, University of California at Berkley, Bancroft Library, M-B-18.

Carey McWilliams Papers, University of California at Los Angeles, 277.

Lazaro De La Garza Collection, University of Texas, Benson Library, Austin, TX.

Papers of Hugh Lenox Scott, Library of Congress, Washington, D.C.

Library and Archives Canada, Department of Militia and Defence, Record Group 13.

Marine Crew Chronik MIM620/CREW, Marineschule Mürwik, Flensburg, Deutschland.

Marineschule Mürwik, Verlustlisten 1914-1915, MIM381, KAI17 040 (Band 3).

The National Archives of the UK, Board of Trade, Commercial and Statistical Department and successors, Inwards Passenger Lists, Kew, Surrey, England, BT26.

National Archives, Washington DC

Record Group 29	Records of the Bureau of the Census, 1790 to 1996
Record Group 36	Records of the U.S. Customs Service, Vessels arriving in New York 1820-1897 and 1897-1957

Record Group 38 Office of Naval Intelligence 1913 to 1924

Record Group 45 Naval Records Collection, Caribbean File 1911 to 1927

Record Group 59 Department of State 1908 to 1927, specifically Papers of Robert Lansing, Volume I and II, Papers relating to the foreign relations of the United States 1914, 1915, 1916 (Latin America), File 812.00 (Mexico).

Record Group 60 Records of the Dept of Justice, Straight Numerical File, 157013, Boxes 1230 to 1236.

Record Group 65 Bureau of Investigation Case Files 1908-1922, Bureau of Investigation Miscellaneous Case Files 1908-1922, Papers of Dr. Heinrich F. Albert, Numbered Correspondence 1914 to 1917, Old German Files, Old Mexican Files.

Record Group 76 Mixed Claims Commission, 1922 to 1941.

Record Group 80 General Records of the Navy 1916 to 1926.

Record Group 85 Records of the Immigration and Naturalization Service.

Record Group 87 Records of the U.S. Secret Service, Daily Reports 1875 to 1936.

Record Group 131 Records of the Alien Property Custodian, Records seized by the APC.

Record Group 165 Records of the War Department, MID Specifically file 9140-1754 (Felix A. Sommerfeld), file 9140-878 (Frederico Stallforth), file 9140-646 (Franz Rintelen).

Record Group 242 German Captured Documents, Foreign Office, Mexiko Band 1 bis 10, "Old German Files."

Record Group 395 Records of the Army Overseas Operations, Mexican Punitive Expedition.

National Archives of the United Kingdom, BT26, Board of Trade: Commercial and Statistical Department and successors: Inwards Passenger Lists, Kew, Surrey.

National Intelligence Center, *American Revolution to World War II,*

Chapter 3, Central Intelligence Reader, http://www.fas.org.

Scott, James Brown, editor, *Diplomatic Correspondence Between the United States and Germany, August 1, 1914 - April 6, 1917* (New York: Oxford University Press, 1918).

Secretaría de Comunicaciones y Obras Públicas, Estadística de ferrocarriles de jurisdicción federal año de 1918 (MéxicoD.F.:Talleres Gráficos de la Nación, 1924).

Staatsarchiv Berlin, Deutsche Dienststelle (WASt), Deutsche Verlustlisten 1914 bis 1917, Berlin, Deutschland.

Staatsarchiv Hamburg, Hamburger Passagierlisten, 1850-1934.

United Nations, *Reports of International Arbitral Awards,* "S. S. 'Edna.' *Disposal of pecuniary claims arising out of the recent war (1914-1918),* United States, Great Britain, Volume III (December, 1934): pp. 1585-1606.

United Nations, *Reports of International Arbitral Awards: Lehigh Valley Railroad Company, Agency of Canadian Car and Foundry Company, Limited, and Various Underwriters (United States) v. Germany (Sabotage Cases), June 15, 1939,* Volume VIII (New York, 2006): pp. 225-460.

United States Census, *Cotton Production and Distribution* (Washington D.C.: Government Printing Office, 1915).

United States Department of Agriculture, *Monthly Crop Reporter, May 10, 1915* (Washington, D.C.: Government Printing Office, 1915).

United States Department of Commerce, *Commerce Reports, Part 3, July, August, September, 1918* (Washington, D.C.: Government Printing Office, 1918).

United States Senate, *Hearing before a Subcommittee of the*

Committee on Foreign Relations, Revolutions in Mexico (Washington D.C.: Government Printing Office, 1913).

United States Senate, Committee of the Judiciary, *Alleged Dye Monopoly, Senate Resolution 77* (Washington D.C.: Government Printing Office, 1922).

United States War Department, *Annual Reports 1915* (Washington, D.C.: Government Printing Office, 1916).

United States Senate, *Investigation of Mexican Affairs, Hearing before a Subcommittee of the Committee of Foreign Relations* (Washington, D.C.: Government Printing Office, 1920).

United States Senate, *Brewing and Liquor Interests and German Propaganda, Subcommittee of the Committee of the Judiciary*, Volume 2 (Washington D.C.: Government Printing Office, 1919).

United States Senate, *Revolutions in Mexico, Hearing before a Subcommittee of the Committee of Foreign Relations* (Washington, D.C.: Government Printing Office, 1912).

Virkus, Frederick, editor, *Immigrant Ancestors: A List of 2,500 Immigrants to America before 1750* (Baltimore: Genealogical Publishing Co., 1964).

YIVO Institute for Jewish Research, New York, Record Group 713, Papers of Herman Bernstein (1876-1935).

AUTOBIOGRAPHICAL WORKS

Albert, Heinrich F., *Aufzeichnungen* (Büxenstein: Self published, 1956).

Bauer, Hermann, *Als Fuehrer der U-Boote im Weltkriege: Der Eintritt der U-Boot-Waffe in die Seekriegsfuehrung* (Leipzig: Köhler und Amelang, 1941).

Boy-Ed, Karl, *Verschwoerer?* (Berlin: Verlag August Scherl GmbH, 1920).

Charles, Heinrich, *The Electro-Individualistic Manifesto: The Anti-Thesis of the Communistic Manifesto by Karl Marx and Friedrich Engels, and the Synthesis of Social-Individualism* (New York: Self published, 1913).

Churchill, Winston S., *The World Crisis, 1911 to 1918*, (London: Odhams Press Limited, 1939).

Count von Bernstorff, Johann Heinrich, *My Three Years in America* (London: Skeffington and Son, approximately 1940).

Count von Bernstorff, Johann Heinrich, *Memoirs of Count Bernstorff* (New York: Random House, 1936).

Dehn, Paul, Dernburg, Bernhard, Hale, William Bayard, Hall, Thomas C. and various editors, *The Truth About Germany: Facts about the War* (New York: The Trow Press, 1914).

Delbrück, Hans, *Delbrück's Modern Military History*, translated by Arden Bucholz (Lincoln: University of Nebraska Press, 1997).

Dernburg, Bernhard, *Search-Lights on the War* (New York: The Fatherland Corporation, 1915).

Fuehr, Karl Alexander, *The Neutrality of Belgium: A Study of the Belgian Case under its Aspects in Political History and International Law* (New York: Funk and Wagnalls Company, 1915).

Gerard, James W., *My first eighty three years in America: Memoirs of James W. Gerard* (Garden City: Doubleday and Company, Inc., 1951).

Gerard, James W., *Face to Face with Kaiserism* (New York: George H. Doran Company, 1918).

Hale, William Bayard, *Germany's Just Cause* (Neww York: The Fatherland Press, 1914).

Hale, William Bayard, *The Case Against Armed Merchantmen*, timely reprints from the New York Press, "The Real Issue in Washington," pp. 6-9, unknown publisher, undated (1915).

Hale, William Bayard, *The Story of a Style* (New York: B. W. Huebsch, 1920).

Jones, John Price, *The German Spy in America: The Secret Plotting of German Spies in the United States and the Inside Story of the Sinking of the Lusitania* (London: Hutchinson and Co., 1917).

Jones, John Price, Hollister, Paul Merrick, *The German Secret Service in America, 1914-1918* (Boston: Small, Maynard and Company, 1918).

Koerver, Joachim, ed., *German Submarine Warfare 1914-1918 in the Eyes of British Intelligence: Selected Sources from the British National Archives Kew* (Berlin: Schaltungsdienst Lange, 2010).

Krumm-Heller, Arnold, *Für Freiheit und Recht: Meine Erlebnisse aus dem mexikanischen Bürgerkriege* (Halle: Otto Thiele Verlag, 1916).

Lansing, Robert, *War Memoirs of Robert Lansing, Secretary of State* (New York: The Bobbs-Merrill Company, 1935).

McClure, Samuel S., *My Autobiography* (New York: Frederick A. Stokes Company, 1914).

Mencken, H. L., *My Life as Author and Editor* (New York: Alfred A. Knopf Inc., 1993).

Muensterberg, Hugo, *The War and America* (New York: D. Appleton and Co., 1914).

Nicolai, Walter, *The German Secret Service, translated with an additional chapter by George Renwick* (London: Stanley Paul and Co., 1924).

Von Papen, Franz, *Memoirs* (New York: E. P. Dutton and Company Inc., 1953).

Rintelen von Kleist, Franz, *The Dark Invader: Wartime Reminiscences of a German Naval Intelligence Officer* (London: Lovat Dickson Limited, 1933).

Rintelen von Kleist, Franz, *The Return of the Dark Invader* (London: Peter Davies Limited, 1935).

Rintelen von Kleist, Franz, *The Dark Invader: Wartime Reminiscences of a German Naval Intelligence Officer*, with an introduction by Reinhard R. Doerries (London: Frank Cass Publishers, 1997).

Rumely, Edward A., *The Gravest 366 Days, Editorials Reprinted from the Evening Mail of New York City* (New York: The New York Evening Mail, 1916).

Scheer, Reinhard, *Germany's High Sea Fleet in the World War* (London: Cassell and Company, 1920).

Scott, Hugh Lenox, *Some Memories of a Soldier* (New York: The Century Company, 1928).

Sperry, Earl Evelyn, Willis, Mason West, *German Plots and Intrigues in the United Stated during the Period of our Neutrality* (Washington D.C.: Committee on Public Information, July 1918).

Steffens, Lincoln, *The Autobiography of Lincoln Steffens* (New York: Harcourt, Brace and Company, 1931).

Tunney, Thomas J., *Throttled: The Detection of the German and Anarchist Bomb Plotters in the United States* (Boston: Small Maynard and Company, 1919).

Viereck, George Sylvester, *Spreading Germs of Hate* (London: Duckworth, 1931).

Von Bethmann-Hollweg, *Reflections on the World War*, Part 1 (London: Thornton Butterworth, Ltd., 1920).

Von der Goltz, Horst, *My Adventures as a German Secret Agent* (New York: Robert M. McBride and Company, 1917).

Von der Goltz, Horst, *Sworn Statement*, Presented to both Houses of Parliament by Command of His Majesty (April 1916).

Von Mach, Edmund, *What Germany Wants* (Boston: Little, Brown and Company, 1914).

Von Schlieffen, Count Alfred, *Cannae* (Fort Leavenworth: The Command and General Staff School Press, 1931).

Von Tirpitz, Alfred, *Erinnerungen* (Berlin: K. F. Koehler Verlag, 1927).

Voska, Emanuel Victor and Irwin, Will, *Spy and Counter-Spy* (London: George G. Harrap and Co Ltd., 1941).

Wilson, Woodrow and Hale, William Bayard, *The New Freedom* (New York: Doubleday, Page and Co., 1913).

Wilson, Henry Lane, *Diplomatic Episodes in Mexico, Belgium and Chile* (Port Washington: Kinnikat Press, 1971, reprint of original from 1927).

Wilson, Henry Lane, "Errors with Reference to Mexico and Events that have occurred there," *International Relations of the United States: The Annals*, Vol. LIV (July 1914).

INDEX

www.ingramcontent.com/pod-product-compliance
Lightning Source LLC
Chambersburg PA
CBHW031941080426
42735CB00007B/216